IGNITE
YOUR
COURAGE

INSPIRING MOMENTS OF
UNTOLD BRAVERY

INTRODUCTION BY

Peter Giesin

Co-Founder and Chief Technology Officer of
Ignite Publishing™ and Longevity Coach

PROJECT LEADERS

Stacey Yates Sellar

Just another human in the middle of
the journey, like you

Karen R. Rosser

Best Selling Author, Former Senior
Army Officer, Acquisition Professional

ADDITIONAL FEATURED AUTHORS

ANA-MARIA TURDEAN • ASHIRA KARPELOWSKY • CHERYL A. RAFTER
CHRISTINA SOMMERS • DEBORAH A. ELLIS • FARRAH SMITH
FELICIA BRIM MOORE • GINA TRIMARCO KLAUDER • JENETTE LONGORIA
JENNY SALIMI • JERMAINE L. BRANTLEY • LADY JB OWEN
LAMEEKA V. HARRIS • LILLIAN SKROVIG DOOIES • MARCIA KLOSTERMANN
MICHIKO COUCHMAN • NAOMI ZION MARK • NOLAN PILLAY
SANDRA VON HOLLEN • STEPHANIE DRUMMOND

PUBLISHED BY IGNITE PUBLISHING™

IGNITE
YOUR
COURAGE

WRITE FOR IGNITE

We trust that after finishing this book, 'Ignite Moments™' will become a part of your vocabulary. You'll begin to think about your own Ignite Moments and the times in your life when you felt ignited to live a different way. If sharing your story feels important, or the idea of writing your Ignite Moment for others to enjoy is percolating to the surface, please reach out to us. We believe every person has a story, and every story deserves to be read. If your words are longing to come forth, we want to be there for you to make it happen. Our desire is to *Ignite a billion lives through a billion words and share seven billion Ignite Moments around the globe.*

GET TO KNOW IGNITE.

Over seven hundred authors have come to us and we have made them international best-sellers in both our compilation books and their own solo projects. People who were terrified to write have succeeded and created outstanding books. Authors who have struggled with writer's block have become victorious.

Individuals who longed to be published but didn't know how to begin have reached best-seller status in a matter of months — delighted, triumphant, and empowered. From homemakers to teenagers, from nomads to millionaires, we have systematically assisted authors in fulfilling their writing goals and reaching their sought-after dreams.

We want to be there to help you become published. Should you desire to write your Ignite Momnet or have an idea for a full book of your own, let us be the ones to help reach your goal. As the leaders of empowerment publishing we know how to take you book and bring it to the world to help precisely the person who needs to read exactly what you have to share. Our programs are easy, fun, efficient and we never own your content or collect royalties. Your story is yours. Our job is to help you share it with as many people as possible.

Learn more about how you can become a published author here: https://igniteyou.life/

GET IGNITE'S
100 WRITING AFFIRMATIONS
EBOOK FOR FREE

Ignite your writing with these inspiring affirmations that were designed to unleash the superstar writer in you. Within this complimentary eBook, you'll find powerful affirmations for you to use daily to gain confidence in yourself and your writing. If you want to get access to this amazing resource, use the QR code below to gain access.

Other internationally best-selling compilation books
by IGNITE for you to enjoy:

———————————

Ignite Your Life for Women

Ignite Your Female Leadership

Ignite Your Parenting

Ignite Your Life for Men

Ignite Your Life for Conscious Leaders

Ignite Your Health and Wellness

Ignite Your Adventurous Spirit

Ignite Female Change Makers

Ignite the Modern Goddess

Ignite Happiness

Ignite Love

Ignite Your Inner Spirit

Ignite the Entrepreneur

Ignite Possibilities

Ignite the Hunger in You

Ignite Your Life for Women (2nd Edition)

Ignite Possibilities (2nd edition)

Ignite Your Wisdom

Ignite Forgiveness

Ignite Your Faith

COURAGE AUTHORS

Ana-Maria Turdean

Ashira Karps

Cheryl Rafter

Christina Sommers

Deborah A. Ellis

Farah Smith

Felecia Moore

Gina Trimarco

JB Owen

Jenette Longoria

Jennifer Salimi

Jermaine Brantley

Karen R. Rosser

Lameeka Harris

Lillian Dooies

Marcia Klostermann

Michi Couchman

Naomi Zion Mark

Nolan Pillay

Sandra Von Hollen

Stacey Sellar

Stephanie Drummond

Publisher's Note: We are delighted to offer the twenty-first compilation book in the IGNITE series. Our mission is to produce inspiring, motivational, and authentic real-life stories that will Ignite your life. Each book contains unique stories told by exceptional authors. They are of the highest caliber to offer engaging, profound, and life-changing examples that will impact the reader. Our mandate is to build a conscious, positive, and supportive community through our books, speaking events, writing workshops, Ignite experiences, podcasts, immersions, a TV show, and our product marketplace. We always welcome new book ideas and new authors onto our platform. Should you desire to be published and featured in an Ignite book, please apply at www.igniteyou.life/ apply or reach out to us at support@igniteyou.life.

Limitation of Liability: Under no circumstances shall Ignite Publishing™, its affiliates, or authors be liable for any indirect, incidental, consequential, special, or exemplary damages arising out of or in connection with your use of any exercises or information contained in this book. Please be advised that if you choose to follow any of the suggestions offered by the authors, you do so of your own accord. It is up to you to seek professional advice before you implement any lifestyle changes. The views, thoughts, and opinions expressed in this text belong solely to the individual authors and not necessarily to the publisher, editorial team, or the experts the authors may reference.

Published and printed by Ignite Publishing™
5569-47th Street Red Deer, AB
Canada, T4N1S1 1-877-677-6115

Editor-in-Chief JB Owen
Book and Cover design by Katie Smetherman, Kristine Joy Magno and Sinisa Poznanovic
Edited by JB Owen, Alex Blake, Michiko Couchman, Mimi Safiyah, Sarah Cross, and Zoe Wong.

Designed in Canada, Printed in China

ISBN: 978-1-7923-8768-5

Ordering Information: Quantity sales. Special discounts are available on quantity purchases by corporations, associations, and others. For details, contact the publisher at the above address. Programs, products, or services provided by the authors are found by contacting them directly.

Los Angeles Tribune
LINKEDIN is a trademark of LinkedIn
STARBUCKS COFFEE is a trademark of STARBUCKS CORPORATION.
BE THE MATCH BIOTHERAPIES is a trademark of the National Marrow Donor Program.
THE CLUBHOUSE is a trademark of Back9Network Inc.
FB is a trademark of Facebook, Inc.

Dedication

This book is dedicated to the many brave souls and dedicated individuals who choose each day to show up in this human experience. It takes courage to be that person, to go forward, and to carry on. The greatest courage we can muster is the willingness to be ourselves. This book is dedicated to each and every one of those courageous spirits who spend their day being who they were born to be.

ANA-MARIA TURDEAN
This story is meant to support you in finding a job that you love.

ASHIRA KARPS
This story is dedicated to my parents, family, and friends, who supported and loved me. To Maria, who is like my second mother, thank you for always believing in me and helping me. To my surgeons and my OT, who helped me along the way. To my special therapist, thank you for helping me navigate my journey. To anyone who has suffered a life-changing physical injury, just remember you can still do anything you want to; you may just have to do it a little differently.

CHERYL RAFTER
To my family who have been on this life journey with me, and created experiences along the way. Friends who love me unconditionally, and I can count on no matter what. To all the people who feel that they have never been worthy, good, or loved enough, yet still have the courage to move on to live their life fully.

CHRISTINA SOMMERS
To my beautiful daughter, you inspired me to find the courage to take my life back and fully heal; now showing you what is possible. To my friends and family who encouraged me and held a vision, I couldn't see for myself in my darkest moments. To all the readers who find a piece of themselves in the story, may you find the courage to take the next steps to find healing on the other side.

Deborah A. Ellis

I dedicate this short story of courage to Evelyn K. Smith, my mother, and anyone who has suffered any form of domestic violence, gun violence, or any kind of violence—intentionally or accidentally. I was accidentally shot at an early age, and I thank my mother and family for their strength, wisdom, and love. To all the people who have helped me become the woman that I am today.

Farrah Smith

Mom, my guiding light, your wisdom on facing fears to unlock potential empowered me to seize chances to transform lives, including my own. You lifted me to that TED stage and remain my greatest source of strength and inspiration on my path of purpose.

Felicia Moore

This story is dedicated to my husband, who always says, "Go for it"! To my daughter, who challenges the creativity in me, and my son, who just tells it like it is. My dad, who will forever be remembered as his daughter's #1 fan. My mom, thank you for always giving the best of you to me. To the ASHS alumni and staff that I had the pleasure of working with, your tenacity and zeal are nothing short of amazing.

Gina Trimarco

I dedicate this to Costa Man, aka David, aka my husband and soulmate. He puts the 'rock' in my 'rockstar' nickname that he's given me. Always supporting, promoting, and loving me exactly as I am. I'm blessed with, grateful for, and humbled by his unconditional and unwavering love. With him by my side, I get to be my best self so that I can help others.

JB OWEN

I dedicate this book to Peter, my adoring husband, who is the most courageous person I know and has given me the courage to always be myself. To all the people who have a dream and find the courage to fulfill it.

JENETTE LONGORIA

I dedicate this story to the Holy Spirit, who gives me the strength to do hard things. Thank you to my family, who are always there to support me. Thank you to my husband for picking me to be your battle buddy on this crazy journey through life. I would have never jumped into the unknown without your faith-filled leadership. A very special thank you to Tammie Miller, whose faith and hospitality provided an opportunity for healing and growth.

JENNIFER SALIMI

I lovingly dedicate this chapter to my dear parents. Your steadfast love and boundless support have instilled in me the confidence to consistently embody my true essence. I'm grateful for your unwavering presence as my pillar of strength, which has empowered me to approach the world with an open heart and a pure soul. No word exists that adequately captures the magnitude of my love for you, so for now, all I can offer is a simple "I love you."

JERMAINE BRANTLEY

To my beloved family and loved ones, thank you for your love and unwavering support. To all those reading my story, I hope you find encouragement and belief in your God-given abilities and strength to travel your journey to succeed in life!
Be blessed!

KAREN R. ROSSER

I dedicate this story to those who have journeyed beyond their imagination and traveled on an unexpected path—those who have embraced fear with a fearless spirit, a resilience of hope, and determination. Continue to illuminate your light and defy the unthinkable.

LAMEEKA HARRIS

I would like to dedicate this chapter to my family, current and those who have come before me. I know it is because of you all that I can live boldly and courageously. A special dedication to my two boys whom I draw so much of my strength from. To my wonderful spouse Daryl, thank you for loving and supporting me through it all. To all the people who have walked this journey with me, thank you all for loving and supporting me.

LILLIAN DOOIES

To my parents and children for their inspiration and encouragement.

MARCIA KLOSTERMANN

Dedicated to my dear family and friends, our extended support network, caregivers, health professionals, and teachers who have all supported us in this journey. We couldn't do this life without you! Thank You!

MICHI COUCHMAN

This story belongs to my Superhero, my Sweet Pea, my Cubby, and the incredible friends and family who supported us and gave us courage, inspiration, and hope.

NOLAN PILLAY

To our unwavering parents, your resilience through life's challenges and unwavering values have shaped us profoundly. Gratitude fills our hearts for your enduring support. To my steadfast siblings, together, we've weathered storms, proving our unbreakable bond. Let's forever stand united. With heartfelt gratitude and eternal love.

NAOMI ZION MARK

I dedicate this chapter to all who have struggled with the agony of childhood abuse, and/or any other seemingly insurmountable troubles. To those who desperately want to overcome, using courage as a driving force to their best days.

SANDRA VON HOLLEN

To my dad and grandparents, thank you for the memories and the love. To my No Matter What friend, may there always be purple butterflies.

STACEY SELLAR

For my sons Dashiel and Declan, who Ignite my courage, curiosity, creativity, love, and laughter every day.

STEPHANIE DRUMMOND

In honor and memory of my mom, Margie C. Brown, who taught me how to have the courage and confidence to face the world.

TESTIMONIALS FROM AUTHORS

Writing a chapter for Ignite Your Courage was a lot of fun. I enjoyed very much both the weekly meetings and the editing sessions. The project gave me the chance to remember long-forgotten events and to improve my writing skills. Thank you very much for this awesome experience.

—Ana-Maria Turdean

Thank you to Steph and the amazing Ignite team for your constant support.

—Ashira Karps

The experience I've had with writing my story has been unbelievable, with the great support and weekly training. This was my first time writing, and the team of people who supported me throughout the process was amazing, teaching me the steps to complete my story. I recommend anyone who is thinking about doing this and thinks that no one wants to hear what you have to say, to jump in and trust the process with this great team of people.

—Cheryl Rafter

God called me to share my story as I walked through my healing journey. When you share your story, it has to be from a healed, resourced state. I never knew how much more healing would happen through the writing process. The way Lady JB and her fantastic team have constructed the creation of these books is fun; it is a learning experience and is bringing one of my dreams to life. Everyone has a story, and this is a perfect way to start.

—Christina Sommers

Collaborating with Ignite Publishing and Lady JB on the impactful Ignite Courage project has been an absolute privilege. Their resolute dedication to sharing transformative Ignite Moments, which propel us toward greatness, was beautifully evident throughout our collaboration. Their unwavering passion for bringing our collective voices to the forefront, and motivating, and empowering others was palpable at every step of the journey. Contributing a chapter allowed me to share my own ignite moment and be part of a truly inspiring initiative that fuels positive change. I am genuinely grateful for the opportunity to work with such a dedicated team committed to a profound mission. I extend my heartfelt gratitude to Ignite Publishing and Lady JB for providing this platform that unites us through our stories and kindles the greatness within each of us.

—Farrah Smith

This has been a rewarding, personable, professional, and insightful experience that I will never forget. Thank you to Ignite for sharing your process with me, it has been empowering and inspiring. The journey of becoming an author is now clearly understood.

—Felicia Moore

Working with the Ignite team and JB has been one of the most amazing experiences in my life and career. They make it easy and joyful to find and show my best self to others. My only regret is that I didn't find them sooner!!! I can't wait for the next project to begin.

—Gina Trimarco

The thought of writing my story was overwhelming at first. The Ignite Team was great as far as offering guidance and support through the whole process. Everyone was friendly and eager to help. Thank you for helping me find my voice and share my story.

—Jenette Longoria

The collaborative journey with the team has been nothing short of amazing. Their talent was remarkable, and their patience was deeply appreciated. This experience has truly been exceptional.

—Jennifer Salimi

There aren't enough words to express how grateful I am to have had the opportunity to work with the Ignite Team, once again. Writing in two books simultaneously can be overwhelming. However, the excellent support you receive from working with a team that motivates you, celebrates your successes with sincere enthusiasm and brings out the best in your writing abilities has been nothing short of amazing! Thank you, Ignite Team, for believing in me when I didn't believe in myself.

—Karen R. Rosser

This has been a journey. I didn't expect so many emotions to come while writing this chapter, but it did. The Ignite team has been amazing! Special thank you to Sarah. That first Kindle with you was amazing. You helped me to outline my story. Mimi!! You are so gifted; thank you so much for helping me find and express those feelings and emotions that I needed to share. JB, you are who you are. Thank you for sprinkling that JB magic in my story.

—Lameeka Harris

Working with Lady JB and the Ignite team has been a fabulous experience for me. The team is caring, supportive, and smart! The editing team helped me take my story to another level - Thank You All! What an amazing journey this has been - I'm forever grateful.

—Marica Klostermann

Ignite helped me discover and hone my talents, passions, and creative drive in the realm of writing. Through their books, I have forged lasting bonds and found endless inspiration.

—Michi Couchman

My ignite journey has been nothing short of an incredible experience. The editing sessions were a joy, and I love JB's beautiful energy. The polishing sessions were my favorite out of the entire editing process. I have many other great memories etched into my consciousness from the experience. Like the moments when my story's seemingly unimportant elements were so skilfully amplified that they danced vividly in my mind as I brought my story together.

—Naomi Zion Mark

To be selected to write another chapter has left me in awe of how compassionate and loving this tribe is. The Ignite Your Courage community and Ignite Publishing is more than just a group—it's a supportive family that empowers each member to overcome their fears and embrace the unknown. From the moment I joined, I felt a genuine sense of belonging that I'd never experienced before. You should join the next chapter, don't think twice!

—Nolan Pillay

Being a part of this book process was a beautiful journey—a chapter I have wanted to make a reality for a long time. The wisdom and guidance from the Ignite team have been absolutely inspiring. This experience has been exactly what I needed to get my writing ignited. I see many more projects on my horizon. Thank you, Ignite team!

—Sandra Von Hollen

Writing gives a speakerphone to the whispers of our soul. Ignite turns the megaphone on and teaches us how to use it. Ignite gives the greatest support- technical and emotional- to make the journey for every writer, from 1st timer to seasoned author, the most amazing experience.

—Stacey Sellar

Contents

WHAT IS AN IGNITE BOOK?

Ignite Publishing has been the leader of Empowerment Publishing for the past half-decade. We sprung onto the scene with a desire to disrupt the publishing industry with books that only tell powerful, authentic, heart-felt stories designed to change lives. As we surpassed our twentieth compilation book, with over 700+ authors published, we feel we are doing just that: empowering others, igniting lives, and making a massive difference on the planet that will inspire generations for centuries to come.

The very word *Ignite* signifies the intention of our books and describes the goal behind each story we share. We see our books as gifts to the world, igniting ideas, thoughts, feelings, and desires in those who read them. Every book we publish is created with the intention to elevate, transform, and *Ignite* the reader toward something greater within themselves. We believe that our books and the stories inside them connect hearts, foster love, bridge gaps, and form a deeper understanding within us. The wonderful stories inside our books are divinely shared so that they become a beacon of empowerment for every person on the planet.

Ignite believes that stories and the genuine sharing of them is the key not only to bringing people together but to healing humanity on a global scale. Stories speak directly to the heart of the reader and touch them in a heartfelt and profound way. Honest and authentic stories open the mind and expand compassion, foster connection, and bring forth the kind of joy that we all desire to have. Stories showcase our commonalities and show how we are more alike than different. They speak of the common denominator we all know, the beautiful human experience.

Each story in this book has been created to encourage you on a deeper level. They are designed to awaken your mind while speaking directly to your heart and instilling a new sense of courage and purpose. As you begin reading an Ignite story, you will find that each one begins with an inspiring *Power Quote*. It is an empowering statement designed to push you forward and challenge you to break outside your comfort zone. Power quotes are phrases that offer insight and motivation. They are meaningful statements intended to Ignite ideas, spark actions, and evoke change. Every power quote is written to activate something in you, so you can be all that you desire to become and, ideally, Ignite another person.

Since this book is all about igniting one's life, each power quote is designed to activate a deeper connection within you. They are written with the intention that whatever you have gone through, or are going through, you can use your inner knowing, to move forward to overcome what might be in your way. The wonderful thing about each story is that it is unique, personal, and intimate. A person's path is unique to them, but the power behind their experience is universal among us all. These stories show a connection to something greater: ourselves. They shine a light on the power within us with the hope they will inspire you.

After the power quote, you will find the author's personal *Intention*. These are the individual insights and genuine wishes the author wants to share with you, as well as their intention for what you will gain from reading their authentic story. Each author came into this book with a desire to IGNITE something in you, and they share that lovingly in their opening intention. From the very beginning, they want you to know they want their story to indeed Ignite something greater in you.

After the intention, you will read the author's transformational *Ignite Moment*. It is a genuine sharing of the author's journey and how they emerge through it with a greater understanding of themselves. Through their unique experiences and circumstances, the authors explain how their Ignite Moment transformed them, awakened them, and set them on a new trajectory in life. They reveal their honest feelings and share their personal discoveries. They give an insightful account of the exact pivotal moment when an inner awakening created a valuable understanding that there was more within themselves.

We all have Ignite Moments that change us, define us, and set us forth on a wonderful new journey of inner exploration. The stories in this book are derived from those moments and are told in the most endearing and empowering way. They show us that *life-altering* situations are designed to impact us in a way that inspires us to step into the person we were born to become. Ignite Moments are universal and transcend all barriers. They allow us to be more connected on a deeper level, showing how we are all One in many ways.

To take each story to another level, you will discover the authors' share exciting *Ignite Action Steps* at the end of every chapter. They want to provide doable actions that you can use to benefit yourself. Each action step is an idea, process, or practice they have used to succeed in their own life. The goal is for you to implement an action step into your life and provoke positive change. Each Ignite Action Step is different and unique, *just like you*, and each has proven to have amazing results when done diligently and consistently.

As you sit down to read this book, know that it is not required that you read it in the traditional way by starting at the beginning and reading through to the end. Many readers flip to a page at random and read from there, trusting that the page they landed on holds the exact story they need to read. Others glance over the table of contents, searching for the title that resonates with them. Some readers will go directly to a story recommended by a friend. However you decide to read this book, we trust it will be right for you. We know that you may read it from cover to cover in one single sitting or pick it up and put it down a dozen times. The way you read an Ignite book is as personal as every story in it, so we give you complete permission to enjoy it in whatever way fits you.

We ask that if a story touches you in some way or inspires your heart, you reach out and tell the author. Your words will mean the world to them. Since our book is all about igniting humanity, we want to foster more of that among all of us. Feel free to share your sentiments with the authors by using their contact information at the end of the book. There isn't an Ignite author who wouldn't love to hear from you and know that somehow their story positively impacted your life. And, if a story speaks to you profoundly, we encourage you to share it with someone special who may need to read it, as that story may just be the exact thing they need to help Ignite their life.

We know you will find a part of your story reflected in the wisdom, wishes, and dreams of the many authors here. Somewhere within these pages will be a reflection of *your* journey and the Ignite Moments you have felt. We know this because Ignite stories represent the stories in all of us. It doesn't matter where you live, your skin color, gender, or how much money you have in your pocket; Ignite stories reflect everyone. They are stories of the human condition; they touch the very essence of what makes us human and our powerful human experience. They bring us together, showing us that our stories do not define us but, instead, refine who we can become.

As you turn the page, we want to welcome you to the Ignite family. We are excited for what is about to happen because we know the stories in this book will inspire transformation. As you dive into the upcoming pages, a million different emotions will fill your heart, and a kindred spirit with our authors will be established. We know that this will be a book that both awakens and inspires, transforms, and motivates.

May you be loved and supported from this page forward, and may all your Ignite Moments be filled with both joyful lessons and heart-filled blessings.

Peter Giesin

INTRODUCTION

BY PETER GIESIN

"Courage is the flame that lights the path of possibilities."

AWAKENING THE COURAGE WITHIN

Courage. It's not just a word; it's a heartbeat, a tremor, a tear, a smile, a leap into the unknown. It's the essence that dwells within us, calling us to rise, to strive, to dare, and to become. It's a force that compels us to embrace the pain, face the fear, and step into the light. Courage is our deepest connection to life, a profound journey into the very core of what it means to be human.

How often have we felt the pull of courage, that inner longing to break free from the ordinary, to reach for something higher, something more profound? How many times have we stood at the crossroads of life, feeling the weight of decision, the fear of failure, the call to adventure? How many tears have we shed in the name of courage? How many triumphs have we celebrated? Courage is our story, our dance, our song.

The stories you find on the pages of *Ignite Your Courage* are not a distant study; instead, they will lead you on a deeply personal, emotional odyssey into the heart of who we are as humans. It's about the moments that define us, the decisions that shape us, the connections that fulfill us. It's about love, loss, hope, despair, dreams, and realities.

Ignite Your Courage is a melange of beautiful and touching tales that delve into the heart of human existence. Each chapter, every line, and word is an ode to our shared journey of love, pain, joy, and discovery. Each unique story resonates on a profoundly personal level, reminding me of my dance with vulnerability and strength. Reflecting on my personal experiences in life, my heart swells with an overwhelming mix of emotions as the many stories remind me of the times when my courage was also put to the test.

My Ironman journey was not just a test of physical endurance for me; it was a deep dive into my soul's depths. Each stroke in the water, every pedal on the cycle, and the relentless steps during the run were interlaced with raw emotion. There were moments of sheer exhaustion, where tears stung my eyes, not from pain but from the surge of emotions, memories of past failures, and the burning desire to prove to myself that I was enough.

Standing outside the Neonatal Intensive Care Unit window, watching my tiny newborn daughter labor for every breath, my heart felt as if it was in a vice grip. It was a cocktail of hope and despair, love and fear. The cold, sterile walls echoed with the soft cries of babies, and every beep of the machines felt like a ticking clock, measuring hope in milliseconds. Every fiber of my being was stretched thin, teetering between breaking down and mustering strength for my little one.

Leaving the farm after high school graduation was akin to tearing away a part of my soul. The sights and sounds I had grown up with were not just memories, but fragments of my identity. The comfort of the familiar, the rustle of leaves, the early morning mist on the fields, and the chorus of farm animals were the lullaby of my childhood. Packing my life into suitcases felt like a betrayal of my roots. The weight of nostalgia was almost unbearable. But intertwined with that was the magnetic pull of the unknown, the allure of the city, and the promises it whispered.

The drive to New York City was a whirlwind of emotions. Every mile was a journey from the past into the future. The rearview mirror seemed to hold a montage of my life, while the road ahead shimmered with potential and new experiences. I remember holding the steering wheel so tight, my knuckles turned white, not from the fear of the journey but from the overwhelming surge of emotions—the heady mix of excitement, fear, and the raw pain of leaving behind a part of oneself.

Many of the emotions I felt throughout those poignant moments are embedded within the pages here. *Ignite Your Courage* is more than just a book; it is a mirror. It reflects the mosaic of emotions we all feel the silent tears, the jubilant laughter, the tremors of fear, and the steady beat of hope. It reminds us that beneath the veneer of strength, we are all beautifully human, raw and real, bound by the threads of emotions that make us alive, that make us feel.

The stories you will find in this book resonate deeply with me, reminding me of the intricate dance of emotions and experiences I've lived through. Commitment, optimism, understanding, resilience, action, growth, and empathy aren't just concepts; they're the very foundation upon which I've built my life.

For me, courage isn't just about dedication; it's an unyielding fire in my belly, a burning passion that has often kept me going when everything else seems bleak. It's the promises I've made to myself during those quiet, introspective nights. When I pair this fierce commitment with optimism, even the loneliest, most desolate hours feel surmountable. There have been nights when I've been enveloped in darkness, drowning in despair, but the glimmer of hope that optimism provides has always been my north star, guiding me toward a new dawn.

Understanding this concept has been a journey of deep introspection. It has transcended the realm of mere compassion for me. It's the quiet tears I've shed, feeling the pain of another, realizing that our stories, though different, are intertwined in the grand tapestry of human existence. It's the scars on my soul, the battles I've fought, the times I've been knocked down, only to rise stronger. It's not just about facing adversity; it's the raw, gut-wrenching pain of being brought to my knees and the exhilarating feeling of standing tall again.

Throughout my life, each step I've taken, every decision, every teardrop, and every laugh line has etched indelible marks on my sands of time. This journey, fraught with transformations, has been the dance of my soul. A dance where I've twirled between past regrets and future hopes, shedding old skins and emerging renewed. Courage has been my compass, connecting me to others and reminding me of shared dreams, collective joys, and the heartbreaks we've all felt so deeply.

With a heart filled with emotions, I've spent countless hours reflecting, hoping to offer insights that might resonate with you, the reader, as you embark on your own journey of courage. I believe you're here because, like me, you've felt the gnawing uncertainties, faced daunting challenges, and sought a guiding light. Perhaps you're searching for that spark, a kindred spirit, or a road map to harness the power of courage. Whatever mysterious twist of fate brought this book into your hands, let it be a beacon to ignite the deepest corners of your heart and soul, pulling you magnetically closer to the dreams you've dared not utter.

In moments of doubt or despair, may courage be the warm embrace you never knew you needed, the whispered encouragement in the still of night. And, let the myriad facets of courage that are shared throughout the book, from its quiet whispers to its roaring cries, be the guiding star you've so fervently yearned for, leading you to moments of unparalleled growth, unshakable strength, and transformative self-discovery.

The Seven Pillars of Courage

Since courage can mean many things to many people, let's delve deeper into the realms within the word C.O.U.R.A.G.E and see how each letter is a testament to our spirit and tenacity, pushing us toward finding our greatest selves. If we were to break down the very essence of courage, it would be:

Commitment + Optimism + Understanding + Resilience + Action + Growth + Empathy

In this ever-shifting world, where challenges loom like giants and the ground beneath feels unsteady, delving into the profound facets of courage becomes our heartfelt sanctuary. These aren't just words; they're the soulful whispers that guide us through the storm. They remind us that commitment is our unwavering anchor, optimism is the hopeful glimmer in the darkest nights, understanding the tender hand that builds bridges, resilience is the quiet force that lifts us after every fall, action is the brave step into unknown horizons, growth is our soul's blossoming, and empathy the warm embrace that tells us we're never alone. Embracing these elements, we not only navigate life's challenges but also touch its very essence, painting our journey with colors of love, strength, and purpose.

From the depths of my heart and the chasm of my experiences, I will share a few Mini Ignite Moments on how I've embraced each facet of courage and used it to move me forward. With courage as a guide, I eagerly invite you to reflect on your own life to witness how every challenge morphs into an opportunity, every wound into a lesson, and every triumph into a testament to our unwavering spirit. May the moment in my life become an odyssey of discovery and profound transformation in your life as you see the many ways courage has inspired me.

COMMITMENT: BEYOND JUST PROMISES

"Courage starts with showing up and letting ourselves be seen."
- Brené Brown

Commitment, in its very essence, is an intense expression of one's courage. When we envision courage, our minds often instantly drift toward grand tales of heroism, warriors in battle, or individuals facing overwhelming odds. Yet, tucked within the ordinary tapestry of life, in its mundane routines and over-looked corners, there exists a form of courage just as profound—the courage of commitment.

This dedication demands a unique brand of bravery. While it might be simpler in some respects, to summon courage in a fleeting, singular moment of uncertainty, it's infinitely more taxing to maintain that same courage con-sistently, over time. It's the difference between sprinting a hundred meters and running a marathon—both demand strength and resilience, but the latter requires a deep-seated commitment.

Think of the countless examples around us: The parent who, without fanfare, dedicates every waking moment to ensure their child's well-being; the writer, who despite countless rejections, remains committed to their craft, believing in the power of their words; or the environmentalist, who, in the face of increas-ing global crises, continues to advocate for the planet. Such commitment isn't about a momentary burst of enthusiasm but rather a sustained flame that burns even in the fiercest winds of adversity.

Commitment carries with it a potent vulnerability. To commit fully is to lay oneself bare to the very real possibility of disappointment or failure. Still, it's this very vulnerability that makes commitment so beautifully courageous. It's a testament to hope, to the unwavering belief in the possibility of a brighter tomorrow, even if today's horizon seems bleak.

Everyone who steadfastly clings to their passion, goals, or relationships has a saga of valor, even if it's not sung aloud. Sometimes, the most profound acts of bravery are witnessed in the quiet, rhythmic heartbeats of a soul deeply committed to a cause, a dream, or another being. The dance of life is enriched and empowered by these beats, and this pulse of commitment crafts the most enduring tales of courage.

Mini Ignite Moment: The Code of Courage and Commitment

Teaching had always been my passion, but it quickly became evident that it couldn't provide for every essential need I had as a parent and single father. With every bill that arrived, every school expense, and every unexpected cost, I felt the weight of my commitment to my 2 children, Jackson and Jorja, deepening.

On one particularly challenging night, surrounded by bills and under the dim glow of my desk lamp, I made one of the hardest decisions of my life. The financial strain was evident, and a return to the IT world, a path I once knew well, became the only way forward. The choice wasn't merely about a career shift—it was an act of courage, a testament to my commitment to my children.

Re-immersing myself in the world of codes, algorithms, and systems took work. I traded my comfortable space at the head of a classroom for late-night shifts in front of glowing computer screens. I remember holding that first paycheck and feeling a cascade of emotions. The comfort of financial security was marred by the sting of a dream temporarily set aside.

But, when I looked into Jorja's hopeful eyes and heard Jackon's infectious laughter, I found the strength to push forward. My children became my anchors, reminding me daily of why I had made the leap. My commitment to them was unwavering, and their trust in me became my guiding light.

I sat hunched over my laptop, and Jorja approached with genuine curiosity about my work. As I explained the world of coding to her and Jackson sat sketching our moment, a profound realization washed over me. I might have stepped away from a traditional classroom but hadn't stopped teaching. My lessons were about courage, perseverance, and the depth of commitment a father has for his children.

Life's curriculum had changed, but the core lesson remained: When faced with challenges, our courage and unwavering commitment to those we love define us. My journey into single fatherhood, underpinned by the strength to shift careers, became my most significant teaching moment. It wasn't just about codes or classroom lectures—it was about living a life that exemplified the values I held dear.

Action Step

Make a Commitment Pledge: *Pledge a commitment to take courageous action for the next month. It could be a personal goal or a promise to someone. Record it, take steps toward it, then revisit it after a month and see how far that commitment has taken you.*

OPTIMISM: THE GOLDEN RAYS OF HOPE

"Optimism is the faith that leads to achievement.
Nothing can be done without hope and confidence."
- Helen Keller

Optimism, in many ways, is the very embodiment of courage. It's not just a positive outlook, but a deeply courageous stance to adopt, especially when surrounded by challenges. It means looking past the immediate hardships, pushing the daunting shadows aside, and firmly believing in our untapped potential. This viewpoint demands the bravery to envision a brighter horizon, to dream beyond current limitations, and to remain undeterred even when towering obstacles stand in our way.

Every drop of your optimism isn't merely a fleeting feeling; it's a testament to the courageous spirit that resides deep within you. It's that resilient whisper echoing in the recesses of your soul, constantly assuring you, *Keep marching forward; there's so much more ahead*, even when the terrain beneath feels unstable. Consider it as your inner compass, your eternal flame, always illuminating the path, always instilling confidence in the unwavering strength you carry within.

Choosing to hold on to optimism is, in itself, a heroic act. It's the decision to keep your gaze fixed on the distant beacon, even when torrential rain blurs your vision. Let this optimism elevate you, making you soar above the densest clouds and steering you toward a destiny bursting with boundless possibilities. And never mistake it for sheer naivety or simple positivity; it's so much more. It's a powerful affirmation of your courage, a reflection of your steadfast commitment to living with unparalleled hope, elegance, and indestructible faith in the journey you've embarked upon.

Mini Ignite Moment: Echoes from the Screen

During the winter of 2013, in a hotel in downtown Detroit, I felt suffocated by my surroundings. The relentless snowstorm outside mirrored the tempest of emotions churning within me. Each gust of wind echoed the whispers of doubt and loneliness that threatened to consume me. The isolation was palpable; only the low hum of the hotel's heating system and the occasional muffled sounds from distant rooms reminded me I wasn't entirely alone.

It was a desolate afternoon as I grappled with thoughts of inadequacy and despair and aimlessly turned on the hotel TV, seeking some form of distraction from the bleak narrative playing in my mind. Most channels were disrupted by the storm, but one seemed clear.

It was a documentary about educators, showcasing their profound impact on young minds. I watched teachers connect with students, igniting passion, hope, and purpose. Something stirred within me as the testimonials from students filled the screen, recounting the life-changing moments these teachers brought into their lives.

And then, in a moment I can only describe as surreal, a voice emerged from the television, distinct from the documentary's narrative. "Peter," it began, resonating with an uncanny familiarity that sent chills down my spine, "Your true calling is to inspire, lead, and shape young minds. Consider this path."

I blinked in disbelief, thinking perhaps my distraught state was playing tricks on my mind. But the voice persisted, gentle yet firm, "You've been seeking purpose and connection, Peter. Teaching can be the conduit."

A glint caught my eye in that harrowing moment: a framed photo of my daughter on the nightstand. Her radiant smile, her eyes gleaming with mischief and love, held a drawing of us—a simple, happy family. The note on the back, written in her childish scribble, read: To Daddy, my hero. I love you. Come back soon!

That simple note cracked the dam within me. Tears, hot and cathartic, flowed freely. Her pure, innocent love pulled me back from the precipice. It was a stark reminder of the lifelines that awaited me, of the reasons to keep pushing forward.

The room, which moments ago had been a space of despair, now felt different. The weight on my chest began to lift. I thought of my daughter's drawing and her message to me, and suddenly it all seemed to connect. She saw me as her hero, her guide. Could I be that for others?

From the chilling atmosphere of that hotel room, a reborn Peter stepped forth, not as the man he once was, but as a powerhouse of confidence and determination. As an educator, he began to impact lives in ways that surpassed even his boldest expectations.

As the relentless snowstorm slowly calmed in the ensuing days, a new resolve solidified within him. By the time he set foot back in New Jersey, his trajectory was set in stone. The corporate ladder no longer enticed him; instead, he was drawn to the world of education. That voice from the TV, real or imagined, had catalyzed a transformation, guiding him to a realm of unparalleled fulfillment.

Action Step

Create a vision board *with images and quotes that fill you with hope. Share it with friends or keep it personal.*

UNDERSTANDING: MORE THAN WORDS

"To understand the heart and mind of a person, look not at what he has already achieved, but at what he aspires to."
- Khalil Gibran

Understanding, in its true essence, is undeniably an act of immense courage. It goes far beyond simply acknowledging another's viewpoint or empathizing with their situation. It demands the boldness to genuinely immerse oneself in another's life experiences, to wholeheartedly embrace their joys and sorrows, and to genuinely perceive the world through their eyes. Understanding isn't just about extending sympathy or showing compassion; it's about forging a courageous and authentic bond, a soulful connection that recognizes and reveres our intrinsic shared human experience.

The understanding you cultivate acts as a resilient bridge, a conduit that seamlessly links you to the hearts and minds of others. It's not merely a passive act; it's an active engagement, a journey of profound discovery. Through this lens of understanding, you gain insights into the souls of those around you and embark on a transformative odyssey of self-awareness. You start to grasp the profound truth that each one of us, despite our unique backgrounds and life stories, is intrinsically intertwined in the intricate tapestry of life.

To truly embrace understanding requires courageously delving beyond superficial perceptions and fleeting judgments. It urges you to navigate the vast oceans of human emotions, traverse the intricate landscapes of varied perspectives, and passionately seek out those golden threads of commonality that weave us all together. This pursuit of understanding, powered by sheer courage and genuine curiosity, becomes your master key—a key that not only unlocks richer, more compassionate interactions with others but also paves the way for a life teeming with depth, fulfillment, and a profound sense of belonging in this vast cosmos.

Mini Ignite Moment: Understanding Across Generations

As I leaned against the old wooden fence, the vast expanse of our family farmland stretched out in front of me, an ever-present reminder of my roots. This landscape, with its lush grass pastures swaying in the gentle breeze, had been the backdrop to my childhood. Yet this visit was over-shadowed by a palpable sense of sorrow. I was here to bid adieu to my father, the man who had always been the anchor to this land and our family.

From my earliest memories, the farm had felt both comforting and constricting. As a young boy, I would often climb the tallest tree or stand atop the barn's roof, looking out at the distant horizon and dreaming of the vast world that awaited. My youthful heart was restless, filled with a burning desire to explore the terrains and tales that lay beyond our farm.

The day I decided to embark on my global journey, the weight of my decision hung heavily between my father and me. "Why would you for-sake all this, son? This land has nourished our family for generations. Everything you need, everything you are, is right here," he had lamented, genuine bewilderment clouding his eyes. I responded with an earnest smile, a mix of excitement and guilt, promising him that I'd be back. While I wanted to wander through bustling foreign streets, hike uncharted trails, and soak up the world's diverse cultures, I silently hoped that one day he'd understand my insatiable curiosity.

My travels became a tapestry of memories: the intoxicating aromas of street food in London, the serene beauty of the Spanish coastal cities, the symphony of languages in a bustling European square, and the profound solitude of the Canadian wilderness. Each experience, each encounter, expanded my understanding of the world and my place in it.

Yet, during a rare moment of reprieve sitting on the front porch watching the sunset over the horizon, I turned to my father, seeking answers. "Dad, in all these years, didn't you ever yearn to see what's beyond these fields?"

He looked at the vastness before us, his face etched with lines of time and toil. "This farm is a living chronicle, son. Your great-grandparents tilled this soil, I played here as a boy, and you, you started your grand adventure from here. While you found purpose in distant lands, my purpose was always here, nurturing the ground, watching the seasons change, and preserving the legacy handed down to me."

In that moment, the gap that had grown between us over the years began to close. I realized how mistaken I'd been, thinking of him as unadventurous. His adventure was different—it was one of dedication, resilience, and deep-rooted love for our ancestral land.

The sky transitioned from hues of amber to a deep blue, with the stars shining down on us. We sat in a comfortable silence, two souls bound by blood and understanding, each on our own unique journey. The beauty of that night was in recognizing that courage and adventure manifest in myriad ways. It was in finding value not just in the paths we choose but also in the ones we don't. And as the night deepened, the connection between a wandering son and his steadfast father was beautifully and irrevocably reaffirmed.

Action Step

Engage in a conversation with someone different from you. Share your learnings and learn from them.

RESILIENCE: THE UNDYING SPIRIT

"Courage doesn't always roar. Sometimes courage is the quiet voice at the end of the day saying, 'I will try again tomorrow.'"
- Mary Anne Radmacher

Resilience is undeniably the epitome of courage in its most dynamic form. It's that relentless spark, that tenacious flame within us that refuses to be extinguished, no matter how fierce the winds of adversity may blow. Resilience is personified by the unwavering inner warrior, one that may be momentarily staggered but rises, time and time again, embodying the essence of endurance and determination. It's about confronting life's multifaceted challenges not with trepidation but with an amalgamation of grace, discernment, and unparalleled fortitude.

Your personal resilience is a stirring testament to the boundless capacities of the human spirit. It paints a vivid narrative of survival, adaptability, and regeneration—it's the art of gathering shattered shards, mending deep-seated scars, evolving from wounds, and sculpting them into magnificent masterpieces of growth and wisdom. An affirmation of the unparalleled courage it takes to metamorphose—to draw beauty from anguish, derive power from vulnerability, and mold sagacity out of past missteps.

Envision resilience as your most valiant compass, leading you through the labyrinth of life with an unwavering hand. Allow it to be your guide, teaching you to not merely endure but to cherish every facet of your journey—the missteps, heartaches, elation, and monumental victories. Each of these moments, these snippets of time, aren't mere happenings; they're intricate chapters of an epic tale. A tale that is uniquely yours, echoing the testament of your inner mettle, your personal evolution, and your unyielding spirit that refuses to be tamed by life's unpredictable tempests.

Mini Ignite Moment: My Lesson on Two Wheels

When my wife approached me with her eyes alight with a fire, I knew all too well that she was about to propose something, "How about a tandem bike ride to Alaska?" I felt my stomach drop. This wasn't just another one of our playful ventures. Her voice quivered with excitement as she painted images of the Yukon and the ethereal Top of the World Highway. But me? I was paralyzed by a silent storm of anxiety and doubt.

It wasn't the daunting distance that gnawed at me but the fear of the unknown, the unspoken trials that lay ahead. Every evening leading up to our departure, as I'd lay in bed, I'd feel an internal tug-of-war. The juxtaposition of her bubbling excitement and my festering apprehensions created a silent chasm between us.

The initial days were hard. Every pedal was a reminder of my internal battle. While she reveled in nature's symphony, often pointing out a hawk soaring or the mesmerizing pattern of stars, my heart was weighed down by a constant murmur of 'what ifs.'

Still, the Yukon, with its relentless rains and treacherous terrains, was where our journey truly began, at least for me. One evening, tied to the bone and struggling with leg cramps, I felt close to breaking. Doubt, like an old ghost, whispered defeat into my ear. Yet, in that very moment of despair, I heard my darling wife's voice. It wasn't her words but the unwavering tone, humming a gentle and inspiring tune in the fading daylight. The uplifting melody reached past my turmoil. Her resilience began to chip away at my walls.

Then came the day our bike faltered. I remember sinking to the ground, overwhelmed by the weight of our predicament. But my wife? She knelt beside the bike, tools in hand, face streaked with sweat and determination, and whispered, "We can do this." Watching her, a realization dawned on me: This journey was less about the path we took and more about the emotional landscapes we traversed together.

By the time the formidable expanse of the Top of the World Highway stretched before us, I felt reborn. The vast Alaskan panorama was magnificent, but the reflection of our combined strength, vulnerability, and resilience truly took my breath away.

Back in our hometown, surrounded by the comforts of familiarity, I found myself reminiscing. The tandem journey was far more than just a physical quest; it was an exploration of our inner terrains. Through biting winds, treacherous paths, and moments of doubt, I discovered the profound depths of resilience.

To me, resilience was no longer just a word. It embodied courage, love, vulnerability, and strength. Every push, every pedal was a testament to the human spirit's ability to rise, even when weighed down by doubt. Thanks to my wife and our shared odyssey, I now know that true resilience is not just enduring but evolving with every challenge and every heartbeat.

Action Step

Create a Resilience Timeline: *Draw a timeline of your life. Mark the highs and lows and reflect on how you bounced back from the lows.*

Action: The Footsteps of Bravery

*"Courage is not the absence of fear, but rather the
assessment that something else is more important than fear."*
- Franklin D. Roosevelt

In its true essence, action stands as the tangible embodiment of courage. It's the culmination of our innermost convictions, manifested in deliberate motion, pushing us toward our aspirations even when shrouded in doubt or overshadowed by fear. Action isn't merely about movement; it's about forging a conscious connection to the wellspring of bravery that resides within us, empowering us to sculpt our destiny and transform our dreams into reality.

Your actions, big or small, echo the resilient chorus of your courageous heart. They represent the strategic, purpose-driven strides you take toward your objectives, signaling your unwavering commitment to fully embrace life's vast expanse with enthusiasm and zeal. With every choice you make, every hurdle you overcome, and every moment you seize, your courage radiates, leaving an indelible mark on the canvas of time.

Approach action with unyielding resolve and spirited determination. Let it become the rhythmic beat that sets the tempo for your life's dance, the guiding star illuminating your journey to aspirations, and the surge of bravery that fuels your onward march. Remember, each action you undertake is akin to penning a chapter in the magnificent narrative of your life. A story in the making unfolds with each step you take, charting a course toward a horizon replete with endless possibilities, profound insights, and a promise of unparalleled fulfillment.

Mini Ignite Moment: A Step into Trust

I've always felt a pull toward giving back. Living in central New Jersey, an undeniable sense of community made me want to contribute in any way I could. That call to service became clear when a close friend went missing on a hike. Thankfully, he was found and rescued, but the experience made me join the local search and rescue team.

During my training, one exercise was particularly memorable. I stood at the edge of a cliff, feeling the weight of the harness around me. My task was simple but terrifying: stepping backward off the edge. Below, it felt like an endless abyss. My heart thudded loudly in my chest, and I could feel my nerves fraying.

"Trust your team," my instructor's voice broke through my hesitation. I could see the conviction in his eyes.

I leaned back with a deep breath and a final prayer, surrendering to the void. A rush of adrenaline followed, but what overwhelmed me was the strong grip of the rope and the security it offered. My team had me, and I felt a profound realization that sometimes courage meant relying on others.

It wasn't long after that the true test came. We received an urgent call about a disabled hiker lost in the New Jersey swamps. The cold was biting, and the night was impenetrably dark. Armed with torches, we ventured into the swamp, the weight of responsibility heavy on our shoulders.

Each hour that passed was a fight against the elements. The mud seemed intent on slowing us down, the cold gnawed at our resolve, and the vastness of the swamp was daunting. Yet, with every step, I drew strength from the team's unity.

By dawn, we found the hiker, cold and frightened but alive. The return journey was no less challenging, but our determination only grew with the weight of a life in our hands. We emerged from the swamp as the first rays of the sun touched the horizon, grateful and victorious.

Back at the camp, as we sat huddled around a fire, I reflected on the night's events. The step off the cliff, the trust I put in my team, and our mission in the swamp underscored the power of collective courage. It was an awakening for me; to understand that bravery wasn't always about facing challenges head-on alone but often about placing faith in those beside you.

Through the search and rescue team, I didn't just gain skills; I learned an invaluable lesson about the essence of action. It wasn't just about moving forward but about moving together, stepping into the unknown with trust and unwavering determination. It's a lesson I carry with me to this day.

Action Step

Make an Action Checklist: *List three actions you've been hesitating to take. Commit to doing one of them this week and the other two the week after that.*

GROWTH: THE UNENDING ASCENT

"Growth is never by mere chance; it's the result of forces working together."
- James Cash Penney

Growth, at its core, is an audacious voyage. It's the bold endeavor of facing adversities head-on, gleaning lessons from setbacks, and relentlessly pushing ourselves beyond the confines of our comfort zones. This journey isn't just about scaling heights or achieving milestones; it's about the deeply intimate process of metamorphosis, of shedding our older selves to emerge renewed, more aligned with our true potential. It's an expedition fueled by the unwavering courage to change, mature, and truly flourish.

Your personal evolution stands as a profound testament to your innate bravery. It encapsulates the myriad experiences you've navigated—the peaks of elation, the valleys of despair, the triumphant successes, and the humbling missteps. Each moment, whether joyous or challenging, acts as a stepping stone, propelling you further on your journey. It showcases your steadfast courage to venture into the unknown, assimilate new insights, and continuously redefine your horizons.

Let the spirit of growth serve as your intrepid compass. Welcome it not just with anticipation but with an expansive heart, insatiable curiosity, and boundless love. Your journey of growth isn't merely a sequence of events or a set trajectory; it's a mesmerizing dance. A dance where each step, each twist and turn, represents a new phase of transformation, unveiling layers of self-discovery and opening doors to a universe brimming with boundless opportunities and untapped potential.

Mini Ignite Moment: Dancing Through Prejudice

When I was a teenager, university felt like a whirlwind. Every corner of the campus was an avenue to a new experience, each day presenting an opportunity to step outside my comfort zone. At nineteen, amidst the tangle of my introversion and societal expectations, I unexpectedly stumbled upon an experience that would define my journey.

It was a Thursday afternoon. I had just finished my physics lecture early, and the quiet hum of the emptying hallways beckoned me to explore parts of the university I hadn't yet ventured into. Without any particular destination in mind, I walked, letting my intuition guide me.

As I turned a corner, the sound of soft piano music caressed my ears, accompanied by the rhythmic pat of feet against wooden floors. Curiosity piqued, I followed the melody and found myself peering through a slightly ajar door into the university's dance studio. Inside, a ballet class was in session. The fluidity and grace of the dancers were spellbinding. Their bodies told stories, each movement a word, each leap a sentence.

Being from a family that cherished soccer and scoffed at dance, I had never considered ballet as something for me. And yet, I was drawn to it at that moment. My heart raced from admiration for the art and an unexpected, buried desire to be a part of it.

The next day, still replaying the beauty of the class in my mind, I mustered the courage to approach the instructor. Ms. Lorraine, a woman with expressive eyes and a demeanor that radiated both warmth and stern discipline, listened to my hesitant request.

"I'd like to join the class. I know it's uncommon for boys, especially someone like me with zero experience, but..." I trailed off, unable to find the words to explain my sudden passion.

She smiled, "Why not?"

And just like that, I was a part of the ballet troupe. The initial weeks were grueling. My body resisted, my mind questioned, and yes, there were whispers. "Did you see? The physics nerd is trying ballet!" "It's such a girl thing; what's he thinking?"

But with every fall, every misstep, I grew. With Ms. Lorraine's guidance and my own persistence, I learned that the journey of growth isn't about external validation but about understanding oneself. My introvertedness, which I thought would be a hindrance, became my strength. I listened more, observed keenly, and took in every detail, which helped me grasp the nuances of ballet.

The final university recital was a testament to my journey. I danced with the troupe, my movements as fluid as any, my heart light, and my spirit free. As the curtain fell and the applause roared, I realized that growth indeed is an audacious voyage. And I had set sail, with ballet shoes as my compass, towards a horizon I hadn't known existed.

Action Step

Develop a **Growth Tree:** Draw a tree with roots representing your past, the trunk of your present, and branches of your future aspirations. Add leaves for each achievement.

Empathy: The Universal Bond
"I believe empathy is the most essential quality of civilization."
- Roger Ebert

Empathy is truly the embodiment of courage, imbued with the soft warmth of human connection. It's not merely the skill to resonate with others but an innate capacity to delve deep into their souls, to genuinely comprehend their emotions, and to reflect back with compassion and understanding. Empathy requires us to muster the bravery to temporarily set aside our own shields, venture into the emotional landscapes of others, and share in their experiences, be it joy or pain.

Your empathy is a testament to your courageous commitment to fostering genuine connections. It is both an honor and a challenge, an opportunity to bridge gaps and a journey into the emotional depths of those around you. It signifies your valor to love unabashedly, extend a healing touch, and be a beacon of solace and understanding in a world often riddled with indifference.

I urge you to wholeheartedly embrace empathy, fortified with the courage to truly see the world through the eyes of others, to lend a listening ear without judgment, and to immerse yourself in their feelings. Let this empathetic spirit guide your interpersonal relationships and the broader choices and paths you undertake in life. You become a vessel of love, understanding, and inspiration by embodying empathy. This isn't just an individual journey; it's a collective movement toward forging a world that thrives on compassion, unity, and an unwavering bond of shared humanity.

Mini Ignite Moment: The Unexpected Lessons

During my teenage years, I took on a summer job that reshaped my perception of life in ways I never imagined. I began working as an orderly at the local old age home, thinking it would be straightforward—changing beds, delivering meals, and occasionally pushing a wheelchair. Little did I know it would be an unforgettable journey through the tapestries of so many lives.

One of my most memorable interactions was with Mr. Thompson, a sprightly octogenarian with twinkling blue eyes. He was an architect in his prime and had traveled the world. Now, his body was frail, but his stories were vibrant. Every day, he'd recount tales of designing skyscrapers in New York or beach houses in the Caribbean. He used to say, "Our bodies might age, but our souls remain evergreen, and stories, well, they keep us alive." Every time he spoke, I felt like I was traveling the world alongside him.

Then there was Mrs. Winters. She used to be a professional dancer. Though age and arthritis had stiffened her limbs, the grace with which she moved, even if just a little, was captivating. She'd show me faded photographs of her dancing days, her eyes sparkling with mischief. She taught me that our passions never truly leave us, even if our abilities fade.

However, the incident that left the most profound impact on me was one with Ms. Rebecca. She didn't talk much but always had a warm smile for everyone. Over time, I realized she had no visitors. One evening, as the sun painted the sky a deep shade of orange, I found her looking frail and shaky. I rushed to her side, trying to make her comfortable. We exchanged no words, but her eyes held a profound sadness and gratitude. As I held her hand, trying to comfort her, she quietly passed away in my arms. The moment was overwhelming—holding onto someone during their last breath, feeling the final heartbeat, and realizing the fragility of life.

The experience at the old age home taught me the impermanence of life and the value of moments. It wasn't about growing old or ending life but rather about cherishing memories, celebrating the past, and living in the present. It taught me to appreciate the people in my life and understand that every phase of life has its beauty and challenges.

As the summer drew to a close, I left the job with not just a paycheck but with life lessons that no school or university could ever impart. Every wrinkle told a story, every sigh held a memory, and every smile was a testament to the spirit of life.

Action Step

Write an Empathy Letter: *Write a letter to someone expressing understanding or apologizing for a past mistake. You decide if you'll send it.*

How Courage Ignites Us All

Each facet of courage is a story, a lesson, a mirror. They are reflections of our struggles and celebrations, our fears and joys, our losses and loves. They are the echoes of our shared journey, resonating with the universal heartbeat of life.

Feel the emotion as you delve into the lives of those who have embodied courage. Experience the tears of a mother's love, the laughter of a child's triumph, the sorrow of a lover's loss, the joy of a dream realized. These are not mere anecdotes; they're pieces of our hearts, whispers of our souls.

Prepare to be moved, challenged, and inspired. This journey into courage is a call to feel deeply, live passionately, and love without reservation. It's an invitation to embrace the extraordinary within the ordinary, to see the miraculous within the mundane.

I invite you to take this journey with me. Open your heart and feel the pulse of courage. Let it wash over you, enveloping you in its warmth, depth, and beauty. Let it guide you, transform you, and empower you.

For courage is not just a virtue; it's an experience, a connection, a celebration. It's the melody that plays in the background of our lives, the rhythm that moves us, the harmony that unites us. The love binds us, the hope that lifts us, the strength that sustains us.

Embrace courage. Let it become a part of you, for it's in courage that we find our true selves, purpose, and joy. In the tapestry of life, courage is the thread that weaves us together, the color that brightens our world, the touch that heals our wounds.

Feel the power of courage. Let it resonate within you, echoing through the chambers of your heart, resonating with the essence of your soul. Let it guide you, challenge you, uplift you. Let it become you.

For in the symphony of life, courage is the melody that will lead you home. It's the song of us all, the song of love, the song of life, the song of humanity.

The multifaceted gem of courage shines brightly in each aspect of our lives. It's not a fleeting emotion but a profound force that shapes our destiny. We create a tapestry rich in courage and humanity through *Commitment, Optimism, Understanding, Resilience, Action, Growth,* and *Empathy.*

Courage is in the dedication we show toward our goals, the faith we have in a brighter future, the empathy we share with others, the resilience we exhibit in the face of adversity, the thoughtful steps we take toward realizing our dreams, the personal development we strive for, and the compassion we extend to others.

It's the understanding that we are all on a unique journey, each facing our own set of challenges and triumphs. And yet, courage unites us. It reminds us that we are all capable of extraordinary feats, boundless love, and incredible transformation. The courage within us is our guiding light, our North Star, leading us toward our true selves.

In the dance of life, we are the artists, the warriors, the dreamers, the lovers. We paint our world with courage, grace, and love. We live with passion, purpose, and unshakable faith in ourselves and our journey.

Courage is not reserved for the heroes of stories and legends; it resides in each one of us. It's in the daily choices we make, the risks we take, the love we share, and the dreams we pursue.

Embrace these facets of courage; let them guide you, inspire you, and transform you. Your journey is unique; your story is beautiful, and your courage is your testament to the incredible being that you are.

Your courage is your legacy, your gift, your eternal flame. It's a force that can move mountains, heal wounds, create miracles, and spread kindness. Let it shine, let it guide, let it be.

For in your heart lies the power of courage, a power that transcends all boundaries, a power that unites, a power that loves. Let your courage be the music you dance to, the wind that lifts your wings, the love that fills your heart.

With courage, you are unstoppable, unbreakable, and unimaginable. You are the best version of yourself. You are love, you are joy, you are life. You are courage!

Lady JB Owen

LADY JB OWEN

"Commitment, clarity, and creativity are the cornerstones of courage."

My intention is to share my humble opinion that the act of courage has 3 distinct cornerstones: commitment, clarity, and creativity. Each is a vital component in the fiber that makes up courage. Each sets the tone, the pace, and the trajectory along the courageous path. Many have said *courage is being afraid and doing it anyway*, **a feat few can often master. With unwavering conviction toward your goal, a clear vision as to your outcome, and the ability to think beyond any self-defined limitation, you will find the courage you need to achieve anything and everything you dream of.**

THE CORNERSTONES OF COURAGE

It is often said that *courage is about having fear and doing it anyway*. Countless self-development authorities have shared, "Push past your fear, conquer your worries, and look fear straight in the eye!" But when your knees are knocking, your hands won't stop shaking, sweat is dripping down your spine, and the hairs are standing up on the back of your neck, none of these antidotes miraculously conjure up the courage you need to carry on. I have never felt fear gripping me with its vice-like claws and simply told myself *to push past it* as if brushing by would make it disappear. Fear has never faded because I *looked it straight in the eye*, nor has my body stopped sweating, trembling, or feeling a pit within my stomach because I was able to *conquer worry* like it was something I could wrestle to the ground. Fear has reared its ugly head multiple times in my life, and I had to have a plan, a strategy, a goal, a vision, and a creative idea on how to outmaneuver its ghastly talons. It wasn't luck, fluke, or unbeguiled grit that led to my success. The ability to overcome any obstacle and transverse those fears came from forging a distinct plan, letting nothing get in my way, and thinking outside the box. I think of those 3 things as the cornerstones of courage; the fundamentals of what we need.

No man has ever climbed Mount Everest by just pushing past his fears. Instead, he meticulously planned, prepared, and performed many tasks that made his courage effectively arrive. No woman has ever gone into labor, eager to deliver her child, with the feelings of looking fear straight in the eye. Instead, she has visualized her baby, committed to the process with conviction, and put her eye on the positive outcome, not the pending fear.

I would be remiss to say that pushing past your fears to leap off a cliff, move to a new city, or start a new job without any pre-planning, preparations, or personal analysis would fall into the realm of foolish, reckless, and asking for hardships. One would not see that as courageous and so *why is the advice around mustering courage tied to making haphazard decisions and taking uncalculated steps?* Those I have seen be the most courageous seem the most committed, clear, and concise. They know what they must do, they look at it from all angles, they see things in an obtainable way, and they know what it is they want to achieve. There seems to be a very distinct recipe for those who perform the most courageous tasks. Think of rescue workers, free divers, brain surgeons, and fire-eaters; they each have a process they go through to ensure their success. It's the actions they take that remove fear and doubt from the equation.

The question then becomes, *do you have to have fear to have courage? Does fear need to come first so that you gain the courage to push past it? Do we feel courage before the fear, or do we feel it after?* I have asked myself these questions throughout my life. I look at my past actions of making bold moves and big decisions only to ponder if it was, in fact, courageous. I contemplate my next steps, dreams, and aspirations, wondering if courage plays a factor. *Am I courageous? Do I use courage to push myself past my fears? Is courage the propelling aspect?*

After a long and tiresome stint of overworking and extreme effort, I knew I needed some personal downtime. Life had been busy, *overly busy*, and my tank needed to be refilled in a new and different way. I wanted to lay on the beach, feel the sun on my face, and have a string of days tied together where I could be free and unencumbered by everything I was doing at work. I decided

I wanted to spend my summer in Mexico, feel the sand in my toes, the salt on my lips, and let the breeze steer me in whatever direction it wanted.

Often in life, we face these pinnacle moments of needing quiet time and self-reflection. We have the desire to stop 'doing' and crave simply *being*. Of course, I faced the inner scrutiny of having such an idea. I wrestled with pushing myself to keep doing more; just get over the feeling of wanting to relax. Many people encouraged me to 'muster on.' Some even said to ignore those internal feelings, and they will go away. When people are telling you one thing, and your body is telling you another, it takes courage to listen to the inner knowing, not the outside noise. With a deep desire to rest for part of my summer, I let the beauty of Mexico dance in my head as I toyed with the idea of how to make it happen.

Yet, also swirling in my mind was the fact that I wanted to spend my summer cycling with my husband as we do every year. We love to ride our 2-seater tandem bicycle to amazing places, see nature up close, and push our physical limits. Cycling is an outstanding way to challenge oneself and persevere through adversity. Each day is testing our physical abilities, adapting to the terrain, and maneuvering through the obstacles that often show up: rainstorms, road construction, and wildlife. Over the past few summers, our cycle trips have involved going long distances and enduring great treks. Each year, we cycle to raise funds for charity and help those in need, and I didn't want to give that up to frolic on the beach selfishly.

As I toggled back and forth on what was best, I found myself seeped in worry. *What would people think if I took the summer off? Who would I be letting down if I didn't rally to raise funds?* I wanted to be happy, but at the same time, I wanted to honor my team, clients, and co-workers, while giving to the charities I had committed to. They say that real courage is tested when you must decide whether to honor others or honor yourself. I believe that real courage is when you find a solution that honors All: you, others, and God's divine direction for your life.

With Mexico calling me to be with Her and cycling tantalizing my soul, I made a clear and creative decision to spend my summer cycling... from Canada to Mexico!

Of course, my husband loved the idea and was instantly on board. He adores adventures as I do and was excited to cycle 4,500 km through 3 countries; Canada, the United States, and Baja Mexico. As quickly as I made the decision and he said yes, others added in their worries, concerns, and objections. Many people felt it was dangerous with the bad roads, the extreme heat, the colossal distance, and not to mention the menacing Mexican cartel. A slew of reasons why *not* to go came pouring in by text, email, and phone calls just days after sharing with everyone. They imposed their fears and worries, wanting to lovingly stop us from following through.

I am not one for listening to others. Maybe that is courageous in itself—not to take on the thoughts of others when you know instinctively what is meant for you. Listening to that intuitive voice that honors your inner conviction is possibly the real test. D*o you persevere, or do you relent? Do you go for it, or do you succumb?* This is the crossroad, the pivotal intersection. This is where the triangulation of the three cornerstones of courage comes filtering in.

First, one must be *clear* and have the *clarity* to see beyond the doubts and hone in on the exact outcome they desire. Courage is having the vision, the knowing, and the picture in your mind of precisely what you are aiming for. It is not indecision; it is precision. It is being so clear on what you choose that nothing else can steer you off the path. Having clarity of your goal and making it crystal clear pushes you toward it. Like a magnet, you are drawn. Everything about your objective is mapped out and defined in your mind, making it easy to achieve. Clarity and inner knowing give you the courage you need to bring the things you wish for into your reality.

I had to be clear on what I wanted both inwardly with myself and outwardly in nature, on our bike, and while dedicated to helping others. I had to let nothing anyone told me about the narrow roads, bad drivers, limited gas stations, and numerous potholes stop me from my desire. I also had to overcome the ridiculous ideas people shared of being kidnapped, accosted, robbed, and chased by so-called 'Mexicana Banditos.' Then there were their fears of us enduring the sweltering heat, facing unprecedented temperatures, and the threat of exhaustion, heat stroke, and even cardiac arrest!

Through all of those discouragements, I had to forge a mighty commitment. I had to decide that, yes, it was going to be hard, but I was willing to put in the work. My husband and I trained at home before our trip. We got our bike in order, our support driver prepared, our follow vehicle filled with needed supplies, and our route thoroughly planned out. It took timing, finances, support, and sacrifice. We had to say no to certain things so we could say yes to our plan. We gave up extra indulgences, saved ahead of time, solicited help from people who believed in our dream, and gained agreement from our kids. Grandparents had to help, the team in the office took on extra work, and through careful preparations and pure commitment to following through, we mapped out every possible obstacle and prepared for each potential setback. Our commitment had to be unwavering despite any unforeseen challenges. With every fiber within our being, we committed to what we wanted. We had to be dedicated, or we would never make it.

When one finds courage, it is cemented within the very foundation of their commitment. Courage is a byproduct of an internal force so devoted to the outcome that nothing can deflect it. The soul has forged a bond with the goal so strongly that through hell or high water, that goal will come to fruition. Whatever needs to be done, will be done in the quest to reach the prize. The possibilities for failure seem insignificant compared to the opportunity for success. It is the commitment that brings forth courage because, through deep, unwavering commitment, you feel the courage to do the impossible.

On a blistering day, twenty-six days into riding with the heat hitting past 110 degrees, we found ourselves climbing yet another hill. The Mexican Baja is part of a group of mountain ranges that stretch 1,500 km (930 mi) from lower California to the southern tip of the peninsula; they are part of the North American Pacific Coast Ranges, which run along the Pacific Coast from Alaska to Mexico. Elevations range from 150 to 3,300 m (500 to 10,834 ft). Throughout our trip, we had crisscrossed back and forth over those steep mountain hills almost 7 times. That day, I wanted to stop. The scorching sun, the unrelenting heat, the ache on my sunburned skin, my parched lips, not to mention sore muscles, flying rock chips, and a crumbling roadside all made it easy to want to quit. But instead of calling it a day and giving in, I reminded myself of my commitment. I took out my phone and started to record a message to myself. *JB, when you want to give up, when it is really hard, when everything seems extremely difficult, and you have all the permission you need to quit, remember this moment. Remember, pushing up this hill. Remember the desire within you to reach the finish line. Draw from your commitment to win, to succeed, to complete what you started. Remind yourself of the goal and get the courage you have within. Yes, you can quit right now, or you can dig deep and recommit.*

Remembering my commitment got me to the top of that hill, and the next hill, and the one after that. Eventually, after thirty-three days and 5,800 km (3,603 mi), we reached our goal triumphantly. We celebrated, posted on social media, and were interviewed by the local newspaper. Almost everyone commented on how scary and dangerous it must have been and how courageous we were to undergo such a treacherous journey on a tandem bike. I didn't think about the courage it took until so many people pointed out how they wouldn't have done it and how frightening it must have been. I didn't feel any of those fears; my commitment was too strong, my clarity unwavering, and when things became extremely difficult, I leaned in and became *creative* to find a solution. I found ways to master my concerns and solve every problem that arose. When we got a flat tire, became lost, ran low on gas, needed to speak a different language, had the military inspect our follow RV, lost track of our driver, faced a rainstorm, a windstorm, and even a hurricane, I used courage to bring forth the courage I needed.

Looking at things from a different angle, thinking outside the box, and being willing to go beyond what I once knew, all instilled a newfound wave of courage that forged a clearer path. I didn't let convention get in my way or what I had done in the past be how I was going to do it moving forward. I had to get out of my old way to find a new way. My mind needed to be creative to be open to unexplored ideas. I had to see it differently if I was going to preserve and succeed. Being creative allows courage to rise. You feel excited, renewed, and enthusiastic to try new things and embark on wild endeavors. Whenever I am asked how I do what I do, I think back to how I felt when the idea first came to me, and usually, that was inspired by doing something in a new way, with a different perspective, sparking innovation and creativity.

For the many who have forged that new trail, stood on the moon, named the stars, found the cures, and invented the impossible, their very essence stood amidst both adversity and creativity. No great invention, galactic finding, or life-changing tool has ever been made outside the realm of courageous creativity. The most daring, who find the answers to the untold and map the path to the unseen, have been brimming, exuberantly with both courage and creativity. They go hand in hand. They exist because together, they achieve greatness.

Sitting on the sand, with the waves crashing before me, the sun overhead, and the pelicans dipping their long beaks into the sea, I take a deep, relaxing breath. I smell the salt air, hear laughter from the frolicking children in the distance, and feel the warmth upon my skin. I have everything I need in this moment. All that is good in the world is around me. All the peace I need, I feel. I lean back to get an extra dose of the sun upon my smiling face. I have accomplished 2 dreams. One to cycle 3 continents, the other to lie on the beach. It took courage in so many ways to be here, to pause and bask in this moment. Courage to be clear, committed, and creative no matter what.

If you want to achieve your dreams, incorporate the 3 cornerstones of courage that will support you in obtaining them. Decide clearly on what you want. Know it, feel it, and describe it in every possible way. Let it be your north star, your guiding light, and your beacon of truth. Make it magnificent and tantalizing. Visualize every detail you need to pull you toward it. Then, get committed beyond reproach. There is no such thing as trying; either you do it, or you don't. It never has to be perfect; it just has to be genuine and from the heart. Give it your all. Be a good student, learn, fail, get up, learn, and fail again. Be ready to work hard and stay focused on what matters most. And, when rough patches and obstacles show up, get creative, be unique, and see it through your own lens, with the willingness to break the mold and smash any limiting box.

When you incorporate these 3 cornerstones of clarity, commitment, and creativity, courage shows up indicatively. Fortitude arrives, perseverance pilots the way, and what was once scary or frightening suddenly seems doable, obtainable, and exciting. You don't have to push through it, worry less, or look anything right in the eye because you have the foundation of a beautiful life, joyously full and blessed from above.

IGNITE ACTION STEPS

It just takes 3 things to find your courage whenever you are feeling apprehensive or afraid. Stop, take a deep breath, and decide you can overcome this, not by grit or sheer will but by wit, wonderment, and total willingness.

Take whatever issue is holding you back and decide to get clear on the direction, result, and outcome you want to achieve. Most people never reach their goals because they don't know what that goal is. Define what you want in a clear and concise way and make it so extraordinary that you *want* to go after it. You don't need courage in the traditional sense because you have switched from fearing it to full-out desiring it.

Once you are clear on what you want, get committed in a way that allows nothing to stop you. Many people think they want something, but they refuse to do what it takes to achieve it. You have to get so committed that no distraction, disappointment, or delay will move you from your goal. The world will test you. The Universe will give you things to see just how committed you are. Persevere. Be unrelenting. Don't give up just when you are so close. Focus on the outcome, the feeling that comes with obtaining what it is you clearly want.

When you are firm on these 2 important steps, hanker down and get creative. Do it like no one else. Be willing to accomplish what others will not. See it from a unique perspective and show up as your life depended on it. The world is attracted to the creative. That dynamic energy attracts equal energy from those who will support you in reaching your stupendous goal.

JB Owen — Canada
Speaker, Author, Publisher, CEO of Ignite, JBO Global inc. & Lotus Liners
www.jbowen.website
www.igniteyou.life
www.lotusliners.com
jbowen
LadyJBOwen

Stacey Yates Sellar

Stacey Yates Sellar

*"Sometimes you don't need more courage;
you just need less fear of judgment."*

**I hope you enjoy this chapter. And if this is the wisdom and nudge you
need, wherever you are, whoever you are, I humbly offer you my story.**

Please Don't Tell Anyone

I run down the street as fast as my chubby little legs and pink flip-flop-covered
feet carry me. I HAVE to get home before. The gooey cherry-cola-colored dye
that drenches my hair is slowly dripping maroon streaks down the side of my
face, past my brow, and down my back. *I don't know if I will make it home in
time...* The light black drape the hairstylist snapped around my neck a mere
30 minutes ago flutters as I run, and between the sweat and the pounding heart
rate, I feel it tightening around my neck. My breath is having trouble escaping
through the narrowing space in my throat, so I claw at the snaps to rip the drape
off. It releases me and falls to the ground as I keep running. I still can't breathe,
and my legs feel weak, but if I can just get home... *Am I going the right way?
I don't know which way to go!* I can tell everyone on the street is staring at me,
aghast and agog, to see this terrified middle-aged, soggy-headed, streaky-faced
woman running like it's the 27th mile of a marathon, and there is a tiger chasing
her. They can see by my pallor that all the blood has left my skin, but what they

can't see is the cause of this terror. The looks on their faces are exactly what I imagined, squinched up in part horror, part confusion, all judgment. "She must be crazy," they realize. They are too afraid to approach me, no one can help me.

I can't believe I am about to do this; tell you my deepest darkest secret. It is a secret I've struggled to hide every day for over forty years, almost my entire life. Most of the people who know me or have met me have no idea how hard I labor to keep it undercover. Every day it writhes like a snake, maneuvering to come to the surface while I negotiate, coerce, and try to tame it. Those few that do know my secret, like my family, don't really know the depths and furrows of it. They can't know the ghostly purrs, prattles, taps, and tugs that only I can hear and feel.

When I first heard of this book about courage, I jumped in immediately, knowing exactly what I would write about. It was obvious; and easy. In 2020, I mustered up the courage to leave an extremely lucrative corporate career in Silicon Valley that I had loved (mostly) for the last sixteen years. My husband and I sold or gave away most of our possessions, and narrowed our wardrobe down to a few suit-cases (not easy for a girl with a shoe addiction). We rented out our beautiful dollar home, took our 6 and 9-year-old boys out of traditional education, and headed off to world school. For anyone not born in the last few years, you will remember that 2020 was not exactly the best time to choose travel, #pandemicshuttheworlddown. While all of that was arduous, the most frightening step was confessing our plan to my uber-enmeshed, money-bewitched, success-driven parents and siblings. If courage is the choice to audaciously and willingly confront uncertainty, intimidation, judgment, danger, and fear, then THIS was courage at its peak.

There was a silent scream from inside as I sat down to write my chapter. The phantom secret sat heavily on my shoulder and kept my hand from writing about leaving Silicon Valley. *This is not the most courageous choice you can make. If you want to truly, deeply, and inspirationally deliver a message about courage, you know what you have to do.*

I knew leaving my job, a great paycheck, my family, friends, and home was a choice I couldn't NOT make. There were so many painful indicators from my job that I couldn't NOT walk away. Silicon Valley had become such an inequitable, avaricious place fueled by over-commitment and never-enoughness, that I couldn't NOT get away from it. I had so much knowledge about the lim-itations of traditional school, I couldn't NOT find a better way to nurture my kids' learning. I couldn't NOT leave. So, in that case, despite the uncertainty and judgment, it doesn't feel that courageous.

But… I can choose not to tell my secret. This will take courage. This is the moment I have been trying to avoid… but have needed my entire life.

You see, I have a full life, complete with academic and career success, a handsome, British husband (whom I married in a castle in Scotland), and 2 healthy boys. We enjoy world travel and alluring experiences. A big, healthy family and a plethora of true friends surround me. My days are filled with laughter, adventure, connection, a love of learning, and risks beyond what most would do. It is what some would call a dream life.

However, I don't let anyone know that there is a crack below what they can see. If my kimono begins to slip and the crack threatens to be revealed, I silently, painfully squirm and shift to get everything back into place. The crack threatens to break open and swallow me whole every day of my life, from the minute I wake up to the minute I close my eyes and even in my dreams when I am trapped in an elevator that turns sideways and upside down. There is no escape.

Sorry if you are hoping my secret includes a gruesome crime of passion or a supernatural alien abduction. I feel myself procrastinating, thinking you will be disappointed that it isn't worthy of such a build-up. And here lies the struggle in real time: I worry, *what will you, the reader, think of me*?

The secret is that I have panic disorder—the constant and chronic fear of having a panic attack. It's a secret because I am embarrassed by it. I am embarrassed because I think—and you probably do too—that I should be able to control it, get over it, just "feel the fear and do it anyway." But I can't. And I have tried. Those pervasive thoughts have plagued me, held me hostage, and quietly tortured me for more than forty years. I was always a nervous child, but my first panic attack was around the age of eleven when I was home alone and out of nowhere felt this terrible fear. Not a slight sense of unease. A feeling of sheer panic, like every terrifying character from every horror movie ever made, was just around the corner and coming for me. The fear surged cold through my veins and stole my breath. I started to hyperventilate as I ran to my neighbor to save me from the phantoms. She was able to calm the nerves but not the thoughts.

We didn't talk about panic attacks in the 1980's. I didn't know what was happening and thought I must be crazy. I didn't want anyone to know I was unstable, so I crammed it down, pushed it below my teen angst, tucked it beneath the depression, and in between my adolescent insecurities. In a span of 10 years, my secret attacks went from yearly to monthly to daily. Despite my best efforts, which included therapy, yoga, and hypnosis, the fear of having a panic attack in public or in a closed space robbed me of vacations, parties, jobs, relationships, and any self-confidence. It took great acts of creativity and resourcefulness to complete my courses and graduate from University. It was a long, lonely death march of avoiding anywhere I might get trapped and be unable to get home to safety, including endless detours to prevent getting captured by panic at a red light. My zone of safety narrowed to just a few places within a mile of my apartment. Then one day, while at work, the imaginary walls began closing so quickly that I felt I only had a narrow escape. The panic pounced, stole my air, drained my blood, and threatened to finally take me to the terror I feared. I quickly but quietly asked someone to drive me home. I hid under my covers, praying the paltry blanket would be able to protect me from all that was about to get me. Fear of nothing but everything at the same time coursed through my veins, and I was too afraid to even move. My brother picked me up and drove me to my parent's house. Afraid to even look out the car window, I curled up in the fetal position for the entire agonizing 8-hour drive. I started to see a psychiatrist who put me on medication, and it was 3 months before I could even go across the street to the neighbor's house. Another month before I could go to the video rental store. Another month before I could drive by myself.

Then began a tedious archaeological dig to find the cause and the cure. The catalyst may have been the devastating earthquake I experienced when I was 3—or being left at the beach when I was 5 (That's okay, Dad. I know 5 kids, 4 friends, 3 dogs, towels, toys, and cumbersome coolers can be a lot to keep track of, I forgive you). Or when I was eleven, being crammed in a small, mouse-like maze of a haunted house where, at the peak of feeling trapped in the claustrophobic cubby, the floor fell out beneath us. An exponential multiplier on top of everything else: my mom. Jane is the most selfless, supportive, genuine woman who will write you a thank you note for your thank you note. But she has a "death story" for every activity you will encounter; crossing the Sahara or a city street, driving at night or driving a golf ball, drinking in a hot tub or eating a hot cheesy sub too fast, being too close to a s'mores flame, or playing any physical game. Just like "There's an APP for that," she has a death story for that! However, the problem with being born sensitive, plus mom's death stories continuously on shuffle and repeat, is that I believed the world wasn't safe.

The cure has been even more elusive than the cause. It has been a slow climb out of a hole I never want to be in again. There were hundreds of rungs on the ladder: cognitive therapy, regression therapy, talk therapy, family therapy, and angel therapy. I had my stars mapped, chakras aligned, allergies eliminated, energy rearranged, my house feng shui'd, and my soul "retrieved." I had my palms, feet, tarot cards, stones, and coffee read (I hate coffee). I had my handwriting analyzed, my horoscope charted, and my psychic energy contacted. I met with numerologists, astrologists, psychics, psychiatrists, and hypnotists. I found my inner animal to the beat of a drum, carried around crystals, and tried daily journaling, hourly affirmations, and nightly prayers. I studied the seventy-two names, the fifteen-minute miracle, the twelve Steps, the 7 great prayers, and so much more. None of those were the cure, but each was a plank of the wobbly bridge that led me here to the adventurous, blessed, yet still imperfect and anxiety-ridden life I live today. I have gone from hiding under the covers to a place where I can travel the world. It takes unrelenting hopeful intention, conscious and sub-conscious intention.

The scene I described at the beginning of this chapter didn't really happen. But that is panic disorder. It is the scene I imagined even before I started my hair appointment. It is the spectacle I envision every time I am beyond my 'safe zone.' Before I even get to my appointment, my familiar thought parasite pops into my head and slowly eats away at any rational truth. *Will I panic while I am there? Will THIS be the time I actually hyperventilate to death or lose my mind?*

The stylist can't tell that while I described the color and cut I like, I am also trying to calm the simmering anxiety that is threatening to make a scene. In these situations, my brain splits, and one part entertains the stylist so she will have no idea that I am on the verge of becoming unhinged. The other is on high alert, trying to cello tape the cracks in the distressed dam so it doesn't burst. My breathing becomes shallow—*tape that*! Blood rushes from my cheeks and arms—*tape it*! My legs feel weak, and I am feeling lightheaded and disoriented—*more tape*! She doesn't pick up that I am extending my exhale to be longer than my inhale to ward off hyperventilation in between our casual "what's new" and "what are you doing this weekend" banter. She is oblivious that I am digging my nails into my fingers to distract my sensations while she sections my hair and slathers on the color. And when she puts on the timer and says, "I will check back in on you in 30 minutes," she has no idea that she just triggered the Now-I-Can't-Leave Panic Button. *If I left now with all this goop in my hair...I would look like a maniac running to get home. But what if the tape doesn't hold? Tape! Tape! Tape!*

A dramatic performance is being played out in the tiny theater for one in my head. There are 2 endings that happen before the hypothetical curtain in my imagination falls; when the tape gives way, the dam bursts, and panic finally drowns me. I will hyperventilate to death in the fetal position on the street in front of leering bystanders, or even worse, I will lose my mind and be taken away in a straight jacket to an insane asylum direct from the 1930s.

In reality, I don't run out of the salon. I tape, tape, tape until she returns and saves me from my worst nightmare *just in time*. Knowing I am almost finished and can go home soon instantly calms my scared system. The paper tiger retreats, the sensations wane, and the sane part of me, returns to take hold of the wheel and get the out-of-control cranial back on the "normal" track. As I leave, ensconcing my mental exhaustion with a cheerful goodbye, I know I have once again successfully hidden the crack and tamed the perpetual panic.

I also know I won't be back. This is what happens when I go to the hair salon alone. This is why I avoid going anywhere by myself. Even if I don't actually have an attack, the fear of one incarcerates me in a relentless game of hide and seek, a neverending attempt to evade the discomfort of what might happen.

And... all the while, very few people know because of one word. *Shame.*

"Shame: A painful emotion resulting from an awareness of inadequacy," as defined by my quick Google search and as adopted by every human. But we need to unravel that definition because this life, this tiny blip, the minuscule measure on a 3.7 billion year timeline of existence, is so short that we can NOT waste it being paralyzed by shame. Because nobody should get to define what is inadequate, normal, or perfect. Shame gave my fear power, control, and advantage. It takes courage to defy shame and judgment- my own and yours- and say out loud, "I am struggling with something."

My eleven-year-old son is my guru right now. I hear him navigate challenging situations daily as he plays with kids in a virtual video game. He often struggles to get them to cooperate in the role-play he is recording for his YouTube channel. When he confidently admits, "I have ADHD, Autism, anxiety, and dyslexia, and when you don't listen, it makes it very stressful for me," I cringe and worry that they will judge and shame him, but they don't. Instead, they are encouraging and supportive, and I am inspired.

I wonder, what would this world be like if there were no judgment and shame? What if we could all freely wear our challenges written on our shirts? "I was abused as a child," or "I have O.C.D.," "I am a perfectionist," "I avoid commitment," "I am a disappointment to my parents," or "I am afraid of crowds." What if sharing our pain so blatantly helped us relate to and be more empathetic toward one another? As we see someone else's challenges displayed, we can nod with a comforting "I got you, hang in there, let me know if you need a hand to squeeze."

I don't have a happily-ever-after ending where I tell you that I found the cause and the cure and live a life free of anxiety. I still live with the disorder and the fear of falling into a horror movie or insane asylum daily. I don't have the 3-step process that will rid you of any challenge because life is a constant obstacle course of challenges. We run into obstacles. We fall apart. We put ourselves back together. We fall apart again... but with a little less mess... but with a little more grace. Rinse. Repeat.

I do know how to live an amazing life in spite of a debilitating disorder. I know I don't have to do it quietly or alone. I don't have to hide under the dark covers. I can wear my challenge "I have a panic disorder" on my shirt with courage, not shame.

This may be the end of my chapter, not my story. My next chapter of life is being written right now, and so is yours. The future is made up of blank pages waiting for us to choose to be the hero of our own journey, despite challenges. It isn't always going to look like the Instagram reel of your dreams, but it can be better than you ever imagined. We must courageously accept, embrace, and not fear our false limitations. We have to come out of the dark and not fear our imperfections being seen! We get to decide if our false flaws are disabilities or superpowers if they help us or hold us back if we are embarrassed or empowered by them. We are stronger than we believe and can handle more than we have been told.

Be brave. Baffle shame. Defy fear. Get out from under the dark covers, share your discomfort, despair, and challenges, and see that you aren't alone. Like a coin, every challenge has 2 sides, and both sides shine when you have the courage to bring them into the light.

IGNITE ACTION STEPS

1. **Be Open. Take action.** Try anything that might bring you clues, clarity, or comfort. Break-throughs may not come in one big fire walk, but rather in baby steps out your door, around the block, or around the world. If you stay open, then every interaction will be a seed for success and survival. Hopeful intention plus intentional motion will take you to places beyond belief when you let it.

2. **Create time and space for healing.** Where can you find more time? For me, it was eliminating social media, reducing Netflix™ binging, and stealing it back from negative people, situations, and thoughts—trade those for healthier relationships, inspirational reading, mindfulness, and meditation.

3. **Have the courage to be stronger than your secret.** Don't give it the power to control you by hiding. If you just want to tell one person without fear of judgment and shame, you can tell me. Here's my email: stacey@happierbytheminute.com.

Stacey Yates Sellar — Around the World
Just another human in the middle of the journey, like you
www.happierbytheminute.com
happierbytheminute
happierbyminute

K.R. ROSSER

"Courage is defying the realms of the unthinkable."

My greatest desire for you, the reader, is to transcend the unthinkable and journey beyond the limits of your imagination. I wish for you to discover yourself, step out of your comfort zone, and live life courageously. Life is not about quitting, and I have learned that when you discover the courage within you, you can shatter the confines of what is conceivable.

SHATTERING THE CONFINES OF WHAT IS CONCEIVABLE

It was 1983, a gallon of gas was $1.24, *Every Breath You Take* by the group Police was the longest #1 single on the radio, McNuggets were an all-time favorite, and I was starting my freshman year of college on the campus of Tuskegee University in Alabama. Coming from the big city of Chicago, it was always assumed that I would attend college close to home. The idea that I would end up making a twelve-hour drive away, in a place I knew nobody, was unthinkable years prior.

The idea of moving so far away started during my senior year of high school while sitting in World History class. The topic for the day was Booker T. Washington, an educator and reformer who taught at the Tuskegee Normal and Industrial Institute (now Tuskegee University) in the late 1800s. I was thoroughly engaged in thought during class and was most intrigued by a man and place I had never heard of. We had never discussed any Black History, so that was my first. I suddenly found myself yearning to find out more about this unknown place. At that moment, a spark was ignited within, which would completely change the direction of my life. It felt like my mind had suddenly expanded beyond my small world.

In between classes I had a break, so I went to the library to find any information I could about Tuskegee and Booker T. Washington. Back then, Google wasn't as popular as it is today. The information was scarce, but it was enough to get me started. Tuskegee was considered a Historically Black College/ University (HBCU). *Geez, I had never heard of that term either and would find out later what it meant to me.* I knew I had a lot of research and reading ahead of me. I would discover other HBCUs all over the United States that I did not know of. The norm for me was to visit some of the predominately white schools within the Midwest. I decided that day that I would have the courage to step outside of the norm and take a different path.

I had always admired my aunt, who attended Washington University in St. Louis, Missouri. Naturally, I thought it would be amazing to follow in her footsteps. However, I didn't get accepted. I was finally beginning to realize that the world was greater than the Midwest. After reading more about Tuskegee and noticing that the student population looked just like me, I requested an application for admission and also filled out the necessary paperwork to apply for student loans. I was so excited and just thought everything would work itself out. I knew there was no way my mom could afford college tuition on her income, yet my decision had been made.

I didn't know much about the South or even where Tuskegee was. However, the name in itself sounded cool to me. I was excited to explore a new chapter in my life and see how things would be on my own. I had visions about what it would be like on a college campus in the South away from home. However, the thought of leaving my high school friends and making new friends, being miles away from my mom, and the comforts of home cast a shadow of anxiousness over me. I was at the point of second-guessing my decision.

Finally, the letter I had been waiting for was in the mailbox. My hands were shaking, and I said a little prayer. I held my breath and ripped it open. I read the first line, *Congratulations on your acceptance to Tuskegee*

Institute. My smile was as wide as the largest ocean. I did a happy dance on my way to tell my mom. She was delighted for me but sad that I would be so far away. At that point, I was in a bubble, care-free, with no idea of how I was going to be able to afford the tuition fees. I just assumed my application for the student loan would be approved and solve all my financial problems.

The car was packed, and the 12-hour journey began. I arrived in the town of Tuskegee, Alabama. I was shocked and tickled to see how primitive the place looked. The town resembled something out of a movie I had seen, but seeing it in person was so surreal. That place was unlike the big city universities I had visited, but that didn't phase me much. It had a certain aura, friendly and welcoming—I guess that's what many call *Southern Hospitality*.

When we reached the campus and my dorm, my mom wasted no time unloading the car. It was nice to have her there with me lending a helping hand as we set my room up. My mom had a twelve-hour drive back home facing her, so she didn't stay long. She gave me her last $20 and said she would send me more money next week when she got paid. We kissed and hugged each other tightly, and I watched the car drive away. Tears formed in my eyes, and I felt alone for the first time in life. I missed my mom already. She was my best friend. I knew I would call home each day on the pay phone until I felt comfortable on my new journey.

As I turned to walk back into the building and into my room, I felt empty and a little afraid. Reality had definitely kicked in; I was on my own.

I went back into my box-sized room, with just enough space for the 2 beds that were bolted to the wall, closets, and 2 desks. I looked out the window for a few minutes and stood there for a while, thinking about life and this new journey I was about to embark upon. I mustered up the courage and decided to walk up and down the halls, greeting everyone as I passed their room. As the day progressed, I met a lot of people from everywhere; Atlanta, California, Florida, and even Chicago, to name a few places. It didn't take long for me to start bonding with others.

Next, I decided to go outside and walk up the hill on campus. I was simply in awe at all of the history on the college campus. The buildings weren't modern; they were historic buildings, and each one had the name of someone significant. They were left in their natural state. I could see the beauty in each one. I could feel what it was like back in the day. It took me a little time to get used to the atmosphere because everything was so different, including the people. The heat from the sun felt different as well.

My first day eating in the cafeteria was a Sunday. I couldn't believe what they were serving. Grits, Fish, and Fried Chicken. Where I come from, we ate grits with bacon, sausage, and eggs. This was my first introduction to some real Southern Cuisine for breakfast.

One afternoon I was walking from class to my dorm room, and I saw a group of student cadets running and singing. I stopped to look at them as they ran by. They were in formation, had on the same uniform, clapping and singing as the guy called out words to a song that they repeated. Everyone was onbeat and energetic, and their voices resonated throughout the campus. I thought to myself, that's nice, but that couldn't be me running these Alabama hills in this Alabama heat. Later I would be told that it was the Army ROTC cadets doing physical training and they were singing cadence while they ran—that would be my first introduction.

A few weeks later, while on campus, I was approached by a guy in an Army uniform. He spoke with me and asked if I had ever thought about joining Army ROTC. I said no. He then asked if I had a minute so he could tell me about it. I said sure. He proceeded to tell me about everything the Army ROTC program offered. He stated the program would pay full tuition, room, and board, and I would receive a monthly stipend. That all sounded good to me, but as young and courageous as I was, I still wasn't sold. I suddenly remembered the cool commercials that flashed in front of me as a child where soldiers jumped out of a perfectly good plane. "Would I be able to jump out of planes if I joined?" I asked him.

He immediately stated he could make that happen. I could complete the scholarship paperwork and start receiving my scholarship during the next school year. I was psyched to think I could jump out of an airplane, but I still had my doubts. I never had any desire to join the Army. My excitement for free-falling from the sky diminished once I thought about the requirement to wear a uniform around campus and run in the hot sun after class. Besides, I would have to add more classes to my schedule, and I was already taking a full class load.

As each day passed, I encountered issues with completing my registration. The Pell Grant I received was insufficient to pay a fourth of the tuition. I would enter my History class and each day be called out of class to go see the registrar. This was the utmost embarrassment, and the *struggle was real!* I eventually went to class early and told the professor, "I'm here, but I know my name is on the list, so I'm going to get a head start over to the registrar's office." This was my way to avoid attention and embarrassment.

Month after month, it seemed I was standing in that long line trying to get some money from somewhere to pay tuition, room, and board. Every day I would need a permission slip to attend classes. I was determined to make it to classes so I could continue to progress and not fall behind. Talk about feeling like a loser without a plan! It was a never-ending story. However, I was determined to find a will and a way to finish what I had started at Tuskegee. That was where I was supposed to be, and I would ensure I stayed there until graduation.

I would eventually get registered on the last day of the semester, which fell on my birthday. I was officially a student, go figure!

Over the Christmas break, I talked with my mom about joining Army ROTC. Her initial response was, "No, no, ma'am!" She said you are in school to get a degree, not to join the Army! I told her about the benefits and that I would have my full tuition paid, room and board, and she wouldn't have to worry about that. She said, "We will see." I kept talking about it over the Christmas break because I was determined to find a way to fulfill my financial obligations.

Christmas break was over, and I was back at that never-ending story of trying to find a way to pay my tuition. I was desperate, so I made the decision to do the unthinkable and joined the Army ROTC program. I received my scholarship, tuition, room and board, and my stipend. All my financial worries were over at last. It released a huge burden, and I was immensely thankful. Unfortunately, it also meant strutting around campus in my ROTC gear and running those Alabama Hills in the Alabama heat!

I never looked back after that. My strong desire to attend Airborne school became a reality, and I completed summer camp. I went on to graduate college and receive my commission as a second lieutenant in the United States Army in May of 1987; It was one of the proudest days of my life.

I always thought I would become a dentist, but I ended up on an unexpected path, courageously stepping into the unknown. My journey and service in the military lasted twenty-four years and allowed me to visit countries all over the world. I was exposed to an incredible variety of cultures and food. I met amazing people who mentored and inspired me. Many are still treasured friendships today. I learned there is a big world out there, much more than Chicago.

I'll admit it wasn't always easy being in the ROTC program. And attending an HBCU showed me the values and principles that were in me but needed to be cultivated. I learned both culture, character, and courage in those years at school and in the army. I found that when I gave my best, the best came out in me. Booker T. Washington's greatest legacy was his commitment and vision to education as the key to true individual freedom and achievement. I believe that my determination and will to continue my education was the key to both freeing and empowering me.

Looking back after serving over 2 decades in the Army, if I had to do this all over again, I wouldn't change a thing. I learned that the world is yours; just tap into it. The Universe presents opportunities, and it is up to you to seize the moment and say *yes*. When you are determined, believe in yourself, and keep going, you can shatter the confines of what is unimaginable.

I encourage you, the reader, to step out on life and make the most of it. Remember, courage is not about being fearless but taking action instead. It is normal to have fear but keep pushing your boundaries through new adventures, challenges, and opportunities that allow you to grow. This will allow you to be more comfortable as you step outside of your comfort zone. If you believe in yourself, you will conceive the unthinkable.

IGNITE ACTION STEPS

- If there is something in life that you want to do, grab life with all your strength. Being courageous doesn't mean that fear is not present but that you take action in spite of what you fear. Change your thinking. Be bold and step outside your comfort zone.

- Define who you are and have the courage to own it. Celebrate your growth.

- Reflect on where you started from and where you want to end up. Keep pushing yourself to go beyond your limits.

- Start journaling and record the outcomes of your courageous actions. Every small step you take builds your courage and strengthens you. You will be surprised at what you can do.

- Take the path of the unexpected. I ended up on a completely different path which brought incredible benefits. The sky's the limit to what you can do.

- Set achievable goals for the one thing you've always wanted to do. Research and enjoy the journey

- Dream big. Dream outside the norm. Transcend the unimaginable. Journey beyond your limits. When you dream big, you invite the same dream to come to you.

Ask yourself the following and answer below…

What legacy would you like to leave?
Are you playing within your comfort zone?
Are you being courageous?
What path are you ready to take?
What will you say yes to?

Karen R. Rosser — United States of America
Best Selling Author,
Former Senior Army Officer,
Acquisition Professional
notsoshy_town

Ashira Karpelowsky

Ashira Karpelowsky

"The way I hold myself up allows me to hold others up, also."

It is my intention that you know that you are not alone. Other people are suffering and have gone through similar events, even if you have not yet met them. I want you to feel reassured that there are individuals who can support you and who understand. I wish for you to see that a positive mindset brings so much happiness. Looking beyond yourself, realizing that you can help others, and bringing a simple smile to someone else's day can lift you immensely and be just the medicine you both need.

The Hand That Made Me

The memory of the day is hazy, and all I see and hear are flashes: my mother's white dress turned red with blood; the panicked muffled voices of the hospital staff. Friday, February 8, 2013, was the day my life changed forever. I was 4 years old at the time, so what I remember is fragmented and chaotic. This is what my mother has told me over the years...

The fateful day started full of celebration and fun as it was my Dad's birthday. A spectacular breakfast was set up, as was the tradition in our home—pancakes, waffles, muffins, croissants, and fresh fruit decorated the kitchen counters. The *Happy Birthday* banner hung triumphantly from the roof. Presents were gratefully unwrapped, though he never asked for anything, and seeing him happy brought us so much joy. But the excitement had to end too quickly, as it was time to head to school.

My mom was a Reception teacher then, so I would go to school with her. On that day, we drove a short distance and found a parking spot. My mom told me to hop out of the car before she parked, as there was a huge oak tree in the way that would prevent me from opening the car door. She put the vehicle into park, and I climbed out. However, my hand was still on the door. Suddenly the car rolled backward, and my hand became stuck between the door and the trunk of the tree. The tires kept rolling backward as my hand was crushed. I screamed a piercing noise that penetrated my mother's heart.

My mom sprang into action. She wrapped her unblemished white dress around my hand, and I watched numbly as the blood seeped into the fabric and dyed the dress a deep crimson. She put me back in the car and rushed me to the nearest hospital, calling a doctor she knew there to let them know what had happened. They assured her there was a bed ready and waiting for me. I don't remember much about entering the emergency room, but I remember feeling drowsy afterward from the medication they administered. The world disappeared as I fell asleep.

My doctor decided that in order to save my hand, the damaged fingers needed to be amputated as they had been so severely broken in the accident that there was no blood flowing into the fingers, and they were starting to turn charcoal black. It was a hugely difficult decision because it was so high risk, yet I am very grateful he had the courage to reshape my hand. The procedure was completed, and so began the journey of having to rewire myself from right-handed to left-handed, from being like everyone else to being different.

I have little memory of my life before that day. I can't remember what writing, drawing, cutting, and coloring was like with my right hand. But when the freak accident occurred, leaving my right hand forever altered, the process of becoming left-handed was seared in my memory. I cannot forget all the months I spent in doctors' offices, hospitals, and physiotherapy rooms.

After the procedure, I made many, many trips to the hospital for check-ups and further surgeries. My mind may have blocked out the accident, but it remembers the cycle of hospital rounds, operations, casts, and bandages, which dominated my reality. It was the *worst*. When I close my eyes now, I can still vividly recall the searing pain as the doctor removed the gauze and the stench of disinfectant as he cleaned and redressed my hand more times than I could count. I can still feel the cold, hard clay from the Occupational Therapist (OT), a tool to help strengthen what would become my dominant hand. After spending an hour trying to mold my hand from the clay, I feel the aching muscles in my left hand. I lost count of the number of times I was hit in the face by the OT's foam ball, as my left hand couldn't catch it. I remember the burning frustration and anger at not being able to perform what were once simple tasks that my right hand allowed me to complete with ease just weeks earlier.

Over time, each session got easier. The searing pain eased. Less disinfectant was required. I started catching more balls than I dropped. The physical adaptation to my new body was taking shape, like the clay I was molding into figurines.

While the doctors and specialists helped me heal physically, I also had a long way to heal mentally and emotionally. As a young child going through medical trauma, I was scared and confused as I contemplated my future. *Wow, this is going to be my new reality. I will have to go back to school, and EVERY-ONE will know me... the girl without 10 fingers.* I felt deep anxiety, knowing everyone would ask what had happened to me.

Once I entered school, I could not help but feel jealous watching other kids my age able to cut and color with whichever hand they chose. I wished I could explain what I was going through to them, as they complained about small annoyances.

Even moments of support were a double-edged sword. My reality was changed, and the expectations of me were also changed. Teachers and well-meaning supporters tried to accommodate me and ensure I was alright. Unfortunately, that attention sometimes invited negativity and bullying from others around me.

Therapy was the lifeline I needed and one of the things that helped me become who I am today. It equipped me with the skills required to build mental strength and resiliency, which continues to assist me in adapting to my new reality and how I function in it.

Even now, I still attend therapy sessions. It's not normal therapy where you just have to sit on a couch and respond to the proverbial 'How does that make you feel?' question from a therapist who scribbles notes as you pour your heart out. I do something called *Art Therapy,* which allows me to be creative. I always find myself making something so random. My emotions spill into my watercolor paintings. Over time the colors I used transformed from dark, depressing images to bright, vibrant outdoor scenes. Being able to express myself creatively helped me process and make sense of my feelings.

Growing up with only 7 and a half fingers was a struggle. My classmates constantly whispered about me. When they saw my hand for the first time, it made me feel unloved as a young girl. I did not know what to do with myself. I asked my parents for a prosthetic hand so I could live a more normal-looking life. As always, filled with love and support, they agreed to help me get one. My dad's friend specialized in making prosthetic limbs, so my parents got to work acquiring me this hand, a hand I thought would be a ticket to acceptance from others.

Then it arrived, and I tried it on. It was a strange, dark beige color that wasn't close to my pale tone. The fingernails were unnatural and hard to look at. It was uncomfortable to put on. In every way imaginable, it didn't fit. Because… it wasn't ME.

I looked down at that prosthetic hand and felt shocked, realizing I didn't want it anymore. I couldn't help but feel upset, wondering if I would ever find the magical cure for my condition. Disappointment gave way to disgust as I questioned myself, my motives, and my future. *Will I ever look better? Will I ever feel like I belong?* To see this fake plastic hand that smelt like rubber left me thinking, *Is this really what I want my hand to look like? Or am I just doing this to make me seem somewhat normal again?* I had wanted that prosthetic to be the answer, but at that moment, I knew with every part of my being that it wasn't. As I looked at my right hand, I started to feel some stronger emotion take over. No, my fingers were never going to grow back on that hand. That hand was different, and different means unique. As I continued looking between my real hand and the plastic one, I felt courage and self-acceptance blossoming. *I may not always like how this hand looks, but I know I love my hand because it is mine.* Nelson Mandela's words resonated deeply within me and have since become my mantra: *Courage is not the absence of fear, but the triumph over it. The brave man is not he who does not feel afraid, but he who conquers that fear.*

I handed the prosthetic to my mom and said confidently, "I don't want it. This isn't what I actually need to heal." My parents smiled at me with admiration as they took the plastic limb away. I was grateful that they supported my wish to be accepted by my peers. But now, I was even more grateful when they unquestioningly allowed me to accept myself just as I was.

The physical changes which left me forever altered, more significantly, left me mentally changed also. Adjusting my mind was like a project—I had to rewire it and find new ways of processing my world and experiences. I had to hardwire my brain for positivity and not negativity. I started doing that work the day I turned the prosthetic down and have been putting in the work ever since.

Multiple people told me that I wouldn't be able to play sports because my hand limited my abilities. Some said I wouldn't be able to catch a ball. But my mom has always said to me, "There's never just one way of doing something; there's always more if you're willing to find those ways." I've been playing netball since I was a young girl. At first, it was immensely difficult to catch the ball, but hours of training and sheer determination meant I found a way to use my hands to play just as well as anyone with 10 fingers.

On the day of my accident, I would not have imagined that I would be standing on a netball court 10 years later, laughing at my inability to perform a ball-skill exercise because of having only one fully functional hand. I found the courage to find humor in my situation. Instead of accepting defeat and sitting on the sideline, I made up my own way of performing the action so that I could complete it just as well as my teammates could. *You don't need 10 fingers to be capable and skilled; sometimes, you just need to be a little more creative!*

In that instance, I was aware that it seemed weird, crazy even, to be laughing at something totally *not* funny, but my perseverance uplifted me. I felt so proud because I saw how far I had come. I had transformed from that little 4-year-old girl who couldn't catch a foam ball and struggled to accept what her life was. Now, I am a fully-skilled netball player who scores goals, even with a few quirks! I had drawn on buckets of courage every step of the way, even to play a simple game. I have learned that limitations are created not by physical differences or lack but by mental obstacles and a negative mindset.

I've discovered that life's circumstances can make maintaining a positive mindset very challenging. Entering high school is daunting for any student, and it was no different for me. As is true for many younger siblings, I entered high school with teachers already being familiar with my name, thanks to my older brother, Idan. Idan has a way of making people love him or hate him. As I entered high school, I felt overwhelmingly like I was not there to write my own story and live my own journey. I was living in the shadow of the reputation already built by my brother—a reputation that didn't necessarily align totally with who I was and what I could offer.

My peers constantly talked about me, and I felt embarrassed to be who I was. It felt like I worked so hard to be myself just for people to bring me back down. I was not going to allow that to happen. I consciously decided to start talking to more people so they could get to know *me* and learn *my* qualities. I was determined to show them that you can't judge me for how I look on the outside or who I am related to but rather get to know me for who I am authentically on the inside.

Before long, my whole school and all my teachers knew me as a kind, sweet, and caring girl. It felt like success. But life has a way of testing us constantly. Just as I started to feel confident about having found my place, life threw me another curveball when my dad, who was highly allergic to bees, was stung

3 times. As a result, he fell into a coma and was unresponsive for more than 3 years. Eventually, he developed an infection and passed away in August 2022, when I was just fourteen years old. My world instantly came crashing down on me.

As if having people whisper about my hand wasn't bad enough, I was a grade 8 student who was introduced to high school by being known as *the girl whose dad was in a coma.* Suddenly I had to grow up quickly; I had to support my Mom and yet continue to succeed at school. I wanted to ease the stress thrust upon my family. Part of my childhood vanished as I needed to find the strength and courage to be there for the people closest to me. At that moment, I was reminded of the true meaning of one of my favorite quotes: *Courage isn't having the strength to go on—it is going on when you don't have strength,* Napoleon Bonaparte.

Even now, 10 years later, I have a vivid, recurring dream of the day of my accident. In the dream, my mother and I are in an empty room. The blackness of the room devours all color. Then there is a bright, white light shining on us. Then flashes of her white dress. The white hospital bed. The white light of the hospital room. And then, my blankie, candy-floss pink and embroidered with my birth date: *19 May 2008.* With my blankie, I am safe and comforted. And then I wake up. It happens like this every time. As with my hand, I am constantly reminded of my past and the trauma I have overcome. It also reminds me of the courage I have drawn upon, without which I wouldn't have become the person I am today.

I am not the same child who lived in pain and overwhelm. I have learned so much about myself. I know I have inner courage and can overcome whatever challenge flows my way. I have proved to myself and others that if I want to do something, I am incredibly capable, despite lacking ten fingers. I was surrounded by so many people who supported me and helped me realize that I was never alone on my journey. My mother was an incredible role model; the doctors and therapists showed me *we all possess amazing potential.*

My positive outlook has enabled me to see the potential in everyone. The way I hold myself up allows me to hold others up, also. Now I know I am strong, resilient, full of courage, and able to tackle anything life throws at me. As Maya Angelou famously said, *I may be changed by what happens to me. But I refuse to be reduced by it.*

It takes courage to step through the pain and suffering, but we can all achieve incredible feats when we harness our courage, believe in ourselves, and, above all, accept ourselves. I don't know how I'm standing here, but the most important thing is that I'm here and standing strong. I don't know what giving up is, and I don't want to know. In a world in which we idolize physical perfection, losing my fingers could have been a reason to focus on misery and self-pity, but instead, I choose to focus on the beauty that life still has to offer me. I am grateful for what I have. I don't believe you need 10 fingers to be awed by a beautiful sunset. You don't need 10 fingers to feel unconditional love from your family members and friends. You don't need 10 fingers to laugh at a friend's joke until you can't breathe. The most important things in life don't require 10 fingers to enjoy at all. In fact, they can be enjoyed to the fullest with much less! I believe that within difficulty lies infinite possibilities if only one has the courage to dream of them. I embrace what makes me unique because I know that imperfection is beautiful, just like the hand that made me.

IGNITE ACTION STEPS

Throughout my journey, many questions arose, and I hope by answering the common ones for me, you will know you are not alone.

Do you feel like no one understands you? There is always someone you could reach out to. Talk to anyone you feel comfortable with, like a friend or family member. When I felt alone, I would allow myself to cry and listen to music, and connect to the lyrics. After that, I would talk to my mom or reach out to my therapist.

Is it ever going to change or always be like this? There is always a light at the end of the tunnel. There will come a moment when things change. Keep going. Catching the foam ball was so hard at the start, but it got easier with practice and patience.

Why me? My mom always told me it was not something I did. It was an accident, and accidents happen to so many people all the time around the world. There is a reason why we go through challenges. For me, it showed me that I have the courage to do things. You can use this fear to fuel you, also.

Ashira Karpelowsky — South Africa
Student, and Public Speaker
ashira_karps

Cheryl A. Rafter

CHERYL A. RAFTER

"We create our life with every breath, every thought, and every word."

The intention of my story is to empower others to know that anything is possible and you don't have to settle. Have the courage to step into the unknown and trust it will all work out in divine order. You are more powerful than you think. Take the leap and know that it is all a part of your journey; it will be worth it to live your dreams with no regrets. I hope my story gives you the strength, and courage to be the powerful, worthy person you are.

THE LEAP FORWARD

Sadness and confusion showed on my face, nervousness sat in my stomach, and heartbreak lay inside my chest as I stared at the tree-lined mountainside rushing by my train window. At 5 years old, I had just been torn away from my beloved grandma, who was my world. Being the first grandchild and living only a few houses away, I was devastated when we were separated. I didn't understand why I was forced to go or why I had to leave.

My parents had chosen to move away to Edmonton, Alberta, from Nanaimo, B.C., and I was already feeling a void in my life because my dad had moved ahead of us to find work. Saying goodbye to my grandma made that void even deeper. I thought that if I were good, maybe I wouldn't have to go. If I could just be good enough, nothing bad would happen. I kept hoping this as the long train ride took me to a whole new world of cold and snow.

Growing up was never easy, being the oldest and caring for my 2 younger sisters. I always needed to be in control and responsible for everything, or so I thought. Throughout my teen years, I was bullied and was barely passing school. I felt alone, worthless, and unloved. Dealing with abuse at home is never easy as a teenager; I was always saving my mom and sisters from the harm my dad was doing to the family. I remained Daddy's Little Girl and kept trying to be good while protecting the people I loved. My focus was rarely on pursuing what made me happy, especially about myself, until in high school, I finally found something I loved and was good at… hairdressing. I took a beauty culture course and had a great teacher who believed in me, which allowed me the confidence to thrive and learn. I was working part-time throughout high school and earning money for myself, which boosted my confidence and self-worth. I could take care of myself and buy the things I wanted. As I carried myself with purpose and positive energy, I was able to draw the attention of others who saw the potential in me and what I was yet to discover. And, those *individuals* would change the trajectory of my life and instill the courage I needed to persevere.

At nineteen, I met the love of my life. He was very handsome and made me feel beautiful, and we had a lot of fun. For the first time, I felt loved; his affection for me felt like it was fortifying my self-worth and self-esteem. As he kept making me feel better about myself, I became more and more attached to him. He was my prince in shining armor, who had come to rescue me from the painful situation at home. But through our twenty years together, it wasn't always a bed of roses. We had many fights and breakups. Each time we were apart, my feelings of unworthiness would creep back in, and take me back to him every time. I kept trying to rebuild things between us because I loved him and knew it would somehow work out if I could just be good.

Before I ever met my Prince Charming, the man I always relied on was taken from me when I was twenty-three. I never expected my dad's death to come so soon; you always think your parents will live a long life. It was a devastating time for me to deal with, as I was very close to my dad despite my difficult upbringing. He was the one who always encouraged me to do better and believe in myself. It took me a long time to get over the fact that I would never see or hear his voice ever again. I regretted that I never got to tell him how I felt and say goodbye to him. For all his faults, I was still Daddy's Little Girl, and I loved him and always tried to make him proud.

I felt the pressure to take care of everything for the family as I always did when he was alive, and it was no different when he passed away. As I wrapped up his affairs and handled his estate, I was concerned about what the future would be like without him and how his passing impacted my siblings. Meanwhile, I struggled with depression and the grief of losing him, turning to drinking and partying a little too much. That put a strain on my relationship with my partner, and things began to unravel.

To add to the difficulties, my 8-year-old nephew came to live with us because he couldn't live with his father. We had decided early on that we did not want children, so welcoming him into our home wasn't easy considering the medical problems and diagnosis of ADHD that he was dealing with. I loved and cared for my nephew, giving him all the support I could to help him cope with his mental state of being. Despite the additional hardships and responsibilities, I was committed to doing the right thing and putting his needs first, ahead of mine, at a very high personal cost.

Then at the age of thirteen, he got into major trouble, and I had to make one of the hardest decisions of my life: sending him to a live-in boys' treatment center. I remember how my sister reacted and thought I was giving up on him. I realized that I would have to deal with the situation alone, as my partner was not supporting me through this terrible time. It was an awful feeling of despair, to see my nephew cry and beg not to go, just as I had when I was forced to leave my grandma all those years ago. It was an extremely emotional and heartbreaking situation, and I felt sad and hopeless. It was like the whole world was against my decision to get him the help he so desperately needed. As I tried to balance the needs of those who were upset with my choice, I had no one looking out for me. I felt lost and alone with no one to talk to.

That event was very rough on my relationship with my common-law husband, who left me feeling abandoned, betrayed, and scared. I had stayed in that mentally controlling relationship because I didn't think I could take care of myself and felt I wasn't worthy of love from anyone else. I depended on him for everything. Each time I got the courage to walk away, I would lose faith in myself and go back, only to find out that he let me come back because *he* felt sorry for *me*.

Turns out, my ex had been having an affair in my own home with someone who was pretending to be my friend. I was devastated and made a fool in front of friends who had tried to tell me the news; news that I didn't want to believe. When I finally realized the truth, I had no choice but to walk away. I became single, turned forty, and lost my job all in the same month. My world would never be the same.

I had spent twenty years being *"We,"* not *"I."* For many years I never felt that I could be my own woman. I allowed myself to be controlled and manipulated, not only in my personal life but professional life. I gave up so much to others and tried to be good all the time, but life was hitting me so hard that I needed to take notice. The anger, despair, and resentment pushed me to the brink. I felt blame and shame at the same time and knew I had to redefine *my* life. I had to find the courage to stand alone, forge my way, and be *good* to me.

A few months after the final breakup, around Christmas time, as I sat in my car late at night, getting ready to go pick up a friend, I had a sudden realization that I could do whatever I wanted without asking anyone's permission. At that moment, I knew that I no longer needed to be dependent on my ex or anyone else. I was moving toward my independence; it was very scary, as I didn't know who I was. I sought to find the powerful, independent woman I knew I could be with this newfound freedom I'd never felt before. I suddenly had the courage and power to make my own choices, and that made me decide that no matter what, I was going to be okay, and there was more to life than I once believed.

It was about 6 months later, after everything was settled, I moved away to Calgary, to find out who *I* was. Moving to a city where I had no friends or job was not easy. I was terrified and had to make a decision to stop driving back to Edmonton in order for me to settle into my new life. I felt I was on the path to being 'good' again, as I opened up to meeting new friends. I even found a man who I thought was true to me, and the familiar feeling of happy butterflies was exciting and encouraging.

That is, until I found out that he had a live-in girlfriend. Again I was heart-broken, and, this time, financially broke also.

I had no choice but to go back to the one thing I knew I was good at, and that was hairdressing. I managed a hair salon that had eleven stylists. In the 2 and a half years that I managed the salon, I took the business to number 1 in sales. That was a big accomplishment and confidence builder for me. I loved working on clients' hair to make them feel good about themselves. I was a great role model for my team, teaching them how to be better hairdressers, and helping them learn and grow personally and professionally. I remember my assistant manager telling me that I have high expectations, and at the same time, bring people up to a higher level. I was back in my element, taking care of others' well-being as I loved to do, and it felt right in my heart.

Then things went wrong again, and I experienced carpal tunnel in not 1, but both wrists. There were complications that led to longer time off work. I went into a bit of depression with being unable to do much and having no control over my recovery time. Again, I felt hopeless, lost, and unworthy, so I sought comfort from another man. And again, he was not good to me; controlling and abusive…true to my past pattern. We both ended up getting involved with the wrong people who were into partying and drugs. I got into financial trouble to the point of being homeless. That was a wake-up call. I mustered the courage to pack up my van and move back to Edmonton because I knew I would not be homeless; that was *not* the life for me.

Moving back in with my mom, with whom I had not lived with since I was eighteen. It was very difficult because I had to admit I failed and couldn't do it alone. I had hit rock bottom financially, emotionally, and mentally. I lost my new vehicle and declared bankruptcy due to being so far in debt. I felt there was no other way out of the mess I had created. I was feeling worthless and ashamed of my actions, along with the bad choices I had made.

It took a little time, but I did manage to get myself back on my feet after a year of staying in my mom's living room and working 2 jobs. Finally, back in my own place, I was excited, feeling confident, and actually believing in myself again. I regained freedom and independence. The feeling of being able to care for myself was powerful, and I knew everything would be alright. The feeling of being able to cook in my own kitchen and have my own space was amazing. That was the independence and freedom I was waiting for. I started to date again, finally avoiding toxic men and finding good people in my life. I was having fun and meeting new friends. Life was good. *I was good.*

Yet, I was feeling a little restless, like there was something else I should be doing. *What was it that I didn't know?* I started looking for answers from the Universe, and even though I'm not religious, I believe in a Higher Power who guides us to our answers. The question was this: *Is this really where I want to be?* Through meditation and stillness, I got my answer: *"No."*

That's when my prayers were answered. I met Darren Jacklin, a success-ful corporate trainer, at a company office training night. I loved his positive energy, confidence, and enthusiasm. We became dear friends and associates as he inspired me to pursue my goals and dream big. At first, I didn't know what that meant. Until one day in March, he called me from the beach where he lives in Vancouver, B.C. I was envious that he was in shorts sitting on the beach as I was in the snow and cold. I hated winters in Alberta and was at a dead-end job, not getting any younger. I always loved B.C.—it was where my life started and where I spent holidays as a kid visiting family and staying with my grandmother.

On that call, he told me, "If you want to change your life, change your environment." I felt like I had finally found an answer to that single encouraging statement. I was overcome with the inner knowing I had been denying myself for far too long. Deep within came the courage to believe: *that there was more out there for me, more that I was worthy of. And that I deserved to have 'good' things in my life.* After so many decades of being good for others, I finally granted myself permission to be and do what was best for me.

After 6 months of planning, I quit my job, put my stuff in storage, and loaded up my personal belongings. I took the leap of faith to move to Vancouver. I knew 1 person there and had no guarantee of a job or anything. I was terrified, leary, and excited all at the same time, *and* doubting whether this was the right choice or not. Darren believed in me when I didn't believe in myself, a true committed friend. I built my new self-confidence and belief on the foundation he had laid down.

As the months went on, I started to meet people and do things I'd never done before. I was sure I had made the right decision. This was a whole new world for me. The first year I was doing different businesses, trying to be an entrepreneur after being an employee all my life. It had its own set of struggles and ups and downs; the biggest was making money consistently. I knew that no one was coming to rescue me, so after about a year of trying to get my business going, I had to realize that I needed to get a job to pay my bills. I felt like a failure and that I was not good enough, but in reality, I was taking care of myself. I learned that I was 100% responsible for my world, and worthy of more. I got back up, found myself a job, put my finances in order *again,* and never looked back.

It takes courage to be unique and be yourself, living life your way and not how anyone else thinks it should be. My belief in myself is very different from twenty years ago. I have a sense of peace, and confidence, and know "I AM" worthy and deserve a great life. I am on my way to being financially free, traveling, and doing what I love. I live in my dream apartment with a view of the ocean, within walking distance of my favorite beach. And, I have even made peace with my imperfect Dad, who I realize is an angel guiding me through life. In the end, through all my struggles, I became a stronger woman who could deal with anything life gave her. All of this built me into the woman who took the LEAP and had the COURAGE to follow her dreams.

It takes a lot of courage to look at yourself and make the changes to grow mentally, emotionally, and spiritually to become a better version of yourself. Know that anything is possible, and you don't have to settle for a life less than what you love. Sometimes in life, you don't think you have the courage to take on what's given to you, but really we are stronger than we think. Trust in the process and know that it will all work out in divine order; it's worth it to live your dreams with no regrets. Follow your heart, it already knows what you desire, be courageous, and take the leap.

IGNITE ACTION STEPS

Do you ever feel like you're not worthy of a life of your dreams? Well, deep down, something happened at a young age that made you think that way. Whether someone told you bad things, an awful event happened, or you just told yourself you weren't enough. We have all been there. Here are a few things that I know worked for me that you could try to help with your belief in yourself:

- Read/Listen to positive affirmations to believe that you deserve anything in life you desire. You are the creator of your world.

- Meditate and ask for guidance from that inner power we all have within us to know you are worthy.

- Spend time with nature, whether that is at the beach or hiking trails, connecting to yourself, and be aware of how you are feeling. Ask yourself if what your mind chatter is saying is actually true.

- Be around people who lift you up and help you to believe in yourself; build that team of people who love you unconditionally.

Cheryl A. Rafter — Canada
Entrepreneur, Connector, Inspirer of Life
cherylrafter.equity@gmail.com
cherylrafter
cheryl-rafter

Jermaine L. Brantley

JERMAINE L. BRANTLEY

"Know yourself, love yourself, and forgive yourself."

My wish for you is to understand that things in life happen that we don't have control over. Don't be discouraged by the outcomes that didn't go according to your plans. Stay focused and keep working towards building yourself and growing through your life's journey. Knowing yourself, being self-aware, and having the courage to face things outside your comfort zone fearlessly, play important roles in overcoming obstacles. Be consistent and work toward your personal goals with an open mind to grow in other areas of your life.

MORE THAN MEETS THE EYE

"Cowabunga!" I jumped my Ninja Turtle® figurine across my bedroom floor, kicking the evil Shredder in his plastic chest as Master Splinter watched proudly. The beeping of my electronic games and the sound effects I created were the soundtrack to my life as an introvert. As the child of a military family who moved to different cities and naval bases throughout the U.S., I always made new friends and left them behind. So, I connected to the things I could keep consistent. Nothing was better than watching my favorite cartoons on TV, playing with my Lego®, and building things. I wanted to be like Mister T, Popeye, and the Transformer, Optimus Prime, the *Strongest* of all Autobots; "More than meets the eye!" In elementary school, while on the naval base, I connected with other military kids by playing on soccer and Tee-ball teams. Sports were fun, but I was more excited about drawing and building model cars and toy jets.

Since kindergarten, I knew I wanted to become an actor, play football for the NFL, and become a fighter pilot like "Maverick" in Top Gun. I didn't know how to make it all happen, but I knew I had to stay focused, work hard, and commit to fulfilling my dreams. Luckily, these were values and skills my parents instilled in me early. As a military child, I had many responsibilities and chores growing up: dusting the furniture, tidying the house, and keeping things in order. That reality facilitated me being organized and staying focused throughout my entire life. I didn't mind waking up early, making my bed every day, and finishing my homework. My parents showed me the value of discipline, focus, and hard work throughout my childhood. I was always willing to learn and do my chores. But of course, as soon as I was done with that work, I was back to building castles and forts connected by zipline with my Lego®.

When I entered high school, I made it my mission to stay focused by working on my future goals. I joined the Junior Reserve Officers' Training Corps (JROTC) and became the maverick of the class earning the highest rank in the east region as a "Colonel" of the Army JROTC. During this time, I joined the school's Aviation Magnet Program, where I learned how to fly airplanes and was at the top of my class. Becoming an aviator has been my passion ever since I was a young boy zooming my model airplanes around my bedroom. However, in order to fly fighter jets, there were specific height requirements, and I was unfortunately too tall to become a fighter pilot. Still, having a leadership mindset in every situation, I always looked at obstacles as something to overcome and not be defeated by when things didn't turn out as planned. Okay, I wouldn't be able to fly fighter jets. That meant it was time to redirect my focus toward the next goal; my dream of making it to the NFL.

Inspired by the athletes in my family, I had wanted to play Varsity football since my freshman year of high school. Since I was chasing the demands of the JROTC, I did not have time to play football and did not become part of the gridiron until my junior year, though most of my teammates had played since their elementary days. Still, my winning mindset and my natural athletic abilities made me a sought-after Defensive Tackle scouted by some of the nation's top universities. I felt like a celebrity being called out of class over the school intercom to meet with recruiters from some of the most prestigious educational institutions in the country. I successfully juggled JROTC and football, all while staying focused on my academics and maintaining a 3.8 GPA throughout my senior year. The world was my oyster, and I was filled with confidence knowing I would be able to accept any of the scholarships that were offered to me by some of the most notable American universities: the University of Southern California, the University of Georgia, and Duke, just to name a few.

Life was sweet until the months leading up to graduation. That was the first time the bottom slipped out from under me. I was informed too late that a full academic ride to college was contingent upon my passing both the SAT and ACT exams, not just one, but both. Because I had not understood the weight of the standardized placement exams and deadlines, I thought my athletic abilities and wonderful GPA would be enough to enter the university of my choosing as long as I scored well on either exam. I had done extremely well on the ACT and figured I was set. I didn't realize that most college acceptances and scholarships were based on the SAT... the test on which I did not perform as well. I also failed to complete the SAT before the deadline to submit it to the Clearinghouse for the scholarship awards to become finalized.

At that moment, I experienced devastation and disappointment over missing out on the scholarships offered to me by all of those elite schools. Negative thoughts started to creep in as I saw every great opportunity and dream slip from my fingers. Graduation was around the corner, and I didn't do well on one of the biggest tests I had ever taken up to that point. It was the first time I had fallen so short, and I was left with a hollow feeling in my chest. To find the courage to keep going, I had to dig down, back to my military upbringing, and remember that what was done was done—collateral *damage*. I knew I wouldn't get where I wanted to go... I wouldn't get *Anywhere* if I felt sorry for myself. I had to shake off the disappointment and not allow the situation to deter me from my goals because I have been and always will be a WINNER. I had to remind myself of my achievements. Although I missed the chance to enter the Ivy League, I still had full scholarship offers from the prestigious West Point Academy and the Citadel Military Academy through my acceleration in the JROTC program.

Attending college and playing football was still an option, as I was offered full scholarships from several schools, such as the University of Hawaii, Baylor University, and North Carolina A&T State University. So, I redirected my focus, took the SAT a second time, and passed with a score of 1070! With that success in my pocket and my options laid out before me, I attended one of the greatest

Historically Black Colleges/ Universities in (HBCUs) in the country, where I was recruited on a full athletic scholarship to play football.

From the moment I entered my freshman year of college, I stayed focused on my studies and never partied or engaged in reckless activities. I maintained that military mindset and structure that was instilled in me ever since my childhood. My friends had waited for the other shoe to drop; for me to go wild and cut loose after so many years of structured self-discipline and achievement. But my mind was always on setting up the future. I applied myself throughout every situation and reminded myself, *Failure was not an option.* I constantly trained hard in the gym and was a top-class athlete, becoming one of A&T's first freshman impact players, and winning the Middle Eastern Athletic Conference Championship as a defensive tackle, all in the first year of school.

Many people saw me as an overachiever and sometimes wondered if it attracted negative attention. I strove to keep myself balanced and humble, but I also knew I had to have the courage to stay true to myself: to know myself, love myself, and forgive myself. Throughout college, I learned the positive impact that mentality has as I encouraged my teammates to have the courage to be genuine and authentic in themselves. I would tell them that being yourself is far more rewarding than pretending to be someone you're not. I was building a level of character, confidence, and respect that benefited not only myself but also those around me. You can never expect someone else to respect or look up to you if you don't respect yourself first. I did my best to exhibit leadership qualities and earned the respect of others throughout my life, from high school in the JROTC to my time in college, where I strived to be a leader and never a follower.

As my senior year at NC A&T rapidly approached, I was on the fast track to fulfilling my dreams of making it to the NFL Drafts. My GPA was great; I was winning championships and was being looked at by several NFL scouts. Without fail, I had worked so hard to make all of my lifelong dreams come to fruition.

Then, I dove for a difficult tackle in one of the last games of my senior year, and my shoulder went numb. I had torn the cartilage in my arm. I kept playing and thought I was doing alright for a few days after. But each time my arm moved: *click, click, click.* My shoulder kept getting stuck, like the gear shift of someone learning to drive a manual car. That unexpected injury immediately threatened my eligibility for the NFL draft.

I was at a low point of defeat, realizing that I may never play football professionally, and for a brief moment, I even doubted myself and my dreams. Yet, as I worked through my disappointment, my doubt started turning into questions about whether the NFL was actually what I wanted. I began to realize I had never really *loved* football like my teammates had; I never felt the passion for it that they did. I had always known it was on me to make my *dreams* become my *Reality*! But now I had to wonder what my dream was. Since childhood, I had told myself a 'story' that I would be a fighter pilot and an NFL great, and I had to execute those goals.

Now, I felt like *a story without words.*

It was time for me to be like Optimus Prime and TRANSFORM. I rearranged my priorities, shifted my focus, and evolved how I applied my self-discipline. I knew that my journey was not over; I needed to be grateful for the many victories I had achieved along the way and remember I could still bring my other dreams to fruition. My setback exposed the people who counted me out and didn't believe in me—those times helped me to learn and grow as a man, teaching me not to allow obstacles or the negative opinions of others to determine the course of my life. I could reflect on my accomplishments and shortcomings and had to forgive others and myself for doubting my God-given gifts and abilities that were always instilled in me throughout my life. When I transformed my outlook, it opened me up to new opportunities.

After graduating from NC A&T, I reached a pivotal point in my life. I was introduced to the entertainment industry when I was cast as a college football player in an independent film, my first time merging my dreams of acting and playing football professionally! Although my childhood dream was to become an actor, I always kept an open mind to learn and expand my knowledge in any field and was willing to work from the ground up, in front of or behind the camera.

In some ways, that was a homecoming for me. As a fourth grader in my elementary school's play, I took on the role of an elderly grandfather; a few years later, I played an intoxicated, happy-go-lucky fellow in the church production. Unlike everyone else, I felt I was right at home on the entertainment stage. And everything felt surreal when I was on location, on the set of my first major motion picture! Each element was music to my ears, from the shuffling sounds of props and costumes to the loud boom of the movie crew shouting, "Quiet on set!" Actors, directors, cameramen, sound, and lighting personnel all steadied themselves to make some movie magic. The mixture of fact and fantasy was so amazing, exhilarating, and at the same time, blessedly humbling.

Once I entered the field of entertainment, I worked in several departments on set. I gained a wealth of knowledge and experience as an actor, stuntman, first-unit movie electrician, and miscellaneous crew member. No matter what role I played, whether in front of the camera or behind the camera, I was eager to provide the imagination and the emotion to help bring out the best in me and in those who were working with me. It was during these moments that I began to feel like one of my favorite superheroes, Optimus Prime. I felt invincible and like a true *transformer*; there is so much more to me than what meets the eye.

Within a relatively short period, I have developed into a sought-after professional stuntman in Hollywood, California. My evolution as a stunt performer was a remarkable opportunity to use my background in athletics and mixed martial arts and has added many credits to my professional portfolio: stunt double for Terry Crews in "Brooklyn Nine-Nine," stunt double in "Lucifer" for D.B. Woodside, and serving as part of the cast and crew on some of the top productions in the entertainment business. I also became a SAG Award Winner for Outstanding Performance By A Stunt Ensemble for the critically acclaimed Marvel movie, Black Panther. Finally, my mental state and mindset were in their PRIME; confident, invincible, and filled with fortitude.

As a Hollywood actor and stuntman, being dedicated, resilient, and respectful of others took me far in my career. Still, the love and passion I have for what I do is the endless motivation driving me to remain successful. I am a very dedicated and passionate professional, and when working with others, I always give my all and show up as a leader and team player. Through my life's journey, I continue to strive for excellence and never settle for anything less. I always believe in remaining humble and never take anyone or anything for granted, including my prior setbacks. Every obstacle I faced in my life helped me to become sharper and wiser. I did not allow it to distract me or cloud my judgment. I found my courage in the face of adversaries and used it to conquer every challenge put before me. I have become the Maverick of my life.

Remember, no one on this earth is immune to obstacles. In fact, you will face many challenges in your lifetime. The question you have to ask yourself is, *"Are you going to sit back and let life pass you by because it's too challenging, or are you going to have the courage to keep fighting until you reach your potential and purpose in life and receive all of the amazing things you worked so hard for?"* The answer you give will be the key ingredient that can help you grow and soar to the highest of heights imaginable and let you finally be in your PRIME.

IGNITE ACTION STEPS

Remember that you have all the things you need to achieve greatness. All you have to do is have the COURAGE to go get it!

Consistency: Identify your purpose, find your motivation, and develop your 'why.' Write it down, so you can keep yourself on track each day.

Outgoing: Sometimes, the things we want most may not manifest in the way we planned. Challenge yourself to have an open mind by trying different jobs because they could develop hidden talents and strengths within you.

Unapologetic: Everyone on earth has a purpose for their lives, so never take your life or anyone else's for granted. You are created to grow from any and all obstacles if you change your thought process to recognize the lessons they teach. You are blessed to be the beacon of light to shine bright for others who may not see their limitless potential but could be inspired by yours.

Rare: Be you. Be bold. Allow any mishaps, mistakes, failed attempts, or set-backs to be your motivation to learn, never give up, and win in the way only YOU can.

Aware: Everyone has different abilities, talents, and learning styles. When you start to map out your career goals, determine your likes and dislikes but always be open to learning something new.

Gratitude: Embrace the work as you chase your dreams because that will make you so much more grateful when they become your Reality.

Efficiency: There are times when we can be our own worst enemy by comparing our talents, skills, accomplishments, and even failures to others. This is self-discouraging and self-defeating, which can result in self-destruction! Choose to be inspired, to be relentless, to be dedicated, and most of all, intentionally focused on the W. I. N. (What's Important Now).

Jermaine Brantley — United States of America
Director, Actor, Stuntman, Entrepreneur
www.imdb.com/name/nm4708409/
Jermaine J Smooth Brantley, Jermaine Brantley
@jermaine_brantley

Gina Trimarco Klauder

GINA TRIMARCO KLAUDER

"To find true love, you must have the courage to love yourself first."

My wish for the reader is to find the courage to leave an unhappy and toxic relationship to find the true love they deserve and desire. Go out and find what you want by knowing *who* you are. Then tell people what you want by *being* that person first.

GET YOUR SH*T TOGETHER TO FIND TRUE LOVE

He asked me what my favorite restaurant was on the "Marshwalk," a popular coastal fishing village in South Carolina that both locals and tourists flock to throughout the year. I hate crowds and loud noise, probably because I make my living speaking in front of large groups of people. When I'm not working, I need to be in serene and calm places. I told him that my favorite restaurant was Costa. Quiet and intimate with great food and off the beaten path. It was also close to the house I was renting. That was important in case I needed to quickly escape a potentially disappointing date.

Frankly, I was nervous about being on a dinner date. It seemed suspect in a weird way because most of my suitors had not offered to take me to dinner. I didn't even care about splitting the bill, but so many of them had only one thing in mind: sex. This was my new life, divorced at age fifty-three and treading water in the new-age dating cesspool.

Granted, I intentionally chose to put myself out there on a dating app, even though most apps were known simply for hooking up. I, on the other hand, was a hopeless romantic because I heard other success stories from my friends about online dating and was optimistic about the possibilities.

My upcoming date with 'Costa Man' seemed too good to be true, but he was the only man who responded to my new and revised online profile, a profile with the headline, *Have Your Shit Together*. My personal description continued with, *I have mine together, and you should too. Be happy with who you are and be secure enough to be with a confident woman who can take care of herself but also needs a man.*

I wrote that profile after a few glasses of wine and a lively conversation with another man I had dated for a minute. We became friends even though it didn't work out. After many odd dates with others, I asked him what about me might scare off men. His response: "You're talented, gorgeous, and don't *need* a man. Eighty percent of the men are scared of you. The twenty percent who will take a chance will get scared off eventually. Men need to feel needed." This enraged me. I shouldn't have to manage the perceptions or insecurities of others just to go on a date.

Within forty-eight hours of posting my revised profile, I was on my way to a proper dinner date with Costa Man. I was skeptical and borderline cynical about this date, but I knew one thing for sure. I knew who I was, and I finally loved me for me. All of the serial dating I had done in a short period of time taught me what I wanted and needed. This 'speed dating' approach, combined with nearly 2 years of therapy, gave me so much clarity and confidence, despite the naysayers who insisted I should have taken a break after leaving my husband. They didn't understand that I was pursuing my lifelong dream. Activity begets results. I wasn't waiting for Mr. Right to find me because there was a good chance his GPS was broken. Mr. Right not only needed to be a willing and equal partner, but he also needed to match my childlike enthusiasm to build a life together.

My ex-husband wasn't that guy. Deep in my heart, I know he didn't have bad intentions. He had his own demons that he couldn't deal with or simply wasn't willing to. Instead, I was often on the receiving end of his unhappiness and insecurities until I was utterly broken, ultimately destroying our marriage. Mine is a story of being unable to see the countless red flags in front of me because my low self-worth blinded me. Those red flags were more like stop signs, and I drove through each one.

The irony is that I manifested my reality, in my opinion, at the age of seventeen. When I told my grade-school-educated, old-fashioned father that I wanted to go to college, his response was, "Why? You're just going to get married and have children." I immediately blurted out loud that I feared I might marry a loser who couldn't support me and our children. My father agreed with my rationale. But my worries were rooted in more than my desire to find meaningful love. I grew up with a sense of financial insecurity and a mindset of scarcity, the product of having a much older father whose health issues, unfortunately, created financial struggles throughout my teen years.

After many failed and toxic relationships, I found myself dating long-distance with a man I thought was what I had always wanted: an attractive, highly educated, well-dressed businessman who came from a family with money. Then one day, I received a phone call from his ex-girlfriend and quickly discovered he had been having an affair with her. I wanted to break up with him, but I loved him. It was so cliché, but I didn't know what else to do. The only way I could start to trust him again was through a marriage proposal and living in the same city. He agreed. Serendipitously, I was offered a job in another city shortly after our engagement, and once he moved there, we started our new life together on neutral ground.

Then the ground gave way. Within eighteen months, the economy crashed, and I lost my job. There we were, both unemployed. I jumped into survival mode. I started a business to generate an income while he appeared mentally paralyzed by the situation. When we moved in together, our fighting was constant and only got worse during the building of my business. We still weren't married because he refused to set a date. Eventually, through couples counseling, we got back on track, and he began to commit truly. He bought a business, and we finally sent out wedding invitations.

Our wedding day was horrible because of the stressors related to his newly acquired business. Instead of being overjoyed and *in love*, we were both on antidepressants, walking through the ceremony like catatonic zombies. I desperately wanted to call it off, but the people around me at the time pushed me to go through with it. "It's just wedding day jitters," they said. So we pushed through the day and faked happiness while I felt like a trapped animal about to face life in a cage. Yet deep down, I knew it was more than cold feet because I asked our wedding officiant to hold off on signing the marriage certificate. I never imagined the "worse" part of "for better or worse" was already upon us. It was time to be married, but it just didn't feel right to me.

We had inherited a rogue employee who embezzled from the business and created constant havoc. This led to a 3-year lawsuit that began a few weeks before our wedding. Not the most ideal way to start a marriage. When the court trial ended, I thought maybe we'd finally get to restart our lives together, but that didn't happen. My husband became a different person. He was angry, depressed, and obsessed with the former employee who attempted to destroy us. He took it out on me often verbally. It was like I became the enemy. He emotionally abandoned me. I started to feel like I was crazy and that I was the one he blamed for everything that went wrong. He chose to spend all his time with other people without me, justifying it to one of our 4 marriage counselors by saying, "She changes the dynamics of a group when she enters a room." He didn't want me around. We were both drinking excessively, which triggered memories of my mother's alcoholism. In drunken stupors, he would become mean and degrading, or even worse, he would ignore me completely.

Shortly after the lawsuit with the rogue employee was resolved, I had several health issues arise, from unexplainable anemia to a broken wrist. Eventually, I moved into our guest room because I couldn't handle the negative energy that flooded out of his pores. I thought the space would help, but it only pushed us further apart. Deep down, I knew I needed to leave him. But each time I thought I found the courage to go, I would get knocked down with a health issue that prevented my departure. With no real support system and insufficient money, I couldn't wrap my head around finding a place to live on my own, which was a legal requirement for filing for divorce.

One day, while lying in a hospital room alone, receiving an emergency blood transfusion, I felt a shift, one that started in my gut and took over my mind. He told a friend that he thought my unexpected illness was something I created or made up. This devastated me. His conflict-avoidant personality caused him to check out on me. What saddened me was the thought of growing old with a husband who couldn't and wouldn't be there for me in times of sickness. I realized that spending the rest of my life with him would be unbearable because health issues would be inevitable, something I had known all too well since childhood. It was clear he wouldn't be the one to advocate for me, and I knew I couldn't live like this for much longer.

I told myself I would leave when I was healthy enough and had enough money, but other excuses constantly interfered. Mostly, I was scared after listening to so many women tell me that getting divorced was the worst thing they ever did. Hearing that it would be impossible to find a decent man was daunting. One woman said she wished she would have just sucked it up and stayed with her husband because of its negative financial impact on her. Hearing these stories terrified me. Instead of realizing that I was strong enough and dared to leave, I convinced myself to stay because that was expected of me as a godly wife. Besides my religious beliefs, I could hear my father's voice replaying: "You don't leave. You work it out." I was so conflicted. I couldn't comprehend how I was supposed to continue to endure the emotional abuse. I was exhausted, vulnerable, and raw. I felt like I was stuck behind a wall that I desperately wanted to climb over but didn't want to risk the elements of the unknown on the other side. Status quo and sadness felt much safer.

The veil of safety lifted when I was recovering from a broken wrist surgery and emergency appendectomy simultaneously. Once again, I was dealing with medical situations, literally single-handedly. Just putting on clothes was a chore for me. It took every ounce of strength to do anything. But I had no choice, as I had to fly to a client's office about a week after my back-to-back surgeries.

I had no idea at the time the impact that business trip would have on the direction of my life. On my flight there, sitting across the aisle from me, was a handsome man. When he began flirting with me, I initially felt embarrassed because I was not myself physically. I was wearing glasses and without any make-up. My hair looked like I just rolled out of bed, and I was dressed in baggy clothes. I felt so ugly because it was just too difficult to put myself together with 1 hand in a sling after surgery.

Here was this man, a former semi-pro football player, over 6 feet tall with blonde hair and crystal blue eyes, flirting with me. It wasn't the first time I was being flirted with, but it was the first time I liked it. I was so broken, looking my worst, and this man saw me and made me blush like a schoolgirl. We didn't exchange business cards, but he managed to find me and my email address on the internet by searching my company's name. He sent me his phone number, and we talked for hours later that night.

This unexpected stranger re-ignited me. I couldn't remember the last time I felt so alive. When I returned from my trip, my husband was dismal and apathetic, as usual, towards me. I had a little swagger after my mid-air reawakening and said, "You know. Men flirt with me when I travel. Just because you don't want me doesn't mean other men don't." This enraged him, which was not what I had hoped for. I hoped he would wake up and see me like another man did; attractive. Instead, he used my comment to punish me for saying such a thing. It was the day before Easter. The next day he decided to spend his day with friends at a bar and told me to make my own plans. He literally abandoned me on holiday, knowing I would end up alone. I was crushed. This reminded me that I did not want to spend the rest of my life this way. I was done being the godly wife and tired of trying to make the best of a bad situation.

Through coaching from my spiritual advisor, I was able to understand that I did everything possible to save my marriage and that God did not expect me to keep fighting. I was no longer conflicted by my religious beliefs. Once relieved of that burden, I found a licensed counselor to help me prepare mentally for starting the divorce process and my exit plan. I learned so much about myself over the next eighteen months of therapy. The real reasons I struggled in my marriage were rooted in the abuse I had endured with my mother, an abuse I was constantly being reminded of through my husband's behavior. I needed to resolve those issues to find my self-worth again. These realizations gave me the courage to set a deadline to move out and officially start the "divorce clock."

Within days of moving into a temporary place with just my clothes and things to run my business, I felt reborn. *Sort of.* Some part of me was sad and still secretly hoping that my husband would realize what he was losing. But I could no longer let him be my problem to solve. I set my sights on growing my business, and suddenly started making money again. People could feel my lightness. Before I knew it, my temporary 6-month lease was about to expire, and I found the next place to live. I knew that making this move into a more permanent home meant that reconciliation was doubtful, and I was ready to start a new life.

While I was on the cusp of greatness, everything came crashing down on me for the next 9 months as the COVID-19 pandemic set in. My business was shuttered, I had no income, and my mother died. I wondered if I should run back and beg my husband to work it out. I didn't have the energy or desire to keep pushing through. I thought maybe all those women who warned me were right. Yet, through faith and my resiliency, I kept reminding myself that I didn't want what I once had. My dream of a happy ending gave me the courage to believe the love and the life I deserved was absolutely possible.

The divorce became final after fifteen months, and a new chapter began. I had a clean slate to build the life I wanted. I got back on track financially and started serial dating. After nearly twenty years with the same man, I had no idea how rough it would be to date again (other than what all those other women had told me), but I looked at dating like a treasure hunt. You must enjoy the search as much as you enjoy finding the treasure, and sometimes you must be willing to ditch the GPS to savor, rather than fear, the journey over the wall.

That jump over the wall is what brought me to the marshwalk. Costa Man, David, had a solid GPS, and his sense of direction was on target. He asked me if I went to church and if I liked banana bread. I was easily impressed by these things. He made a dinner reservation at Costa, and that is where we first met face-to-face. I was nervous to see him, but the conversation was easy, real, and fun. He was handsome, a gentleman, kind, transparent, and funny. We walked to our cars after dinner, where he gave me the banana bread he had made and asked me if he could kiss me. That was a first. Of course, I said yes because I needed to know if we had chemistry.

Boy, did we. 1 year later, on the anniversary of our first date, we got married. We are so equally yoked in the most beautiful way. He is my best friend and the true love of my life. While therapy healed me and my self-worth issues, David shows me the unconditional love I always craved. I learned that I had lost myself and my belief in my personal value, and when I decided I was worth it, life became golden and grand.

If you're unhappy and questioning yourself or judging your choices and decisions, you may want to get your sh*t together and climb over to the other side of the wall. What I mean by that is, you may want to figure out who *you* are and what *you* want. The journey might feel painful, but it is worth it because you will find a life of joy and peace when you value yourself, define your needs, and determine what is most important to you. When you pursue exactly what you want in life, you get it. Be clear with your intent. Speak your truth. Follow your unique GPS, and seek the treasurers that are just waiting for you to discover.

IGNITE ACTION STEPS

- **Seek counseling or therapy**. Use the support of a professional to help you work on the things you can't see on your own.

- **Create a detailed list** of attributes you need and want in a partner. By defining exactly what you want, you will attract exactly what you asked for.

- **Write a dating profile**, describing who *you* are and what *you* want. Date a lot to refine your needs and desires in a mate. Then re-write your dating profile after dating a few people making sure you show up being yourself.

Gina Trimarco Klauder — United States of America
Speaker, Sales Coach, Trainer, Improv Comic, Author, Podcaster
www.ginatrimarco.com
🅕 *ginatrimarcoimprovised*
🅞 *ginatrimarco*
🅛 *ginatrimarco*

Sandra Von Hollen

SANDRA VON HOLLEN

"YOU are the Magic Sauce!!"

My dear Reader, I wholeheartedly believe that practicing gratitude daily has the power to transform the course of your life, no matter the challenges you may face. Even amidst grief and sorrow, you will discover rays of hope illuminating your path. Embrace courage and step boldly into the person you aspire to be—the best version of yourself! You are capable of experiencing life's journey with resilience and grace. The world awaits your greatness!

ONE PURPLE BUTTERFLY

On a fateful day in July 1977, the irreversible loss of my childhood unfolded, forever shifting the trajectory of my life. In hindsight, many years later, that pivotal day remains etched in my memory as a turning point where grief and courage converged, leading me to a profound understanding of my own resilience. With this in mind, let me tell you my story of finding courage from the ashes of grief.

As a 9-year-old, I was awakened, just after midnight at home, to my mom's shrilling screams and cries. Consumed by fear, I bolted upright in my bed, my heart racing. My cousin, lying next to me, was equally terrified and awake. We debated who was going to see what was the cause of such commotion. UGH! It was me. As I made my way down the narrow, dimly lit hallway, I could hear my mom's sobs and the familiar voices of my Grampa and Uncle. I stood in the doorway to the living room, out of breath with fear. Finally, they noticed me. Grampa approached and wrapped me in his protective arms. Then, he delivered the dreadful news that my Dad was never coming home again. Dad and his friend had been hit head-on by a drunk driver and were killed instantly. I was shattered and ran to my cousin. I screamed at her. "MY DAD IS DEAD!"

I went to my little brother's room next door to deliver the heart-wrenching news that our Dad was never coming home. We cried together on his bed, not knowing what our lives would look like but knowing they would be very different from that moment forward.

3 crying children returned to the living room where Grampa sat, overcome with grief. We were overflowing with deep emotions, anger, and many questions. Such as, *How could this have happened? Why wasn't he home?* He should have come home earlier, as we were leaving for a family reunion in the morning. That was the looming question I repeated for many years to follow. *Dad, why didn't you come home earlier that night? You'd still be here with us.* The "what if's" would continue for years.

Eventually, we gathered a few things and made our way to the police car, which was waiting to take us to Grampa's house. The police car ride seemed to take forever, like we were stuck in a bad dream. When I think back now, I have no idea how we all fit into that car.

As my grandparents' house filled with devastated relatives and dear friends, I clung to my little brother, and in this time we forged an unbreakable bond. That day in July marked the end of my childhood as I knew it. The trajectory of my life forever changed with the devastation etched into my soul. It was my first and very tragic encounter with grief. Little did I know that it would be something I carried with me for a lifetime.

As I went through my teenage years and early twenties, the constant grip of grief was ever-present and evident in everything I did. The feelings of loss, anger, and sadness resided deep in my heart—I used alcohol to numb the anguish and to try to cope. Of course, the alcohol did nothing good and led me down a path of many poor decisions to find the love I was missing. The weekly bar trips with friends seemed so fun at the time. And, many Sundays were wasted recovering from a hangover.

The feeling of not being enough and the lack of self-esteem was something I would struggle with for many years. I had adopted many insecurities, all leading to a feeling of unworthiness.

Amidst my newfound reality, my relationship with my mom changed as she navigated her new reality of parenting all on her own. My grandparents became my guiding lights as I grew up. They were extraordinary individuals helping me through all of life's lessons. I spent much of my time with them. On weekends I'd go to their house and play cards, learn how to knit/crochet with Gramma, or just absorb their company and visits. I found solace in their presence; they were my confidants, my everything.

When I was thirty, my Gramma passed away from cancer. I was blessed to be able to be there with her as she crossed over. Saying goodbye to Gram was incredibly difficult and took my breath away on more than one occasion. Grampa passed after a medical procedure a few years later, and I regretted not being there for him. I wish I would have stayed at the hospital with him that night. Instead, I received a call from my Uncle that Grampa was gone. It was an unexpected call that shocked me to the core.

The summer before Grampa passed, my uncle, the dad of my cousin who was with me the night my father died, was killed in a car accident. I was called to the accident scene and, along with my stepfather, identified my uncle as he lay motionless on the side of the highway. That was one of the hardest things I've ever had to do. We drove to the nearby hospital from the accident scene to be with my aunt and cousin. She was there for me when my father passed, and death again intertwined with our fate.

As my grief accumulated, I felt like drowning in it. Dark days seemed never-ending, and I suffered from an undiagnosed illness for nearly a year. I would constantly lose my voice, my chest ached, and I would have no energy. It was hard even to keep my house clean. Day-to-day chores seemed overwhelming.

As my life progressed, my incredible husband and 3 kids kept me busy with fun adventures and the blessing of watching them grow up. I poured my heart and soul into caring for my family. I would tell the kids stories about my dad and my grandparents. I emphasized just how important these incredible individuals were to me. I spoke of the fabulous garden where Grampa grew the most delicious green peas in the world. I would share my Gramma's many talents; crocheting, painting, and quilt-making. I talked about how my Gram was my best friend and that I was the luckiest person to have had them for my grandparents. I was truly blessed. I am who I am today because of them.

The stories were plentiful, as my memories of the most special people in my life are true treasures. However, I could never get through a story without that heaviness in my chest, that big lump in my throat, and the tears threatening to spill over. I failed to realize that this was grief, unprocessed and unresolved.

I had boxes of precious memories in my garage, though I would never open them. Every time I glanced up at those boxes, I would feel the tightness in my throat, that all too familiar ache in my heart, and those darn tears would well up. *Ugh, I just couldn't kick this mountain of grief!*

As I entered my early fifties, a newfound flame ignited within, compelling me to embark on a transformative journey toward self-improvement. Amid that journey, I was introduced to 2 extraordinary women who unveiled the secrets of Feng Shui, unraveling a practice that would lead my life into a new era. They taught me; *Where the focus goes, the energy flows.*

I was facilitating classes at my holistic wellness store, where we would bring in people with different skills each week to teach and offer the community interesting and engaging experiences. That particular Feng Shui class was a weekend class diving into the power of our possessions—2 days of understanding energy and the vibration of our home and environments. Typically, I would facilitate the classes and not participate. However, these ladies insisted that I become an active participant. They reassured me that everything would be taken care of during the class, allowing me to focus on my own growth and healing.

I am so grateful they encouraged me to boldly step into my greatness.

During that weekend's class, I learned all things Feng Shui—including the 9 sections of the Bagua map and each section's significance. I discovered what each room represents in a home or space. For example, the furthest left corner from the front door is the wealth area, and the closest right corner is the travel section. According to the Bagua map, my garage represents the travel section of my home. In my garage, I have so many things that I accumulated along my life journey. Including Gramma's unfinished paintings, *oh gosh, she would not be happy that I still have those!* She would say, "Get rid of those terrible pieces." Yet, to me, they were fragments of her, unfinished but still precious.

I learned that energy needs to flow in every room of your home. When we hang onto items that no longer serve us or live in too much clutter, we create stuck energy.

Inspired by my newfound understanding, I took the assignment of decluttering and clearing out the items that were weighing me down. I opened the boxes and meticulously sifted through those treasures. As I uncovered Gram's unfinished paintings, I took some moments to remember her in her painting clothes and basked in that familiar paint smell. Surprisingly, instead of sadness, I felt comfort and peace. As I bid farewell to those unfinished pieces, I know she smiled. In those moments, I released decades of bottled-up anguish and replaced them with feelings of gratitude and joy.

I discovered that *grief is a part of life, it differs for everyone, but it doesn't have to be the story that defines us.* That awakened the beginning of my journey to unpack the grief I had carried for far too long. Taking that leap of faith and participating in that class was my first step toward courage. My first endeavor into the new chapter of an improved and healing me. No more being consumed by grief, instead, living in profound gratitude every single day.

The week after I cleaned out the garage and sifted through my grandparent's treasures, letting many of them go, I won a cruise. *Whaaattt???*

Remember, according to the Bagua map, my garage is the travel zone in my home. I cleared out the clutter so the energy could flow, and the Universe rewarded me with the cruise! *Yes, it did!* From that moment on, I was captivated by the power of Feng Shui. Since then, I have implemented Feng Shui in the rest of our home and our business. I have experienced an accumulation of great things happening in my life since letting go and moving on.

I continued to pursue other self-development modalities. I embraced guided meditation and writing in gratitude journals, which I continue as my everyday practice. I have stepped out in courage and realized my worth. I am worthy of accepting what's best for me, making me my best for family, friends, and business associates. Through raising my consciousness, I also hired a life coach. I immersed myself in books and put into practice the profound knowledge I learned from those pages. High-quality nutrition has also become an integral part of my well-being. I am improving in mind, body, and spirit. My entire life feels like it has been released and given back to me.

Now in my mid-fifties, with the recent passing of my very dear friend, I am reminded of the beautiful impact one person can create. She was my 'no matter what friend' for over 3 decades! In one of our final visits, we made a pact that if we got to choose what we were when we returned to this earth after we had passed, she would return as a purple butterfly. At the time, we didn't realize the significance that would have for her family and friends. Since our pact, purple butterflies have shown up in symbols, images, and many magical ways. They are testimony to a lady that made a huge impact in the lives of so many. Her absence on this physical plane will be missed unmeasurably. Knowing the abundant love we all shared will have her memory live on forever.

Her ripple carries on, one purple butterfly at a time.

With the loss of my friend, I have found myself so grateful for all the incredible memories I have of our friendship. Yes, it's still painful, but the love and memories outweigh the darkness grief can bring. Grief is an enigmatic creature and differs with each person you lose. When left unaddressed and unacknowledged, a tight grip on one's spirit continues. When you embrace and surrender to it, *you get to choose to see the rays of hope illuminating your path.*

As I took those first courageous steps to master my grief after losing her, this became the turning point in my life—a pivotal moment that led me to embrace a new mindset, habits, and practices—rebuilding a life worth living through self-development and gratitude. I am no longer a victim of my grief but a master of it, transforming my pain into purpose.

When we take the first step of courage to say YES to becoming our very best selves, It truly is a beautiful transition. Through the messy unpacking of grief and feelings of unworthiness—putting the broken, jagged pieces of ourselves back together is a beautiful process of pain, anger, hurt, and many *AHA* moments!!

Taking that very first courageous step toward change is undoubtedly the most challenging. Do it despite your fear, embrace the messiness, be willing to fail, and learn. Be open to growing and becoming better. The time for transformation is now. Once you embark on the journey of becoming the best version of yourself, you will witness the profound effect it creates. Your greatness will radiate and touch the lives of others.

Embrace your courage, my friend, and witness the incredible ripple of transformation that awaits you on the other side.

Ignite Action Steps:

- **Learn the methods of Feng Shui.** Seek out the Bagua map and implement just a few simple practices. You will be inspired by the changes that start to show up in your life. Begin with 1 room at a time and revel in the new life you are creating.

- **Start Meditating.** Use guided meditations to discover the wonder of what meditation does for your heart, brain, and well-being. Through meditation, you will learn to quiet your racing thoughts, the value of slowing down, and the importance of breath.

- **Let go and release.** Clear the clutter that no longer serves you and may be weighing you down. Take a moment to cherish those items, bless them and send them on their way.

- **Start a Daily Journal of Gratitude.** Begin your day by writing 3-5 things you are grateful for. At first, you may only find gratitude in the air you breathe, your morning coffee, or the gorgeous sunrise. As you begin the habit of gratitude, you will find so much to be grateful for. It's a magnificent process to witness unfolding. Living your life through the eyes of gratitude is truly a blessed way to live!

Through gratitude, I acknowledge that I have been blessed to be present to raise my children into adulthood. Growing old is not a privilege given to everyone. Make the most of every day and cherish your incredible memories with your loved ones.

Sandra Von Hollen — Canada
CEO Alberta Laser Engraving, Ignite the Light, Wellness Coach
www.albertalaserengraving.ca
www.ignitethelight.ca
www.sandravonhollen.com
sandra kells-vonhollen
sandra._vh

Deborah A. Ellis

DEBORAH A. ELLIS

"Respect and Expect. If you get a Reject—
Defect and Resurrect with Greatness."

I intend to inspire and motivate you in a way that ignites your ability to see, do, and have whatever your heart desires; to be carefree, at peace, and let go of yesterday and look forward to your best day ahead. It is my hope you will challenge whatever frightens you from achieving your goals or next accomplishments. I graciously authorize new confidence for you to live your best life.

DOUBLE DIMPLE

I can remember the hot sun on my face, adding heat to stinging pain as I lay on the ground in shock, bleeding from the right cheek. I was a 7-year-old little girl growing up in the countryside of Middlesex County, Virginia, when I was accidentally shot in the face by my brother playing Cowboys and Indians. A real gun fell from under the mattress that we were playing on and that's when my life took a turn toward life or death.

Miraculously, and filled with fear, we had the courage to run up the long dirt road for help at a nearby family member's home. My mother was working, and our area was too poor for there to be phones in every home. So, my uncle ran to her workplace and summoned her with the news. As any other mother would do in panic, she sped home to rescue me, driving fast, turning wildly into the driveway while crying. My eyes followed the overwhelm, nervousness, and shock of my family members frantically reacting to my injury. I just laid, crying, waiting until my mother arrived, and when she did, she quickly said, "Put her in the back seat." My brother was eagerly trying to get in as she took off with both back doors still open and me bleeding profusely, holding a honey bun that someone gave me to stop crying.

Within ten minutes, we had pulled into the doctor's office, and my mother, without hesitation, took me straight inside. After a brief exam, I was rushed off to Richmond Memorial Hospital with sirens blaring a warning: "Life-threatening! Move out of the way!" The last thing I remember was a doctor standing over me saying, "Bye-bye," while placing a mask over my face in the operating room.

I woke up with a stiff face as the bullet was still lodged in my palate. My mother was beside me, anxious to know my prognosis. I remember people saying how lucky I was to be alive; that I could have been blinded or worse killed. The horrible pain, the worry on my mother's face, and the sounds of people wondering if I would die ... that was the first time I had to tap into my courage. I couldn't talk for weeks, and the recovery took months before I was able to eat properly and feel somewhat normal again. Yet, I survived still being the same happy little girl down the country road, playing with my brother and sisters, making mud pies, and enjoying fruit from our apple, pear, and fig trees, while picking blackberries along the roadside. People would later identify me by my right cheek because it looked like I had a double dimple from the gunshot. I courageously embraced it as a part of me.

My mother and stepfather, however, were struggling with jobs to make ends meet as I was healing and life was going on day by day. It was around that time my stepfather decided to move us an hour and a half north to Hampton, Virginia so that we could have a better education. Our new home was nothing like living down the dirt road. We lived on a main street that ran like a major fairway toward Langley Air Force Base, one of the biggest landmarks of the area. We were still very country at heart as we played up and down the backyards with neighborhood kids catching tadpoles, crabbing with chicken necks, and inter-mingling with classmates from the adjoining affluent Air Force neighborhood. The two divided neighborhoods were only a short walk from our elementary school, where we all got along and respected one another.

However, in our home, things were quite different from the magical expe-riences I'd had outdoors with my friends. Courage was educating me in new ways. One day, I saw my stepfather pointing the same gun I was accidentally shot with, at my mother's head while she was holding my baby sister. The screams and tears pouring down our faces weren't magic; they were tragic. As the domestic and verbal abuse toward my mother continued, I became fearless in my own mind. I said to myself, *I don't like that, and no one will ever treat me that way.* That conviction gave me a sense at an early age that I wanted none of that for my life or for my four sisters and brother.

My brother taught me courage in other ways, though perhaps not the healthiest. He was the eldest and most mischievous, born with larceny in his heart. He was the worst criminal, but he was also good with his hands and could fix broken things, like radios, stereos, and cars. He liked to dress sharp and was a very handsome young man who just needed guidance and acceptance from a father figure. That was something he could not get from my stepfather, who abused him just as cruelly as he did my mother. The years of the bad relationship between him and my stepfather brought my brother and I closer, and made the two of us more brave.

That's when our twelve and fourteen-year-old minds gave us the misguided courage we needed to one day decide we were going to kill our stepfather with the same gun I was shot with, the same gun he'd waved at our mother. That was, of course, my brother's idea. The plan was to be on top of the shed when my stepfather came home and shoot him when he got out of his old green Cadillac with the Batman fins. We lay on our bellies perched atop the detached shed, hidden behind some trees, waiting for him to pull into the driveway. We had been waiting at least half an hour when our stepfather finally arrived.

"Shoot him," my brother whispered.

"I thought you were going to shoot him!" I said back, scared we would soon be discovered.

We were still on top of the shed, disagreeing when my stepfather was already in the house. Thank God, no one found out. That became our secret, and we kept it from everyone for years. As we grew older, my brother kept making unfortunate decisions, and I watched him choose drugs again and again. I told him I was sure he was going to die a long, difficult death. He eventually left home shortly after high school and joined the Army Reserves. I hoped he might turn his life around. But instead, his life was tragically shortened after driving late one night and having a head-on collision with a tractor-trailer driver. I felt devastated that I had lost my only brother, but I used my courage to keep going.

During my three years in high school, I signed up for the nursing program that was offered through a local vocational-technical program (VOTECH). My counselor told me it would be a great career start, and I felt the excitement of having a job where I could earn *good money* after watching my brother earn *bad money*. I excelled in the nursing courses, and that became the beginning of providing for myself and my future. I also worked summer jobs to keep adding to my finances. That was when my perspective shifted, and I felt like I would make it in life as I was learning skills that could support my independence. At such a young age, I could even buy a Buick LeSabre, a full-size family car, and it was better than the adults' cars on my street.

My stepfather decided to take my car as his own without my permission, and my heart could take no more. I remembered my courage; my promise to myself that I would not be abused by him any longer. So, I ran away and stayed with a few friends, hiding in their bedrooms at night. Of course, their parents knew I was there and let my mother know that I was okay. I lived that way during my eleventh-grade summer until I amazingly found a one-bedroom apartment with a small living room and adjoining kitchen, bedroom, and bathroom, and that then became my home.

After high school graduation, I found myself in Missouri for Army Basic Training, preparing to enter Fort Sam Houston in Texas as a Combat Medic. I joined people from all over the United States at basic training as we endured being yelled at and shuffled around in the cold by drill sergeants. Everyone was stressed at first, but as we got used to the routine, it was more of a mind game. It was less about courage and more about survival at that point. We knew the drill sergeants' job was to teach us teamwork, discipline, weapons, physical training, and more while developing us into soldiers before we entered specialized training in our career fields.

My first assignment was working on Labor and Delivery, then I primarily worked as an Allergy and Immunology Specialist. Then I moved into staff positions, joining War Fighters in XVIII Airborne Corp Surgeons Office. No, I was not Airborne, nor did I ever want to jump out of planes. I had plenty else to be brave about. Being a medic, I had to dig even deeper than ever before just to keep doing my job. I witnessed a decapitation after a Persian missile blew up. I witnessed a mid-air collision and the ensuing ground collision at Pope Air Force Base in North Carolina that killed twenty-four members of the U.S. Army's 82nd Airborne Division. Another terrible incident I went through as a medic was providing support after a sniper wounded nineteen soldiers and killed one of them.

My time in the Army wasn't all bad, though. The cohesion, opportunities, and education I experienced were a big plus. I completed a Bachelor of Science and Security Management, a master's degree, traveled, and met people from all over the world. And what I enjoyed the most, my biggest reason to be courageous, was the birth of my daughter (who now serves in the Army as a Labor and Delivery Nurse).

Reflecting on my own life as I watched my daughter grow, I realized that there are many courageous phases to life from infancy to adulthood. There are times when you have no choice but to accept what is at hand or happening in your life. As a child, so many decisions were made for me, and being brave looked a lot like getting by. The magical thing is you don't stay a child forever. In time, you get to see that your ideas of what's good for you are none of anyone's business unless they can help you along the way.

In my teenage years, I learned courage through life's lessons. I wanted a better life for myself and wasn't willing to settle. I was determined not to be a victim or victimized, which meant standing up for myself and being strong.

With each step I took in my adulthood, I made decisions and choices for my own health and wealth. Life will offer you the bitter taste of lemons and the sweet taste of lemonade, but I had to decide what was best for me, asking myself, *Is this all that I am worth?*

I always pose this question to inquire what one feels they are worth. By asking this question, it opens the possibility for more to unfold and a positive outcome to be revealed. I have found that the words we speak empower us. There is life and death in the power of the tongue. The words you speak can either elevate you or tear you down.

From everything I have learned, I choose to use my courage to speak positivity into my life, and that is exactly what I now do. I feel empowered through affirmations, saying:

- I AM *Enough*
- I AM *Valuable*
- I AM *Grateful*
- I AM *Determine*
- I AM *Intentional*
- I AM *Rejuvenated* to live my best life every day

Through my growth and after serving twenty years in the Army and retiring, by faith and grace, I have been afforded better opportunities, jobs, mentors, entrepreneurship, and investment. And, I have blessed, inspired, motivated, and mentored others. I have come so far from the long dirt road and those childhood dreams I envisioned for myself. My courage drove me to aspire for the best life and taught me to work hard and do what it takes to achieve it.

Incredibly, my mother has come just as far. She had always taught us to work and use our money for what we wanted, and I saw her do the same; getting her 'Ph.D. in life,' gaining her independence with her own career, and enjoying retirement. Her greatest reward is loving her children and never comparing us to one another. Her heart is so big and she gives endlessly—she is one of the most courageous people I know. There was never a time I couldn't talk to my mother, even when she was going through her own difficulties.

I remember asking my mother, "How did you endure life's tribulations?" She simply said, "The mornings would come, and I had my children to take care of. It was not about me for a long time." If that's not courage, I don't know what is. And, that is the courage I keep living each day. From all the life lessons and wisdom I have learned, I see the beauty and essence just like a caterpillar that turns into a beautiful butterfly after a long sleep in its cocoon. I am so grateful for how my life has turned out after almost losing it, and the double dimple of my smile is proof that life emerges courageously through unexpected tragedies.

The world requires fearlessness to overcome the things that challenge our nerves, emotions, fears, doubts, and expectations. Enjoy being all that you are. Become courageous and bask in the fruits of your labor to make the impossible possible. Push through limitations because great things come through hard work and perseverance. Find your worth and honor your value. You tell people how to treat you and set the tone for the respect you receive. Be confident in who you are, and life will give you the blessings you desire.

Ignite Action Steps:

RESPECT yourself enough that others don't have a choice but to do the same.

R = Release anything or anyone that does not serve your good—resentment, jealousy or anger, and all negativity. Allow your spirit to be at peace and your internal organs to rest. You need them to survive.

E = Everyday wake up giving thanks for a new dawn, another chance to be great, to be at peace, and to love.

S = Self-Respect and respect for others. Value yourself and your beliefs and bring no harm to others; be respectful of others despite your differences. Treat people the way you would want to be treated.

P = Plan your intentions and know your purpose, being consistent from start to finish. The old saying is that it is not a plan unless it is written. Be your own architect and see it in your mind until it is a reality. Keep a daily calendar, journal, or notes available to stay on track.

E = Exercise your faith and body to speak the same healthy language, find an activity you like and switch them up until you have one you enjoy. Read and recite your affirmations and your devotions, eat to live and not live to eat, exercise to fuel your energy, and sustain your day. The benefits of exercise are endless.

C= ChAmp versus ChUmp; another way of saying don't have pity parties but champion your way through the day, through your goals, and know that sometimes losing is winning. Take baby steps and write out your plans, prioritize what you can do now, and know that every plan is a process and it takes time.

T= Ta-da, Tenaciously take action and be responsible. Teach others how to treat you, tell people how you feel; no one does mind reading 1-0-1. Don't let a misunderstanding keep you from achieving your goals, have the courage to say *I was wrong, you were right,* or whatever needs to be said.

Deborah A Ellis — United States of America
Security Program Management, Veteran, Author, Property Management
deborah.a.ellis
deborahellis4x

Nolan Pillay

NOLAN PILLAY

"Life does not have to end where you started!"

I want you, the reader, to know that by learning to embrace life as a blessing with an empowering mindset, you can greatly enhance your overall perspective and well-being. Adopting this attitude will allow you to shift your focus from dwelling on hardships and challenges to recognizing the inherent value and beauty in every experience. To those who are reading this, I urge you not to let any system turn you into a victim. Instead, embrace every challenge and obstacle as a chance to learn and evolve as an individual. Believe me, you'll experience a profound transformation. Just dare to think differently, and you'll become a game changer. Embrace these hurdles and difficulties as they propel you to become the best version of yourself.

FROM SAMOOSA BOY TO CEO

The alarm clock went off. It was 5 AM, cold and dark. I was so unmotivated to move—some mornings, I was even in tears, wishing I could lay in my warm floor bed a little longer. But we didn't have a choice; our survival depended on me getting out of bed. As a 10-year-old Indian boy, my siblings and I used to go out early every morning selling Indian delicacies, including the most delicious Samoosa that our mum used to make. Life was very simple back then. If you did not make a sale, it just meant we would not have money to buy groceries for our supper or lunch the next day. I remember times when dinner was just a glass of water or a cup of tea. My stomach would growl with hunger, but I blocked it out of my mind as there was no other option.

There was a mixture of pride and shame when we went out. I noticed the judgment on people's faces when they opened the door to me with my basket of delicacies in hand, ready to be sold. Yet, I was glad to be helping my family. The excitement when making a sale was so fulfilling that it motivated us to venture out daily. It was a proud moment, and we all celebrated together.

Our family was made up of 7, including Mum, Dad, 2 sisters, and 3 brothers. We also had a few dogs through the years. Our home was a 1-bedroom brick house with the lounge made into a bedroom for the children, divided by a makeshift curtain and a bedsheet on a string. The toilets were outside, a few meters away, so we had to brave the trip, no matter the weather. Our wash basin was a small steel bowl, and charcoal was toothpaste for us when we could not afford the luxury. Life was not easy in South Africa, but we were grateful that we had our family together.

As a young boy, I recall some days going to school with torn shoes or no jersey on a bitter, rainy day. Other children used to make fun of us all the time… something people call bullying these days. It was hurtful, and it took a lot of courage not to start fighting those mean kids. We knew what would happen if we did—getting into fights would mean a beating from our parents *and* from the school principal, so we did not take the risk and accepted what came our way.

Dad used to work as a waiter back then and Mum worked in a shoe factory, earning small salaries that could barely cover the household bills. We would often try to watch the neighbor's TV through a small gap in the fence until we were spotted and the door would slam in our faces. We thought, *How cruel can people be?* Some days, we found ourselves without electricity and had to study using a very small candle. Our parents always enforced that we get a good education as this would help us to get better jobs. Though, I often ponder whether this was really true, as my strong values got me to where I am now. Looking back, I see value in education, but I didn't do well at school and still managed to become successful.

As far back as I can remember, South Africa was going through something called Apartheid, a system of institutionalized racial segregation and discrimination that was enforced from 1948 to the early 1990s. The term "apartheid" is an Afrikaans word meaning "apartness," and the policy aimed to maintain the dominance of the white minority population over the black majority. The South African government enacted a series of laws separating people based on race and ethnic background. The primary racial groups were classified as White, Black, Colored (mixed-race), and Indian/Asian. Each group was subjected to different legal and social restrictions, with Whites receiving preferential treatment, while the other racial groups faced varying degrees of discrimination and marginalization. Racial classification determined where individuals could live, work, and receive education. Non-white individuals were required to carry passbooks that contained personal information and proof of permission to be in certain areas. These were called Dompass, literally meaning the "stupid pass" or domestic passport. These laws restricted our movement and employment opportunities.

Once when I was about fourteen years old, I recall being beaten with a baton by a white Afrikaner policeman because I was in the city center after curfew. His baton was made of thick, hard plastic and could cause bruising or even more severe wounds, including bone fractures, nerve or muscle damage, and internal injuries. Luckily, my muscles took the impact, but it still caused me excruciating pain that was felt for days. I was angry, scared, and wanted to scream out and fight back but knew the consequences if I did. I cannot even recall why I was there in the first place, but it was a lesson well learned. You had to be courageous enough that even when being beaten, you accepted it and did not try to defend yourself, or else you would end up in prison.

Still, to this day, being an Indian in South Africa is extremely difficult as we are always in the middle and lose many benefits through various systems implemented by the government. African Blacks get priority. As an Indian, it feels like we fell through the gaps in society and do not have access to the same opportunities. We are either not black enough or not white enough. It's a sad state of affairs, but we do our best to become successful. Nothing will hold us back as we believe in our God-given potential.

During my school days, I recall being an excellent sportsman, excelling in athletics, basketball, football, cricket, and tennis. Seriously, I was really good, but unfortunately, the apartheid system prevented me from representing my country professionally. No black person was allowed to play sports for his or her country back then. It almost broke me as I knew the potential I had. It took courage to watch those non-black citizens partake in sports at a higher level, knowing I could have done better than many of them. At times, I do ponder the thought of how far I could have gone in sports. I feel strongly that this could have been my career choice, and I could have retired successfully. *The apartheid robbed me!*

Since the door of professional sports was closed to me, academics had to be my pathway toward a future filled with success. I wrote my matric exam at seventeen, and my courage was tested again! At that stage in my life, I believed that I was a solid student academically. Throughout the years, I had good grades, even in accelerated courses. There were no signs that my education was dropping. After I wrote my exams, I did the normal thing anyone my age would do—celebrate with my friends and wait until results day. Back then, the outcome of our exam used to appear in the local newspaper. The big day arrived, and we all excitedly went to the newspaper offices to check our results. I started to go through the paper, page by page, but could not find my name. I called my friend to check, and he said, "Sorry, your name is not there." This could only mean one thing… that I failed!

I was in tears. I stood in a corner, overwhelmed and sobbing because my name did not appear. I was embarrassed that I let myself and my family down. I then decided that I would go the next day to the school to find out what was going on. I met with the Principal, who I sensed by this time knew that I had failed but played along until, eventually, he told me the hard truth. It wasn't a misprint. I was left in dismay, totally gutted at that point. I was too embarrassed to face my parents or the close-knit community we stayed in. People used to judge us, and I knew they would call me a failure. Gossip came naturally to them, they always looked for something or someone to discuss. I turned my back to the Principal and started to walk home with just one thought on my mind: end my life.

I got home, took a lot of tablets (not sure how many), and woke up in the hospital to realize that I also failed at my suicide. The nurses and doctors were in the ward looking at me in disbelief, making me feel even more guilty about what I had just attempted. They had given me something extremely salty to drink, which caused me to bring up all the tablets at the same time. I discovered that this was the method they used when a person overdosed. Everyone was asking me randomly why I did it, and each time I had to explain that I failed and did not want to go on with life. My parents and siblings were upset with me, but they later understood. Today I can relate to this journey with a smile as I am grateful to have survived that phase of my life.

Eventually, I got discharged and faced the community. My family was very supportive of me, but the working world was less so. Without a matric pass, companies don't normally hire you. I started to look at my options, and eventually I asked a friend whose dad worked in a factory. I told him that I would take on *any* job without feeling ashamed. After all, I had started out as a 'Samoosa Boy.' I truly believed that God was on my side and that very same year, in December, I got a job as a packer and sweeper in the factory. It involved packing soup in boxes at the end of the production line. I was nothing but grateful that I could earn money and help my parents with household expenses.

I couldn't help but wonder if this was all life had in store for me. My daily attire was white overalls and a broken broom handle. Meanwhile, I used to watch my seniors daily, dressed up in smart clothes, carrying files around, in meetings, and wondered if I could be like them. Be careful what you put out into the Universe. During one of my twelve-hour night shifts, a voice asked me, "Is this where you want to be for the rest of your life, Nolan?" It was so real, like this voice was reading my mind and shouting down at me. I don't know if it was God or my Higher Purpose, but the question was valid. My immediate answer was, "No." I instantly paused, fluctuating between thoughts of inspiration (*I CAN do more*) and self-doubt (*I'm just a packer sweeper and don't have my matric*). Fear bounced around in my head and threatened to keep me standing still as I wondered whether I had what it took to pursue a real career. Yet the voice kept asking, again and again, "Do you want to be here?" and I couldn't deny the answer in my heart. "No." As I embraced the truth, new courage began to grow in me, and I knew I could improve my life if I tried.

That was the moment everything in my life started to change. I decided to do something and use my courage to help me fulfill my dreams. My plan was to work overtime and start to fund my own studies, moving the financial strain away from my parents. Slowly, this allowed me to grow within the manufacturing company all the way from a sweeper to a Technical Engineering Buyer, a promotion which meant my wife, my 2 children, and I needed to move from our home city to the business hub in Johannesburg. We had to pack up within 3 months and be exposed to a new environment, new schools, and everything that comes with a major move. My career lasted thirteen years in the same company, and I made it my duty to gain as much knowledge as I could, becoming an SAP Specialist, one of the highest certifications in the IT industry.

I have been working for the last thirty years, finding my place with major corporations both locally and internationally, but corporate South Africa was still a challenge. Although we thought that the apartheid regime had left us behind, it was still very much alive. Imagine getting to your workplace and having to work as a "team member" when your colleagues always had hidden agendas. Although I was in a senior position, I was often left out of key decision-making meetings. This upset me and continued until I tapped into my courage and spoke up about it. Yet the more I voiced myself, the more I realized that my local colleagues would go to the project lead above me. I listened to the inappropriate mocking and negative sharing about our country from some of my white colleagues, while I held my tongue. It was like being fourteen all over again, having to find the courage to chin up while experiencing discrimination. I could not believe that in the year 2019 racism was still present.

I persisted and worked hard. For me, acquiring the necessary skills to excel in my job was more important. Unfortunately, promotions or increases were not part of my benefits as an Indian. However, that did not stop me from doing my job to the best of my ability and going the extra mile. I realized that this was a major plus for me, as it taught me to become more resilient and not play the victim or engage in a self-pity mindset. I knew I could and would do much better in life. Nothing would stop me from becoming a successful human and supporting my teammates' success. I was always very eager to share my knowledge with other colleagues.

What I did not realize was that these colleagues would take me for granted and use the knowledge I shared to take over my job. I traveled twice a month internationally, getting paid a good salary, enjoying the benefits, and reporting to the New York office. They did not like this. I could sense the enviousness when I walked into impromptu meetings, and the room went quiet. I had to adopt a strong mindset coupled with good human values to face the days that followed as I wondered how I would provide for my family. All I knew for sure was I could not handle being in an unsupportive environment anymore!

After thinking about my career carefully, I once more tapped into the courage it took to try something new. I decided that I would opt to leave the corporate world, knowing that something better was out there for me, even if I wasn't sure what it was. It took me about 3 months to start finding myself again after leaving my long-standing position. I could see the light within, the possibilities before me, now I needed to take action!

In order to find my purpose, I revisited my past. Growing up in poverty amidst inhumane conditions, something always took me back to my roots. I then looked at the values that had been instilled in me, and "humanity" was always at the forefront of my mind. I asked myself, *How can I impact humanity? How can I make a difference?* I was discovering more about myself, recognizing I needed to do something that allowed me to feel fulfilled and, at the same time, influence change. I started to connect my values to my life's purpose, something that was staring at me, but to which I was blinded. Then, at last, I remembered the work I had begun years earlier and left on the back burner. I reignited my mission of serving humanity.

I am now the CEO of StraightTalkWithNolan, which includes personal mastery coaching and training. I offer courses and tools to help people reach their optimal success. I have also become the founder of the non-profit company, "Be the BEST version of YOURSELF Foundation," created solely to serve humanity. Every year, we embark on different projects that serve humanity. Next year, you will find us climbing Mount Kilimanjaro again, raising funds for cancer, mental wellness, and the start of our Community Skills Village. Looking back, this 10-year-old Samoosa Boy was always courageous enough to stay the course and never quit on his or his dreams. Today he has been featured in some of the biggest platforms globally, including Ignite Humanity™ TV and the Los Angeles Tribune™. It is all because he knows and lives to prove that *life does not end where you started.*

IGNITE ACTION STEPS

I believe that racism will always be here until we educate people to see humans first, not race or skin color. It is through our actions that we can make a difference.

Embrace Courage in Adversity - Many of us faced numerous challenges and difficult circumstances, from poverty and hunger to racial discrimination and limited opportunities. Rather than succumbing to despair or self-pity, demonstrate resilience and the will to keep going, even in the toughest times. You can do it by believing in yourself!

Seek Opportunities for Personal Growth - Despite facing setbacks and limited educational opportunities, show determination to improve your circumstances. Allow yourself to actively seek opportunities for personal growth and education. This can involve investing time and effort into learning new skills, pursuing education, or taking on challenges that can push your current boundaries.

Serve Humanity and Find Purpose - Go on a journey of self-discovery and connect with your core values, particularly the value of positively impacting humanity. Consider finding purpose and meaning in your life by aligning your actions and efforts with serving others. This can manifest in various ways, such as starting a non-profit organization, participating in community projects, or using one's talents and skills to make a positive difference in the world.

Nolan Pillay — South Africa
Mindset Specialist, Professional Speaker, Coach, Mental Health Advocate,
International Best Selling Author, Philanthropist and Partner to the Napo-
leon Hill Foundation
www.nolanpillay360.com
www.straighttalkwithnolan.com
www.soulmindbodyinstitute.com
www.bethebestversionofyourself.co.za
nolan.pillay.37
nolanpillay360
nolanpillay

Farrah Smith

Farrah Smith

"Fear should not paralyze us but ignite us,
calling us to step into the realm of extraordinary potential and
forge a life illuminated by purpose and passion."

My intention is to inspire and empower others facing fear and self-doubt to embrace their potential. By vulnerably sharing my own inner battles, I aim to convey that even the bravest among us contend with insecurity. My core message is that living courageously requires daily practice—but it allows us to overcome obstacles, conquer fear, and lead lives of meaning and purpose. I hope readers walk away believing in their inner fortitude to achieve greatness despite life's challenges.

From Fear to Purpose

It felt like the physical world was shrinking around me. The open park trails, beautiful Southern California beaches, and my beloved horse stables were all closed due to the COVID-19 pandemic and the resulting stay-at-home orders. All my usual sources of tranquility and rejuvenation vanished overnight. As a dedicated fundraiser constantly on the move, my bustling calendar, once filled with important meetings and vibrant events, was also wiped clean. The days stretched out endlessly, lacking human connection and the activities that normally brought me joy and fulfillment. As time passed, the monotony of each day weighed heavily on me. The hours gaped empty before me as I grappled with a gnawing feeling of purposelessness, desperate for relief.

One afternoon, while idly staring at my computer screen, desperate for a distraction from my reality, in a serendipitous moment, an ad flashed across the screen: *How To Land A TEDx Talk & Spread Your Message To Millions In As Little As 30 Days*. My heart skipped a beat. Public speaking was one of my greatest fears, but doing a TEDx talk was a long-held aspiration. Until that moment, it had remained a distant dream, tucked securely in the realm of "someday when I have more availability." But now, with nothing but time, a new question loomed before me: *Did I possess the courage to seize this extraordinary opportunity?*

If I landed my dream talk, I would face a formidable challenge—bearing my life's raw, unfiltered truth on the daunting TED stage. I would stand exposed before the crowd, revealing not just my triumphs but also my deepest struggles. The prospect both exhilarated and terrified me. It called for a level of vulnerability I had never allowed myself publicly. It would demand extraordinary courage to overcome my fear of judgment and failure, which were formidable opponents.

I agonized over the *Learn More* button for days, my cursor hovering as I paced my apartment, my heart racing. I would think, *Why am I going to do this to myself on top of everything else?* A voice of caution whispered in my ear, urging me to stay within the confines of my comfort zone, convincing me that boredom and isolation were preferable to putting myself through something so challenging and scary. Yet, amidst the overwhelming self-doubt, another voice refused to be silenced. The gentle whisper of my intuition, that quiet yet insistent inner guide, reminded me that the very thing I feared held the key to the relief I was seeking. My mind teetered on the precipice of a decision, *Would I choose the refuge of comfort or the call of purpose?*

Then, one day while walking to my local spiritual church, a realization struck me with immense force:

I had been staying home during the pandemic because I wanted to live, but 10 years prior, I had been staying home because I wanted to die.

I desperately longed for a more meaningful life while suffering from the worst bout of depression I had ever experienced. A sadness crippling me to my very core had left me sitting at that same church a decade before, not knowing how I would overcome the emptiness I was feeling inside.

That poignant experience would become the opening to my talk, a story of resilience, triumph over darkness, and the revelation of a life illuminated by pursuing my passions. I deeply yearned to guide others on a similar path, helping them navigate their own struggles and adversity toward a more fulfilling existence. Fueled by this mission, I rushed home, opened my laptop, and finally clicked the *Learn More* button, eagerly enrolling in the course.

Fortunately, I had encountered numerous stories of highly qualified individuals who had faced multiple rejections in the demanding TEDx application process before finally earning their spot on the stage. Drawing inspiration from their resilience, I made a personal commitment not to let doubts about my chances overshadow my dedication, even if it meant braving a hundred resounding "no's." Rejection had become a familiar companion on my professional journey, and I was prepared to embrace its presence if it meant eventually succeeding. Little did I anticipate the extraordinary surprise the universe had in store for me—on my third application, I received the coveted "yes."

After hearing the voicemail from the organizer congratulating me and requesting a call back to discuss the next steps, a whirlwind of emotions washed over me: a mixture of gratitude and joy, quickly followed by a wave of terror and feeling physically ill. A single thought echoed through my mind, *Oh my God, this is really happening.* An insidious voice of self-doubt was in my head, making me question my ability to rise to the magnitude of the opportunity.

Thoughts of backing out lingered, but as the initial shock subsided, an unwavering determination took hold, fueled by the wisdom imparted by my mother. She told me fear should not be avoided or suppressed but rather embraced as a gateway to something extraordinary. She went on to say that the opportunities that intimidate us are often the ones that can propel us to unimaginable heights, infusing our lives with profound meaning and enabling us to leave an indelible mark on the world. It became clear to me that the fear I had been feeling was a sign that this was *my* moment, and I had to seize it. I had summoned the courage to pursue my dream, and it was time to embrace the challenges that lay ahead wholeheartedly.

I was filled with anticipation as I prepared for my first call with the head of the TEDx team. I imagined the conversation flowing effortlessly and envisioned him enthusiastically embracing my idea. However, my initial excitement quickly faded as he meticulously analyzed my talk, focusing on the section delving into my mental health. His concern was etched across his face as he explained TED's strict guidelines regarding discussing this sensitive topic. He said he felt it was best to avoid the subject and suggested

I remove that part of my message. My heart sank, and I thought, *but that was the whole point of my talk!*

I had known the pressure of hiding my mental health struggles and the damage this could do. I felt it was important for others to see someone who looked like they had it all put together with an amazing career and life—standing on stage admitting to their pain. The thought of compromising or giving up on sharing my most challenging struggle was inconceivable.

In an attempt to advocate for my personal mission to share that part of my story, I sent the organizer a link to Tim Ferriss' talk, which fearlessly delved into the depths of suicide and the overcoming of emotional lows. It defied the very rules that had been sent to me. Perplexed, I questioned how Tim Ferris had managed to deliver his talk when I couldn't. The organizer simply replied, "You are not Tim Ferris." Part of me wanted to be angry, but another part anticipated his response.

My stomach sank as I pictured my talk falling short of the inspiring and meaningful speech I had envisioned. I attempted to craft an alternate version, omitting that significant portion of my journey, but it felt incomplete, leaving me in panic. After days of wrestling with self-doubt and enduring agonizing mental back-and-forth, I firmly committed to delivering the talk that resonated deepest within my heart. Through countless phone calls, emails, and an exhausting number of edits, the organizer and I finally reached a revision that authentically addressed my struggles while adhering to TED's guidelines. I took a deep breath as I felt an immense sense of relief. I was proud of myself for not giving up on that integral part of my mission—utilizing this extraordinary platform to support others on a similar path.

Just when I felt like I had calmed down and settled into the experience, the fear of vulnerability began to resurface, and the urge to retreat started gnawing at me again. *But I had fought fiercely for this opportunity and topic. How was I back at questioning myself?* The entire process had become an unrelenting whirlwind, pushing me to the limits of my endurance and tempting me to throw in the towel. During one particularly difficult day, I reached out to a trusted friend, seeking solace and understanding in my overwhelming fear. However, instead of providing comfort, he posed a simple yet powerful question that struck a deep chord within me: "If this endeavor brings you so much misery, why do it?"

What he didn't know was that my deeper inner turmoil went beyond stage fright. It stemmed from the fear of revealing my battles with clinical depression and the darkest moments of my life when thoughts of suicide consumed me.

The mere thought of confessing them on such a public platform filled me with terror. I had kept these struggles hidden, with only a select few aware of my journey. My mind raced with apprehensions: *What if my employer disapproved? What if I lost the respect of my colleagues? What if my vulnerability hindered my chances of finding love or securing future job opportunities?* The weight of worrying about all the ways this talk could negatively impact me became overwhelming.

However, his blunt question about why I would willingly choose to do something that made me so uncomfortable served as a profound reminder. It reignited my sense of purpose and reaffirmed that the value of this experience went far beyond my reputation or personal comfort. Deep within me resided a story with the power to ignite hope and inspire transformative change in the lives of those who would listen. It was imperative for me to continually remind myself that this talk was a calling to serve, and it needed to transcend my ego. So, I fully committed to cultivating every ounce of courage to uplift and assist others, no matter how scary it felt. I knew this was my moment to step into the realm of my highest potential and do something extraordinary for myself and humanity.

On the day of my talk, a powerful quote by Mark Twain echoed in my mind: "Courage is not the absence of fear but acting in spite of it." After dedicating countless hours to memorizing my speech and building confidence to address the vulnerable subject matter, the grip of my deep-seated fear of public speaking remained relentless. The physical manifestations were undeniable—my racing heart, clammy palms, and an overwhelming sense of impending failure. However, in that pivotal moment, I reminded myself of my remarkable journey and the significance of the message I was about to share. I refused to allow fear to seize control and undermine my efforts. It became crucial for me to regain command over my physical state so that my words could be delivered with the unwavering strength and conviction that resided within my heart.

Luckily, as a certified life coach, I was equipped with techniques to regulate my nervous system and counter the overwhelming effects of fear and anxiety. One technique that had scientific backing was the "Superhero Pose." Despite my initial reservations about how I might appear standing backstage with my chest out and hands on my hips, I was desperate to find a way to calm down. Embodying a powerful stance has been shown to reduce stress hormones and boost confidence, so it is worth a try. As I contemplated adopting the pose, something remarkable happened—I noticed another speaker already standing in the superhero pose before me!

It was reassuring to see Dr. Mary Wilde, a highly educated and well-respected figure in the field of resilience, embracing the same technique to combat her own fears. I was surprised and comforted by the fact that even she was scared at that moment. It served as a beautiful example of the message I was about to share. Courage is often perceived as impressive, powerful, and self-assured from the outside, but on the inside, it can be accompanied by stress, anxiety, and overwhelming self-doubt. The people we admire may look like they are never scared, but fear is an intrinsic part of our human experience. We all encounter moments of uncertainty and apprehension. What distinguishes those who accomplish their boldest dreams from those who don't is how they respond to those feelings. So, with Mark Twain's words echoing in my mind, I carried my fear onto the TEDx stage, allowing it to dissipate under the radiant lights.

In the following months, I was incredibly moved by the emails and messages I received from friends and strangers alike. Their words revealed my speech's impact on them—how it moved them to tears, resonated within their hearts, and sparked a renewed sense of hope within their souls. Most touchingly, individuals who were grappling with their own mental health challenges expressed feeling less alone and inspired to persevere in their journeys. I realized that everything I had set out to achieve had been accomplished, all because I refused to let fear win.

Baring my soul on the TEDx stage has taught me a profound truth: courage is not an exclusive trait, but a potent force that resides within each and every one of us, patiently waiting to be summoned. When we embrace our fear and vulnerability, we unlock the potential to overcome doubt and achieve extraordinary things. Courage is not confined to acts of grand heroism; it manifests in the small, transformative moments that shape our lives. Whether it's summoning the bravery to leave an unfulfilling job, embarking on the journey of starting a dream business, or realizing a long-held aspiration, my sincere hope is that by sharing my story, I can inspire others to tap into their own inner reservoirs of strength and resilience and forge paths illuminated by profound meaning and purpose.

IGNITE ACTION STEPS

- **Discover Your Purpose:** Take dedicated time for self-reflection, exploring your interests, values, and passions. Engage in journaling to capture moments when you feel most alive and connected. This deep introspection will help unveil your true purpose and guide your path forward.

- **Set Meaningful Goals:** Define clear and actionable goals that align with your purpose. Break them down into smaller, achievable steps to make progress more manageable. Setting well-defined goals creates a sense of direction and focus that propels you toward meaningful accomplishments.

- **Cultivate Self-Coaching Skills**: Develop effective techniques to navigate challenges and overcome obstacles. Nurture a growth mindset that empowers you to take charge of your personal and professional development, understanding that challenges and failures are learning opportunities.

- **Take Courageous Action:** Recognize that fear is a natural part of pursuing your purpose. Rather than allowing fear to hold you back, take action in spite of it. Step outside your comfort zone, challenge limiting beliefs, and cultivate resilience. Each intentional step forward builds your courage and propels you closer to your goals.

- **Embody Your Inner Strength:** Utilize practical tools and techniques for self-regulation when faced with fear or anxiety. Incorporate practices such as deep breathing, visualization, or adopting empowering body postures like the "Superhero Pose" to manage stress and boost confidence. By mastering fear management, you can rise to the occasion and seize those moments that have the potential to create meaningful change in your life and the lives of others.

Farrah Smith — United States of America
Charity Director, Life Coach
www.coachfarrah.com
coachfarrahsmith
coachfarrahsmith

Christina Sommers

Christina Sommers

"One day, one moment, one breath at a time,
you will build up the courage to overcome."

I intend to show you that you can be courageous and take back your life while finding joy in the journey. I recognize too many people stay stuck because of fear. My deepest desire is to come alongside you and offer my story—share my courage—and help anyone who desires to love their life once again. I hope that you can step into your authentic true self through your inner strength and courage.

The Woman At the Top of the Stairs

One morning, more so than other mornings, anxiety held my breath hostage in my chest as I began my daily ritual. Sleepily, I headed down the stairs, wondering if I would find my husband there, and if I did, *would he still be alive?* That question was followed by one that hit me like a ton of bricks. *How did I end up here? How did I let my life get this bad?* I am unsure what made this morning different from others, but I remember very clearly thinking to myself, *Why would God allow me to survive a head-on collision to live a life in hell?*

Up until that point, I had been just merely surviving everyday life. I was trying to keep the peace in my home by any means, which often came in the form of self-sacrifice: walking on eggshells, anticipating what my husband would want and when, and most of all, not showing any emotion of my own. Any time I tried to communicate my needs or ask for compromise, it became clear I should have kept my mouth shut. I constantly had to hide my sadness and frustration. Even my moments of happiness or expressive joy were immediately suppressed if they didn't match his energy at the time.

When I think back, it always was a toxic relationship; I just didn't see it. Often, when one is involved in an unhealthy relationship, you get there without even realizing it's happening—until it's too late. You feel like you are stuck.

When I was a young child, I dreamed that if I ever got married, it would be for life. I envisioned the white picket fence, a quaint house, and a happy family. If I ever had a child, my child would have a loving, caring, present father. My parents divorced when I was 4, and although I got to see my dad regularly, I often wondered how different it would have been if he had always been there. Therefore, I felt I should keep enduring, trying, and coping if there was even the possibility of creating that picture-perfect future for my child.

My husband and I were married for 10 years, together for seventeen. During that time, we split up 3 times before the ultimate separation and divorce. The story was always the same. Once we were apart, he would put in the effort to turn things around. I would hear him saying all the right words: "I'm going to do better," "I got a job and am working hard," "Give me another chance." He would love-bomb me with affection and praise and keep me believing he could truly change. So, I would trust him again, care about him again, and love him again. Then, within a year, he would start to slip, and things would get incredibly volatile… *again.* We fought constantly about everything, especially if I disagreed with him. His voice would get louder and louder, his chest puffing bigger with each hurtful word. He would bring his fist crashing into the wall beside my head; just days after, he told me how lucky I was that he didn't beat me. The efforts to gaslight me eroded my confidence as I helplessly tried to figure out how to cope. I began to ask myself: *Am I stupid? Am I crazy? Did this actually happen?* I had to keep a journal to remind myself that the problems were not all in my head.

Anyone in this position would seek a safe space to heal—a way to climb out—and I did. During our first separation, just after I gave birth to our daughter, I found my faith. Initially, I was tangled more in the rules of religion rather than leaning on the spiritual aspects and my personal relationship with God. With my faith journey, becoming a Christian, I was trying my best to be *a good*

Christian wife. I often hung onto the rules, morals, and values I heard, often keeping me stuck.

The last 2 years before our final separation was the worst it ever had been. When my daughter was only thirteen, she and I were in a head-on collision just 10 minutes from our home at the time, on our way back from a fun visit with family in Virginia Beach. My husband was supposed to go with us on the trip but did not because his plans weren't working out the way he wanted. My daughter was spared major physical injuries, but I lost consciousness at the scene. Major injuries included suffering from a collapsed lung and internal bleeding, and my leg, hip, knee, and ankle were shattered. I was in a coma for 4 days and spent over a month in the hospital and 4 months not able to put weight on my legs, having to do rehabilitation before I could *learn* how to walk again.

After the accident, I think my husband felt guilty because if he had gone, I would have been in the passenger seat and not sustained the severity of the injuries I did. His coping mechanism after the accident was returning to his drug addiction, which progressively worsened. He kept it hidden for a very long time, or at least the severity of it. While healing, I noticed his short visits, distracted behavior, and lack of empathy. I felt I had to stay with him because I couldn't take care of myself as I recovered, but ultimately I knew the time had come for me to muster the courage and take my life back.

I finally decided to leave a year after the accident. Then, we learned that his father passed away. I thought, *what kind of wife would leave her husband right after his father passed?* So I held on. I went into survival mode. I focused on my recovery as much as I could. I did what I could to keep the peace. I tried to do all the things people suggested. For example, I set boundaries, but they are only good if you enforce them. I prayed for him; I prayed for me; I prayed for us. I completely relied on my relationship with God. I tried to be a good example. I tried to communicate better about our issues, but every time I tried, he always asked me, "Who is putting these ideas in your head?" indicating I wasn't smart enough to work through our problems.

Even though I sensed I needed to leave, I stayed through the funeral and put in another 6 months. I worked for a business that allowed me to relocate during that time. Initially, I thought this would be the opportunity to separate and find freedom. Yet he convinced me that he should come along and create space between him and the source of his drugs; it would be a fresh start. He indicated he wanted to kick the addiction and that moving would be the perfect opportunity. There I was, fooled again.

From the outside looking in, it appeared that our daughter and he had an excellent relationship, and I did not want to get in the way of that. I felt I could sacrifice myself to keep them connected and continued to convince myself it wasn't that bad.

The next stop was central New York, where we were both originally from. He always hinted he wanted to move back, and when we were there to visit family, he became convinced. We found the cutest house on that visit, made an offer, and there we went. We were moving further away from the source of the addiction, and we were both sure this might be the answer. But all it did was add fuel to the fire and worsen the problems. More than ever, I knew I had to find a way out as I had reached the depths—the bottom of my life's staircase.

Even the places where I sought freedom from my pain were keeping me trapped. There is such a stigma about divorce, especially among Christians. Whenever I felt like God was releasing me to leave, I would hear a sermon on the sanctity of marriage; that when your marriage is failing, do 'these' things to make it work. You can fill in the blank with everything recommended; I tried them all. Every time I tried something new, things only got worse. Sometimes there would be testimony about how God healed a person's spouse, and they were set free. I kept hoping and praying that mine would get better, also. I was stuck in this marriage between my childhood dreams and wanting to be the good Christian wife who could one day share her testimony about how God healed her husband and saved their marriage.

Instead, I am sharing my testimony about how God has given me the courage to leave my marriage, find my strength, and refuse to settle.

The first step came that fateful day when I woke up dreading going downstairs; my husband was at a point in his addiction where I genuinely believed he was trying to kill himself. He was in so much pain, and drugs were the only way he found the slightest bit of relief. But I never knew what I would find each day when I woke up and went downstairs. Consistently, I found him passed out, and the work began to clean up the aftermath of the night before. I found myself crying out to God, in a way I never had before, saying, "You can heal him, you can heal us, I know you can...so why won't you? Why aren't you fixing this?" I heard God in the depths of my spirit; *You're right, I can, but I can't force him. It has to be his choice.* Just like that... one step up the stairs.

One particular scripture I felt was preventing me from moving forward is Malachi 2:16, where the words, *I hate divorce, says the Lord God of Israel* are contained. I didn't want to disappoint God. *If He hated divorce and I got divorced, what would that mean for me?* Then I came across an article explaining the meaning of that scripture. I learned that God put that scripture there because, during that period, men were divorcing their wives for no reason, essentially leaving them destitute, and God didn't like seeing his daughters being hurt. If I accepted this interpretation, I would believe that God would not be mad at me for getting divorced; God never wants to see his children stay in a harmful environment—this became my next step up.

During the last and final argument, I finally saw how our conflicts negatively impacted our daughter. She was in another room, but I could see her from where I stood. I caught a glimpse of her face, and the mask she had learned to wear so well cracked just the tiniest bit. I could see on her face the pain she was feeling—the fear of our conversation escalating. I became aware that day that my daughter was hurting more than I could see and that her safety was my pressing concern. The chains finally broke, all at once, as new courage ignited within me, and I began the journey back to the top of the stairs. I finally knew there was no more *trying* to make it work. For the sake of myself and, more importantly, my daughter, I needed to get us out of this relationship. I did not want to see her hurt. I didn't want to see me hurt. It was time for the vicious cycle to end for good.

I began the journey back up the stairs of reclaiming my life. I knew God allowed me to survive my car accident for a bigger purpose, and it was not just merely to survive everyday life so that I could endure and persevere through whatever that day held. God brought me to this point to take back my life and thrive; to summon my inner strength; to live a life I love, and to find peace and joy every day.

Shortly after our separation, I thought I would have the peace and joy I longed for. But, instead, that was where the true healing journey began. I kept myself busy as a way to cope; the problem was the moment I stopped moving, all I heard were the lies spewed at me over the years. I was a shell of a person; I didn't know what I liked and didn't like. I was severely overweight, and my mobility was very limited due to the car accident. Healing takes trial and error; the key is ensuring you include the body, mind, and spirit. I started moving my body by taking nature walks and participating in workout programs. I also have been working on cleaning up my nutrition by reducing the amount of processed foods and replacing them with real whole foods. I learned about journaling and meditation practices, which I have incorporated into my morning routine. EFT (Emotional Freedom Technique) and breathwork are 2 amazing modalities I utilize most frequently. It took time, but eventually, I felt I'd found my courage and triumphed over my hardships.

Looking back, had I been aware of the repercussions of abuse, I may have decided to leave sooner. I might have made different choices if I knew what a healthy relationship looked like. When I left, I didn't realize I was being courageous. I saw it as a matter of survival as I began my healing journey. Now I know that it *did* take courage to take that step and that it came from an inner knowing that God wanted more for me. He gave me the courage and the strength to *take my life back*, to find peace and joy, to thrive and love the life He gave me to live. Now, each morning when I wake up, I feel peace and joy in my chest because of the woman I know I finally found at the top of the stairs.

It takes courage to go out and try new things and learn what you do and don't like. I am continuing to learn about the abundance of resources available. The healing process takes work, but it is worth it; the steps may be presented as simple, but they yield amazing results through commitment. Healing is never linear: expect challenges and know there are various tools you can use when facing each one. They always get easier when you work through them.

It is incredibly important to do your *own* work first. Too often, we see the issues with the other person and simply want *them* to change. We all carry our own stuff, so if you start working on yourself first, you can be an example and invite your partner to mirror your efforts. It is then up to them. In any relationship, it takes 2; if 1 is willing to show up and the other isn't, it may be time to be courageous and take the next step up. Remember, you cannot change someone, no matter how much you want to; you can only change yourself.

It's amazing how our perception of certain concepts changes as we grow through life's events. When thinking about courage, I thought it was reserved for those who faced some of life's significant challenges and heroically came out on the other side. But we exhibit many small moments of courage in our everyday lives. No matter how big or small, you exemplify courage if you face your fears. And you deserve to celebrate your courageous self.

Learning how to be courageous is a journey where you offer yourself grace if you don't show up in the manner you expected, and you celebrate yourself when you give it your best.

IGNITE ACTION STEPS

- **Healing involves your body, mind, and spirit**
  - **Body** - nutrition & movement.
  - **Mind** - personal development, community, create a toolbox of resources.
  - **Spirit** - spending time in prayer and meditation, connecting with God.

- **Give yourself grace**; healing is a journey; it will ebb and flow. Be gentle with yourself in the challenging periods and celebrate the smallest wins.

- **Create a toolbox**; there are plenty of various healing modalities, tools, and resources available. Through trial and error, give them a try, the ones that work, keep them handy in your toolbox; the ones that don't work, let them go. Remember, not all the tools will work in every situation; you may need to put the ones that always used to work on the shelf and pull a different tool out.

- **Establish a self-care routine that works for you**, and make it non-negotiable. Keep your toolbox handy for when you become extra triggered, you don't have time, or you just have an off day. *It happens; you're human.* Give yourself permission to take it one step at a time.

- **You have everything within you to make the best decision** *for* **you**; know that in many circumstances, it takes staying in the situation to find the courage to leave that situation. I am only sharing my story so you don't feel so alone in yours, and if the only thing you are waiting for is permission—permission is granted. If it is your faith keeping you stuck, know that being mistreated is not God's desire for you.

Christina Sommers — United States of America
Podcaster, Emotional Wellness Coach, Author
www.reloadinchrist.com
🅕 reloadinchrist or Christina Sommers
🅘 @reloadinchrist

Marcia Klostermann

MARCIA KLOSTERMANN

"Fight with all your Strength; Love with all your Heart."

I hope my story helps you find the courage to survive the toughest of times and gracefully surrender when there are no answers. I hope you'll fight the good fight by being a courageous warrior for yourself and your loved ones, but know when it's time to set the armor aside and live life to the fullest.

THE WARRIOR PACT: TO LOVE AND PROTECT FOREVER

"And it's a—Boy!" the doctors announce excitedly. How amazing, my first child! Rather than being thrilled, I hold back my excitement until basic questions are answered: "Are there 10 fingers and 10 toes? Are you sure everything is okay?"

The concern spews clearly from my mouth in spite of being extremely groggy from the anesthesia. An hour earlier, the doctors said that if we didn't do a C-section, both the baby's life and mine would be in danger. After losing 2 infants to miscarriage over previous years, I'm on pins and needles, afraid that I might suffer a third heartbreaking loss. I need to hear the doctors tell me that everything is fine, as I can't wait to see my baby, Spencer, finally in my arms.

Instead, before laying eyes on my sweet baby, a nurse takes me out of the OR, in my hospital bed, to my designated room. I keep begging to see Spencer, but the medical team has much to accomplish in the typical post-operative process. "It will be an hour," they say, asking me to be patient. Nervously I wait, my body shaking from the cold. I feel like I'm serving a life sentence in an ice chamber for a crime I never committed. The medical team is working hard to take good care of me, but as a new Mom, I want my baby in my arms immediately!

Eventually, the nurse lays Spencer's tiny body on my chest. I knew he would be small due to lower-than-normal amniotic fluid during my pregnancy—I was prepared for that, but he was only 5 lbs 10 ounces… and I was already worried. We lock eyes, Mother and Son. I feel the earth move within an instant as I look into those beautiful hazel reflections of light and life. I know I will love this sweet boy forever with an amazing connection bonding us for eternity.

Unexpectedly, another force beckons my attention. A powerful knowing, an energy telling me that something isn't right with my precious son. I begin to feel a sense of vibration—an all-encompassing sensation and the atmosphere around us becomes very strange. *Is it just in my mind?* I sense and hear a deep noise—it's increasing louder and stronger all around me. Suddenly I see white lights brighter than the human eye can handle. *Oh my God. Am I going to die? Is Spencer going to die? Is this the End?* I look away, the extreme white light changes to a rainbow of glorious colors! I'm afraid but amazed at what is happening before me. Time is irrelevant—what seems to be an hour passes in mere seconds. I hear an immense Voice speak without saying a word: *Life will be very hard with this precious child. Do you accept him and this difficult life?* Hearing that message from such a powerful vibration had me in awe and responding immediately, "Of course I do! I will always take care of him—I'm his Mother!"

The Voice responds, *Very well, so be it. Take care and go on your way.*

I am instantly back at the very spot, the exact moment looking into Spencer's eyes. Of course, I never physically left, but I knew I had been on a spiritual, transformational journey. I saw the light, heard the voice, and felt my body wake up differently. It was a sacred encounter and an incredible gift, one I know will change my life forever. Still locked in that miraculous gaze with Spencer, my sweet and magical child—who is my direct connection with God—I marvel at the moment that just occurred. How lucky and blessed am I to play this human role of "being Spencer's Mom"?

And so it is—I'm Spencer's Protector, his Life's Warrior, no matter what comes our way. I made a pact with God, not knowing how much armor I would need to fight this fight.

Within days, Baby Spencer is struggling with the basics of being human, mainly with getting nourishment. He's fine for a short period of time, then he's sick and throwing up for days on end. Being a cautious, high-achieving Mom, I'm all over it, communicating with our doctor and trying to assess the root of the problem. At 6 weeks of age, Spencer's pediatrician told me the vomiting was likely due to my breast milk, and we should continue trying different formulas (I had already tried 3). He added, "Marcia, you're a nervous first-time Mom, which is likely part of the problem." I think, *What? Oh, that was the wrong thing to say to me. I'm his mom, I know Spencer is sick!* Every ounce of my Being is filled with exasperation over the doctor's patronizing comment.

In an instant, the Voice I heard when I first locked eyes with Spencer carries me to another dimension of strength. Even though I'm a new mother, I find my words—words that empower me. I courageously state, "I'm a very focused Mom who will do anything for her son. I think your comment and analysis are inaccurate because you truly don't know what's wrong. I'm going to get another opinion, and by the way... you're FIRED!" *Deep breath! Way to go, Warrior Marcia!* I stood up to a doctor who wasn't truly helping us. I rose to the occasion for Spencer, for myself, and for all young mothers and parents who are trying to navigate their way through a healthcare crisis. The warrior in me won my first battle, with armor provided from the heavens above.

A few short days later, an ultrasound and a new pediatrician's perspective means Spencer is scheduled for emergency surgery due to a rare issue called *pyloric stenosis*: the tightening of the wall around the small intestine. Babies can die from malnutrition and starvation if it's not diagnosed early enough. Spencer was vomiting because there was no place for the food to go. Of course, I'm angry and frustrated about the time we lost dealing with a doctor who wasn't attentive. But I'm also thankful the warrior in me worked hard to seek another opinion and found the source of his issue. Spencer makes it through surgery, and we carry on as partners in our battle. I envision life being better now that we both made it through this difficult challenge.

Except the Voice had said, "*Life* is going to be hard." The Voice was right... the following weeks and months continued to be filled with chaos, fear, and sadness. From the time of Spencer's *pyloric stenosis* surgery to the age of fifteen months, he has been in the hospital for over forty-five days and nights. I began to feel like a doctor myself, learning to deal with: RSV (respiratory syncytial virus), pneumonia, mastoiditis (an aggressive infection on the ear's mastoid bone), requiring surgery and IV antibiotics for 3 months. His eyes were beginning to cross due to strabismus (surgery and long-term patching required), flu, lymphedema, bronchitis... you name it, he had it. Including seizures, both basic and grand mal, which are exceptionally scary. It's horrific and heartbreaking when your child goes into a physical, uncontrollable spiral. Seeing Spencer go through all of this sends me into a frenzy until I finally learn how to control his seizures with medicine.

None of this is what I expected or dreamed of when I thought about becoming a Mom. My rosy visions were of a happy, healthy child. I envisioned hearing my baby giggle, laugh, and play peek-a-boo. It's so sad when dreams are crushed before our eyes as life takes the pen and rewrites the script.

From an overall progress standpoint, Spencer is definitely behind the curve. I speak with experts who specialize in childhood development. I hear statements like: "Your son is not thriving," or "Spencer is developmentally delayed." *Really? What was your first clue? I have barely breathed for fifteen months. Spencer needs help. I need a lifeline.* We discuss whether it is situational or whether there is something inherently wrong. Spencer should be sitting up by now, he should be crawling. He's not doing any of that. I need to know what's wrong with my son, and, more importantly, how to help him.

We continue to pursue experts in all categories: genetics, neurology, cardiovascular, and orthopedic. Spencer displays so many issues across the board, that I feel like I'm playing Pac-Man®, trying to beat the villain that pops its head up at every moment. I cannot understand why it's so difficult to diagnose something in this day and age. In my heart, I'm falling apart because my sweet baby is so sick, and nobody understands why. In my head, I think, *I just want to go to work, where I have some control. I can't keep up with all of this!* At my job, while everyone is extremely supportive of me and my "sick child," I'm still expected to perform, which I do in spite of my armor being severely dented. We learn to dig deep when we have to get through the darkest days.

Finally, after mounds of admissions paperwork, Spencer is approved for a full assessment at one of the most recognized medical systems in the world, the Mayo Clinic in Rochester, Minnesota. We travel there and stay at a hotel nearby. I'm thrilled to be working with this team. They analyze Spencer for 3 days, doing exorbitant amounts of bloodwork, physical and mental analysis, and even a DNA skin graft. I'm thankful for the thorough effort they are making to uncover the root of Spencer's health concerns. The outcome of the evaluation, the answer I've been looking for, is near—I'm feeling nervous yet optimistic. Once I know what's wrong, I'll do anything to make it right.

The doors close to the sterile conference room. White coats flutter about. I count 8 specialists in the room to discuss my sweet Spencer. It feels ominous. *What will the outcome be? Maybe I don't want to know.* I sense gloom seeping across the room as the senior geneticist shares their findings and completely alters my life:

> "We have done extensive analysis on your son. We are very, very sorry to inform you that we believe he has Mucolipidosis Level III (MLIII), a severe, regressive, progressive syndrome that will end his life. He will be dead by the age of 3. Take him home, love him, and enjoy the time you have left. We are so sorry."

"WHAT? What are you talking about?" I cry out. "How can this be happening to Spencer, my innocent little boy?" The experts share more information based on their analysis. I want to negotiate, like I do at work. Surely I can make things right like I typically do. I long for the light, the knowing, the clarity in wearing the armor and being the warrior Spencer needs, but my knees buckle under the news, and my heart tears open in agony. I feel myself begging inside, *Spencer has to LIVE! Just lessen the sentence, please! Let him live to be at least 10 years old. Okay, I'll take 5 years! Please, God, just give us more TIME!*

Grappling with this diagnosis means I'll be burying my darling son in eighteen short months. After more discussion and fact-sharing by the medical team, it was obvious that there was no lengthening of his life-span or prognosis. There will be no scraped knees, baseball practice, or teenage acne. They robbed me of graduation, girlfriends, a wedding, and grandkids. I was getting none of it. Period.

With the air sucked out of my chest, all I could do was latch onto a single glimmer of hope.

"I heard you say, 'We *believe* it to be MLIII.' Are you not 100% sure?" I asked painstakingly.

"We are 97% sure." The senior geneticist responded.

Clinging to desperation, I look at them and say, "Well then, there's a 3% chance you're wrong! I'm going to focus on that."

That's it, it's all I had: 3%. I cry out to God and the Universe. *Where are YOU, and where is that Voice that gave me strength? Why can't you make this right?* I hear nothing as I sob and shriek all the way home to the new HELL I call my life. The Warrior, my inner strength, has been stomped out. I can barely stand up, much less gather my armor and fight again. My days are filled with a deep fog of despair. I am numb. I don't feel. I don't care. I just carry on through another minute, hour, day. I try to work, cook, clean, pay bills, and care for Spencer. Always, there's the negotiation with God: *Please take me. Leave Spencer alone.*

Friends and family are with us in our battle; they love Spencer and are so sad about his situation. Some try to share words of wisdom or guidance. In many cases, it backfires because grief at this level is so personal, raw, and intimate—something that is truly between ourselves and God. When you are faced with losing a child or losing something you love so tenderly, you change; you lose a part of yourself as well, long before death actually happens.

Deep in my own conflict and frustration with God, I received a phone call from my sister. "How's your day going?" she starts, in the typical friendly way. My tone tells her that I don't want to talk, and my spirit is hollow. She knows; she understands. In a way atypical for my sister, she finds the words that completely change my life:

> "Marcia, I've never heard you sound like this before. Your heart and soul must be destitute. I'm just going to say, though, if losing Spencer takes you down, and we lose you too, then his life was for nothing. Please keep fighting for Spencer, but also fight for you! We need you and your beautiful spirit with us."

My heart skips a beat. *Oh my God, she's right!* I can't fall apart or die inside, it only lessens everything Spencer and I stand for. As hard as it may be, I need to find the courage to live, be strong, be the mother he needs, and survive. I make a soul-defining decision to gather my armor and continue fighting for not just him, but for *myself*: to live life to the fullest, to give from my heart, no matter what. I will not let myself or Spencer down. His death is not an ending. Spencer's life is a gift, regardless of the timeline. Our lives and souls together are so precious, and bonded, no matter how much time we have.

I also know I need to find the courage to surrender—and make peace with God. But I'm only human; my heart aches realizing that I will have to carry on alone without my beautiful boy. So, I embrace every moment we have. Spencer rolls on the floor, smiles frequently, and makes sounds and noises—he's not able to communicate with words, but I know what he's trying to say—he's very descriptive with non-verbal cues! He obviously doesn't understand what's going on with this horrific diagnosis of his physical body, but has a quiet peace encircling him which gives us both strength. Spencer seems to be content, and our days are somewhat calm as I hold the torch and carry on.

Sixteen months after the MLIII diagnosis, the most amazing event occurs. I'm preparing dinner in my cozy kitchen when the phone rings. It was an unexpected call from Spencer's new geneticist at the University of Minnesota, now engaged in his long-term care. What they share completely impacted my life:

> "Marcia, we're calling to inform you that Spencer does NOT have Muco-lipidosis III. I repeat, he does NOT have MLIII!"
>
> Gasping, I drop the phone, fall to the floor, and cry out in gut-wrenching relief, *OH MY GOD, OH MY GOD—IS THIS REAL? THANK YOU, LORD!* The 3% margin won, the diagnosis was WRONG!! Spencer's death sentence has been obliterated!

Every cell in my body is invigorated that this is actually happening. No, it isn't a dream—the MLIII nightmare is over. After catching my breath, I pick up the phone again… the Specialist and I candidly discuss the amazing outcome of this misdiagnosis. As I gather my thoughts, I wonder out loud, "So what IS wrong? What does Spencer have?"

The Specialist made the next comment very clear: "You need to prepare yourself for the fact that you may never find out. That's genetics. If we haven't figured it out at this point, there's a strong likelihood we will never know."

Those words hit like a ton of bricks falling *again* on my heart and on my dreams of helping Spencer. *How can I fix something if I don't know what that something is?* The amazing news of Spencer not having MLIII was exhilarating, and I count my blessings. But not knowing a diagnosis would be a challenge for me, the wearied warrior who wasn't willing to surrender just yet.

Over the next few years, I continued working with geneticists in the area, doing test after test trying to determine a diagnosis. Everything comes back negative, and every doctor says we'll probably never know the syndrome. I'm exhausted, and I know Spencer is tired of being poked and prodded. I finally made a decision to "let it go" and to move FORWARD! *If God wants me to know, God will let me know.*

I realize I can't fix everything. I'm missing out on my life, and I am missing out on the essence of Spencer's pure spirit by focusing on the issues I cannot change. *Enough!* Spencer and I have a life to live and many other dreams to pursue—it's time to make positive things happen. Courageously, the warrior decides *life is for living.*

Living is what we finally began to do… I always wanted to adopt a little girl from China… I began putting my energy into that process. I realize that moving on from toxic relationships is necessary. I leave my dysfunctional marriage after trying for years to make it all work. I take a new position at my job, and I feel a zest for life and a joy in my spirit. I also make a conscious choice to be strong and healthy for both myself and for Spencer's care.

When asked by acquaintances about "What's wrong with Spencer," I smile and comment: "He has Spencer Syndrome. It's his own syndrome because he's one in a hundred million!"

Surviving the incorrect MLIII terminal diagnosis was transformational; however, my surrender to *not knowing* the diagnosis for Spencer was also one of the greatest challenges I've overcome in my life.

Over time, my work takes us to a new city filled with exciting opportunities, new friends, and, of course, new doctors for Spencer. I had always hoped, in my wildest dreams, that someday a specialist, with a fresh perspective, would nail the diagnosis. Spencer is now thirteen years old, so I've been chasing a mystery syndrome for thirteen years that was not meant to be revealed. Until one day, a new neurologist examines Spencer meticulously and then quietly leaves the exam room. Spencer and I wait; I wonder what this doctor will reveal. 5 minutes later, with a print-out in hand, he confidently states:

"It is Cornelia de Lange Syndrome."

I'm confused and say, "Excuse me? Are you saying you have a diagnosis?"

"Yes!" He explains in great detail about this rare syndrome. The unknown abyss is quelched—Spencer Syndrome, at long last, gets a real name. Glory be to God!

I begin to cry, not frantically but with tears of resolve. After years of trying to label Spencer's condition, this amazing doctor confirmed a diagnosis in less than twenty minutes and with minimal effort. Thirteen years of floating in the abyss is over!

As we move forward, life with Spencer is definitely interesting, challenging, and inspiring. He is intellectually disabled but he's the wisest person I know because of his old soul. He's unable to talk, but he has touched thousands of people by never saying a word. He's unable to walk, which was very difficult to accept, knowing he would never run, jump, or play like other kids—but we battled on and have a cool wheelchair, van, and lift system for mobility. Spencer is now a handsome, twenty-four-year-old with the longest eyelashes you've ever seen! He is a charmer and a cheeky guy! He's his own, beautiful person, a warrior himself, having quietly fought so many battles throughout the years. In watching him, I have seen the essence of courage go beyond the meaning of the word. His fight, fortitude, and fabulous determination to live life and be exactly who he is has changed me fundamentally as a person. Despite the hardships he has endured, he is a fighter and full of zest for life. If I had to define courage, I'd say look at my son. Spencer is the definition of how to keep living life, and I'm absolutely honored to be his Mother.

Thankfully, Cornelia De Lange Syndrome is a quieter, gentler syndrome. Spencer will have the amount of time on this planet that he and God choose. I can forever be at peace knowing I did everything I could to fight the good fight. Finally, this Warrior Mom hangs her armor up and learns how to simply *be a Mom*.

As the Voice predicted, "Life is going to be Hard." It has been hard, but that doesn't mean life hasn't been good. When we make a pact with God to say yes to our lives, including the hardships, it becomes the foundation of our strength and courage. It carries us through the toughest of times… fighting with all of our strength, loving with all our heart. Let love and courage guide you through your greatest challenges, and listen to that warrior voice within you. When you need courage, seek, and you shall find it… Your inner strength, your *Voice,* will carry you when you can't carry yourself.

IGNITE ACTION STEPS

Find the Courage to Surrender when necessary. You can't fix everything—learn to let go. The knowledge, information, and people will come to you when the time is right. "When the Student is ready, the Teacher will appear." (Buddha)

Share—Learn—Grow. Find a support group—share information, and your struggles. You're not meant to be on an island… Information is Power!

Keep moving forward. Grieve your losses and struggles in life. When you're ready, make the decision to continue moving forward—it's the only way *through.*

Trust your gut and follow your instincts. You know when something isn't right with yourself, your child, or a loved one. Stay the course—follow it through to a better place.

Find Joy through the tough times. The more we love, the more we suffer loss; that's part of being human. Living with joy is also why we're here—Choose it intentionally!

Marcia Klostermann — United States of America
Warrior Mom, Author, World Traveler, Advocate for People with
Disabilities, Telecommunications Executive
Marcia Klostermann
Marcia Klostermann
Marcia Klostermann

Stephanie Drummond

STEPHANIE DRUMMOND

"Courage is the ability to embrace the strength you have within."

Look at your challenges; see what drives you to face them. Do you draw from within yourself, or do you use other means to handle those tests? Do you have the courage to utilize the goodness and strength inside of you? My hope is you will see uncertainty doesn't need to be fear-based. It can be eye-opening, interesting, and can lead you on a new life path. After all, it's uncertain. May you move beyond your existing boundaries, embracing the reality that what is frightening can also be refreshing. Society often conditions us to believe uncertainty is scary, but take a chance yourself and move with a brave mind ignited by the spark inside of you.

BEYOND BOUNDS

The last brown box was being loaded onto the giant moving truck headed for the local storage facility that would be its temporary home. Its final destination, and mine, was actually half a world away. Looking around my near-empty apartment in Sacramento, CA, I reflected back on how this move came about. Never in my wildest dreams did I ever imagine relocating to London. Not only was I leaving, but I was going alone to a land that was virtually unknown to me. All I really knew about London was that it's the home of the royal family, their fish and chips are world-renowned, and there is a pub on every corner. *Will I fit in? Can I find my way around a metropolitan city, and learn about a new culture and a new job?* My head starts swimming, and immediately doubts creep in, making me rethink this bold move. *Stop it! Get out of your head. You got this! It's time to make your dreams come true.* Picking up the phone, I called the only person who could reassure me and remind me to pull on everything within myself: my mom. Margie Brown, a daughter of the south, was raised in a tiny town where the corner store was the post office, grocer, and local gathering place all in one.

At a young age, my mother bravely left segregated Georgia and made her way to the bright lights of the big city of Philadelphia, PA. My mom met and married a Navy man. Shortly after they welcomed their first child, a son, my dad was sent to Morocco as part of his Navy service. Mom joined Dad a few months later. That meant traveling to a new country away from family, friends, her job as a nurse, and everything she knew. She could have chosen the easy road and stayed with her parents in Georgia, but she chose to face the challenges and joys of living in a new country with her husband and son. She drew from within herself the courage to embrace a new adventure and set an example that I would one day follow.

There in the Northern African land of heat, spices, and vibrant color, is where my life began. After 2 years in Morocco, the Navy relocated our family back across the Atlantic to Philadelphia, then eventually to Spain, and finally to the sunny beaches of San Diego, California. I was born into and raised with the mindset of seeing every new location and a fun adventure for most of my childhood.

That sense of adventure would take on a different shape for me as a teenager as my inner core had propelled me forward to face the unknown. In my elementary years, I fit in as the social butterfly. But junior high school was a whole new world! I felt like I was in a fishbowl with kids who did not know me. Some of the students were intimidating, some were nice, some were nonchalant, and others paid me no attention. No one prepared me for the shock of that challenging environment. Needless to say, I did not do well in the 7th and 8th grades. After a trying year and a nasty fight with another student, my parents thought it best to send me to a private school. In the 9th grade, I was a new student again, entering Christian High for the next 3 years.

The first day at my new school, I woke up with butterflies in my stomach. Mom had prepared a big breakfast: homemade biscuits, bacon, eggs, and fried apples. The house smelled like Sunday morning. I came to the breakfast table in an almost zombie-like state. The unknown of what the new school would be like was starting to gnaw at me, and I was unsure I could eat the wonderful feast before me. To make matters more daunting, my new school dress code required that I wear dresses that fell below my knees or lower. I rarely wore dresses; when I did, they were thigh-length or higher. The dress code police had ripped away my teenage identity! Was I going to a monastery or a high school? Feeling defeated over how I looked in this granny dress and the uncertainty of this new school, I slowly ate breakfast.

My mom saw my downcast face and tried to reassure me everything was going to be fine. She told me to be myself and make friends in no time. She made it sound simple, but I soon found reason to question her assurance. As I entered the school for my first day, I found myself at the welcoming assembly for over five hundred students. I also discovered I was the only African American in the entire student body! I stood among the other students and began looking around at faces that were unlike mine. Flushed with waves of uncertainty at what my future held while standing in the courtyard, I knew it was up to me to either forge ahead and make the best of this uncomfortable situation where there was no turning back, or shrink into someone I did not want to become. I chose to rise above my present circumstances and excel academically, adding the title of 'exemplary student' to my distinction of being the school's first African American student, in drill team, drama, and on the cheerleading squad.

I kept that title of academic excellence all throughout high school and into my college years at San Diego State. I earned a degree in psychology before landing a job at General Dynamics, where I would meet the man who became my husband.

Yet 5 years after we married, I once again found myself back at a crossroad that caused me to find deep-rooted determination to rise above my situation. As we increasingly realized the irreconcilable differences between us, we had to accept the hard cold fact that our marriage was over. It was the end of a dream that, since my childhood, had been something I longed for.

I felt like a failure, broken, crushed, and at a low point in my mid-twenties. There were days I walked around in a daze. *How did we get here? How do we break this news to our families? Do we have to divide our mutual friends? Do we just kiss and say goodbye?* The label of 'divorcee' was so unreal to me, and it felt smothering. I needed to escape from the crushing feeling all around me. Despite the fact San Diego was my core, my identity, and held so much of who I was, at that moment, I knew I couldn't stay. The city had become tied to the idea of losing a significant part of myself, and it was more than I could face.

A new city and a fresh start seemed like the solution. I accepted a new job in Dayton, Ohio. It was a place I had never visited, yet I took the job without hesitation. What a move of gumption to leave everything I know and love behind, including my family. Although this was all scary to me, I knew I also had a strong foundation for taking this challenge on. After all, I grew up moving all over the world, I had tackled uneasy school environments that once seemed alien, and above all, I was my mother's daughter. Remembering these things was key to facing and embracing my fears.

Although we were going our separate ways, my ex-husband graciously agreed to move me across the country to Ohio driving a U-haul. The funny thing about U-Hauls is they hold secrets. The U-Haul that carried me from San Diego to Dayton, Ohio, held my thoughts, dreams, fears, and questions. If only those walls on wheels could talk.

Road trips are a time of adventure and wanderlust for me, and that drive was going to be just that, an adventure for certain. Early on a sunny January morning, with my black Honda Civic hitched to the U-Haul, and all of my belongings inside, my ex-husband and I climbed into the cab with the black faux leather bench seats and felt like this was our last hoorah.

Driving across the country, we were like 2 roommates on vacation. Moments of laughter about the roughness of the ride, reflections of the beautiful landscape, and our giddiness reminded me of the good parts of our marriage. The radio was filled with nothing but country songs, and from time to time, we belted out a tune or 2o only to bend over in laughter at how we needed to keep our day jobs as we sounded awful. If the walls of the truck could speak, they would share how I glanced at my ex-husband at times and thought to myself, *WHAT AM I DOING?* There were long stretches of silence. I reflected on my failure, and my heart sank from frustration and pure sadness. Marriages fail daily, but how could this be happening to us? Failure was not supposed to be an option, but here I was, sitting in a U-haul, driving to a new state to start my new single life. I thought, *Let's turn this truck around, admit things were hasty, and give our life another try.* I did still love him, after all.

Arriving on a snowy morning in Ohio, my emotions ranged from joy to sadness and sheer fear. Would I be able to make a new life on my own? These questions and feelings echoed in my head as I drove my ex-to-be to the airport. I looked at him with sadness mixed with a sense of profound peace as he exited the car. He wished me nothing but love and a wonderful life. Tears streamed down my face. Saying goodbye was not as easy as I had tried to convince myself it would be. As the car door closed and he walked into the terminal, I felt my past leaving and my new life lay ahead.

Dayton was a place where I grew from being a naive young lady into a full-grown woman. Defying my thoughts, taking this leap was the launch pad enabling me to bet on myself and God even when fear gripped me. I spent 6 years growing and becoming my own person again, drawing on my inner strength to define who I was on my own. Through a professional connection and an interesting turn of events, I would eventually return to California. However, I was amid farmland and mountains rather than coastal beaches this time. And it was in Sacramento I found the courage to pursue the biggest adventure I had yet to take on… London.

London was enriching and eye-opening. My mom's daily pearls of wisdom, prayers, and love ingrained a sense of pride and tenacity in my soul as I navigated the foreign landscape of Tube rides, afternoon tea, Marmite sandwiches, and driving on the opposite side of the road. The courage to move there was one of the best decisions I could have made. I flourished, grew, traveled, and found my true self.

Then, twenty-five years after I first left Dayton, I returned for a reunion weekend with dear friends. It was during that weekend when my inner core was shattered. On March 14, 2022, a ringing phone awakened me out of a deep sleep. *Am I dreaming?* Who was calling me at such an early hour of 5:30 AM? I answered, "Hello?" but all I heard was crying, followed by crushing words, "Stephanie, she's gone. Your mom is gone." My beautiful mother, the woman who was my all in all, the one who pushed me beyond myself and my biggest cheerleader, had departed from this life.

Numbness blanketed me. *My mother is gone? I am heading back to Georgia next week to see her. She has dialysis today. This must be a mistake.* We had chatted the day before, and she sounded weak and tired but otherwise fine. In an instant, I felt like an orphan with no immediate family. Before I could fully process my loss, the phone rang again. The nursing home needed information. Then the funeral home wanted to know where her final items should go. *For goodness sake, can I please have some time to let this soak in?*

I did not want to disturb everyone in the house, so I sat for a long time with the suffocating sorrow, unable to cry. I was with my mom 2 weeks ago, not realizing it would be our last visit. I wondered with a heavy pain in my chest, Who will I call to chat, share my secrets, and *laugh at old memories? Who would pray for me daily and love me so fiercely? Who will give me the courage I need to carry on?*

The hour-and-a-half flight from Ohio to Virginia seems like an eternity. I'm numb for the majority of the trip. As I left the airport and headed home, I called a friend who had recently lost her mom for words of wisdom as I had entered a club none of us wanted to be in; the motherless-daughter club. My friend's warm words of empathy and sympathy give me strength to face the rough days ahead.

Walking into my quiet house alone, filled with pain, took me back to the first day at my private high school… the feeling of being alone and uncertain of the future. I was hit by a lightning bolt as I realized that my mother had been preparing me all my life for this bitter time. From my teenage years in high school as the only African American student, to going through a divorce, to moving overseas alone more than once. In living and recalling all the lessons she taught me, I realized I could never truly lose my mother. Because of her, I have the personal tools needed to face the challenges of grief and anything else forever. I cried myself to sleep, my tears of sorrow and wistful gratitude mixing together as I drown in my memories of my mom and the valuable life lessons she gave me.

Gripped by the waves of grief, depression, and deep pain, I knew the only way I could function and move forward was to get professional counseling and join a grief support group. The months of learning coping tools and being able to openly share what was on my heart with a neutral individual saved me. A friend and I had an overseas trip planned for a small group in the fall, and the preparations gave me activities outside of my 9-5 job so I would not fall into the cycle of despair. I forced myself to socialize with a small group of friends who gave me a safe space to cry, be angry, or sit in silence without feeling like a burden. In the back of my mind, I could hear my mom's voice whispering to me not to wallow over her passing because I had so much life yet to live. I heard her encouraging me to celebrate her life by being the best version of myself. She imparted to me all I needed to live courageously.

Losing my mom wasn't easy, but it showed me that I could flourish in life using what she taught and imparted to me. My life experiences have also given me many rich lessons to draw from. My life is joyous and bountiful, despite my loss. I have used my fortitude to preserve, my desire to live authentically to foster my accomplishments, and my willingness to exemplify courage to mirror those lessons to others.

In this life, we all face various challenges, small ones, big ones, good and bad, but how one chooses to face them is significant. Inside of us is a rich pool from which to select what is needed to meet what is given to us. Choose to courageously pull from your inner strength even when it's very uncomfortable. The depths of your life's well expands each time you draw from its richness.

IGNITE ACTION STEPS

- During my courage journey, it has been vital for me to pull from within myself. How can you do this as well?

- Prayer is vital for knowing yourself, so pray the way it feels best for you every day.

- Assess the challenge and then make an action plan to best tackle each step ahead.

- Make an action plan based on the situation, remembering the plan can change anytime. Be willing to pivot with courage and trust it always works out.

- Give yourself grace. Don't be so hard on yourself. When it feels overwhelming, breathe. Take a big breath in, it will help.

- Seek advice from trusted individuals or professionals in their field. Such advice can be exactly what you need to hear and motivate you.

- Draw on the tools within your internal toolkit to guide you. We all have the tools within us for exactly what we need.

Stephanie A. Drummond — United States of America
Program Manager/Coordinator
@trveldiva

Jenette Longoria

JENETTE LONGORIA

"Just because it scares you doesn't mean it should stop you."

People tend to think that courage is the magical power you obtain when undertaking a noble quest. Like it's a token, you must find and pick up along the way. I've come to define courage as the ability to choose the pursuit of purpose over logic when you are afraid. It's simply making a choice of what's more important to you, what you want more. *Do I want to move toward my purpose or stay in my comfort zone?* Courage is about making a choice that something is more important to you than the 'logical' option, going against what appears to make sense because there's something you need more... something you desire more.

DON'T STOP WITH SKETCHES

My face had nothing but a blank stare—somewhere between a deer in headlights and a child caught in a lie. Inside I was screaming with fear. All the questions were rolling through my mind like a digital message marquee over a Broadway theater. *How are we going to survive? Are you going to see this through? What the heck is happening?*

My husband had just told me he was fed up with working in the toxic world of disgruntled employees and business owners who had no ambition beyond paying their monthly bills. He explained how he found an online trainer out of Canada. He wanted to quit his job and invest in a sales course. He could work on his own time and make more money than he would be working for somebody else.

Was this even real? We were sitting in the van, waiting in the parking lot of our kids' dentist's office. I could barely concentrate on his words over the dull roar coming from the back seats. A minute ago, I was thinking about how we would get all 3 kids through their appointments. It had been such a regular Tuesday. Suddenly, I was face to face with one of those blockbuster movie moments where the character's life is about to change entirely based on just 1 decision.

What was I supposed to do? I knew that I couldn't ask him to stay at a place where he was anxious and discouraged. He would hate me. I would hate me. I looked him in the eyes and told him we'd be alright. I assured him that I would support his decision and we'd make it work, whatever that looked like. Clearly, the Holy Spirit had taken over and allowed these words to come out of my mouth. At that time in my life, I was not capable of facing such a big unknown with that level of peace. My words came from a place of calm and trust. They did not represent the wave of horror crashing over my mind; panic, instability, and longing for control.

Let me back up a bit...

When we were first married, we had been living tightly wrapped in our comfort zone, even if it was below the common societal standard of comfort. We were inexperienced at this family thing and we misused just about every resource we got our hands on. Life was a bit of a trainwreck for a while. Once we came up for air and realized our limited options, we decided to get a better hold on ourselves. We found a great Bible-believing church and, not too long after, signed up for a Financial Peace class. We took our lessons from it and started doing life differently.

That was the first step in working on ourselves as individuals, a decision to take intentional action and create change. We were sick of having our options dictated by our resources—or lack thereof. We were ready to unlock opportunities that were previously beyond our reach.

We had no clue how much opportunity our choice was about to create. But in hindsight, it makes a lot of sense that I was open-minded about my husband leaving the traditional workforce to join the 'gig economy' in search of the laptop lifestyle. No one was prepared for what would come next, but we'd all soon find out that this is how the world was about to shift.

The feeling of peace and trust was fleeting. Despite the course being my husband's path, I was involved by virtue of being his wife. I was being asked to put my faith in a sales guy telling people to learn, grow, and watch all of his content. He had built an army of followers with almost religious devotion, removing anyone from his kingdom who would dare question or oppose him. I wanted to support my husband's personal development, but I wasn't buying all the hype. I felt I was surrounded by idiots who had drunk the Kool-aid.

Eventually, I was slowly dragged, kicking and screaming, down the rabbit hole. Before long, I succumbed to the philosophy, "If you can't beat 'em, join 'em." I was taking the course, doing the homework, and gearing up for my fame and fortune in sales. While this opportunity did not turn out to be the be-all-end-all of awesome we had foreseen, it taught us a lot. Mostly about ourselves and what we really wanted in life. Following the end of the sales training, a copywriting class was offered. They defined it as *Sales in Print*. I saw it as 'my' path. So, I invested in a new skill while at the same time rekindling an old passion for writing.

Growing up, my talent for writing was never celebrated as much as my more tangible artistic skills like ceramics, woodworking, and sculpture. There was a certain beam of pride that my mother displayed when she was able to walk visitors around the house, showing off the dish set, the pottery on the mantel, or the welded sculpture in the office. And that was fair. Writing had always come easily for me, but I was never spectacular at it. I had never invested in the skill like I had some of my other abilities.

Now that I had a 2, 4, and 6-year-old, there was little time for 3-dimensional art or even simple crafting. I wasn't able to express myself through artistic outlets like I once had. There just wasn't enough time in the day. So the idea of using a skill I enjoyed to pursue a career opportunity was exciting. It was fulfilling to create again and actually make money doing it. Being a mom is fantastic, but as any parent can tell you, it's a thankless job. You love them. They're worth it. But it still leaves a little bit of a hole in your identity as an adult to repeat mindless tasks of cleaning and recleaning the same messes every day without any personal growth or noticeable progress.

I was entering completely unknown territory after being a stay-at-home mom for 6 years. I was re-entering the workforce as an entrepreneur with my own copywriting business. It was exhilarating and terrifying all at the same time. I had learned new skills, and I had confidence in my own ability, but I had to enlist the confidence of others to pay me for it. I had to talk to and network with business owners, explaining what a Copywriter was and how I could help them. That what I had to offer was valuable enough for them to pay me well. I had such a hard time approaching people and saying, "I'm a Copywriter!" It didn't feel real, and it scared the crap out of me! I had never published any-thing, but here I was, as a ghostwriter explaining to others how I could help them tell their stories. Oddly enough, I always found it easier to help others support what they were achieving than to bring one of my own dreams to life.

Trying to prioritize others' successes and keep all the balls in the air for months got to be more than I could handle. I was supplementing our family's income with my meager little business, and I had no faith in myself to reach the level I had dreamed of. I was constantly angry, stressed, and blowing up at everyone around me. Working from home, that "everyone" was my family. I had completely switched gears from '*momming*' to *writing,* and everything else was trivial. I had to prove I could be successful—to myself more than to anyone else. I was seeking self-worth in what I could do or provide for others. I had no idea how to handle or compartmentalize the waves of emotion and resistance that come with growth, so I found myself reacting to everything. The tiniest inconvenience would set me off, screaming and throwing a 5-alarm adult temper tantrum. It was like I had lost control of myself and become someone that I didn't want to be.

I knew this was not a sustainable way of life. I knew something had to give, and though the last thing I wanted to do was deal with any of these unknown feelings, it was time to make a choice. *Did I want to seem put together and in control while my emotions ate away at me? Or was I willing to admit that all the unknowns had become too big for me to manage on my own?*

I signed up for another class at church. This one focused on accepting who I was and my limitations and learning how to give the rest to God. It was meant for life's hurts, habits, and hang-ups. I ended up discovering a lot about myself. Apparently, I had a lot of shame about my "prodigal daughter" phase that I'd never faced. That decade or so of rebellion when I had decided to make every wrong decision I could because *Why not? It's my life.* Since returning to God and the life I knew I was called to, I have lived in the shadow of those poor judgments. They played over and over in my head. Even though I was not the same person I had once been, I was unable to forgive myself for doing stupid things to seek the approval of others.

Somewhere along the line, I had attached my self-worth to being accepted or fitting in. I desired so badly to belong somewhere that I could never seem to find. I was trying to recreate myself but felt like I still didn't make the cut because of the guilt I carried from my previous behavior. I was constantly afraid that people who knew me earlier in life would pop out of the woodwork with evidence to convict me as a fraud of the person I was working to become. I was caught in limbo, not finding my place in either direction.

My revelation came through words spoken by our pastor's wife. She always says, "God put inside of you everything you need to face what you will go through in your life. Just be who God created you to be." As the words sank in, a feeling of warm self-acceptance started to flow over me. Those aspects of myself I had hidden away in shame… I began to sit with them and examine them. I'd spent so long doing things to seek the approval of others, but my actions didn't fit who I really was or what I stood for. This created guilt in knowing that my previous behavior didn't align with who I wanted to be.

Slowly, I felt the forgiveness toward myself grow… *You have value as a person. You don't have to hide from who you are.* I was able to start recognizing the internal attacks on my character when they happened. As I would talk through what I was feeling, the voice in my head that was trying to stop me would get quieter. *You can be okay with the choices you made back then because that's the knowledge you had at the time. Now that you have grown, you can use the knowledge you've learned to make different decisions.* My heart rate would slow back down, returning to a sustainable rhythm. The fog of chaotic panic in my head would lift, giving way to a visible path where I could plant my next step. Eventually, grace came. It was like the vice grip that had been clamped on my shoulders was being loosened, and the tension was lighter. *You can release it; you don't have to carry this pain of regret anymore. Those years were just the sketches of the beautiful masterpiece God is creating through your life. It's okay to give yourself grace.*

It took me a long time to embrace the fact that I am enough. I didn't need to do anything or prove anything. No amount of work or effort was going to make me more valuable as a person. It was terrifying to imagine a day when I could look at anyone from my past and tell them that the person I used to be is not the person I am today. That I do not have to dwell on my moments (or years) of bad judgment. And that I will not let my past define whether or not I reach my full potential.

For the first time in a long time, I gave myself permission to fully trust myself. It became my mantra on the days when I was so fraught with imposter syndrome that even the thought of getting out of bed was too overwhelming. *[Deep breath]. God gave you the skills to get where you are at. He put you in the exact place where you are supposed to be, doing the exact thing you are supposed to be doing. You've got this!*

I finally believe it. After several years of working on myself, I am able to believe that I am enough. The person I am today, the person I am becoming, is enough. It's so freeing to truly step into my own identity as me. To understand, accept, and own who I am. Not just what I can do. It didn't always look pretty. In fact, sometimes, it looked downright pathetic. Waves of fear, uncontrollable feelings, and outbursts had threatened to tear my marriage and my whole life apart. I had to fight myself to not destroy everything I was working toward. I used my courage and made the decision to crawl out of bed and face the day.

Now, most days, I am able to respond instead of reacting. There are still those days when I totally lose my crap, but I can look back and recognize what went wrong. I choose to work on myself when everything inside of me says to *run from this unknown pain*. I can go a little further than before. I am able to separate the replays of fear in my head from reality and decide which will get my attention. I can now confidently tell others, "I am a copywriter, an editor, and a ghostwriter. I help people share their message." It took a while. I had to step out and do it in order to know that I actually could. I think Bob Goff said it best in his book, *Everybody Always*. "What we actually want is that extra nudge of confidence from God and the opportunity to move forward courageously to do those things we already know how to do."

Long ago, God had given me the skills and everything I needed for this path. I just had to get over my own shame and get out of my way to believe it. I needed a reason to do something hard, then see the confidence I gained from succeeding at it. As I look back on my story from this point in the journey—because it's not the end. I'm not *there* yet, and honestly, I don't know if I will ever be. I realized that there was an underlying theme in each step—that I *had* to make a decision.

I've come to define courage as the ability to choose the pursuit of purpose over logic when you are afraid. I had to choose which was more important to me, being comfortable or fulfilling my purpose. In each situation, despite the smart, safe, or logical choice, I had to decide to take action to reach what I wanted. Each time I had to choose to take an action that made my life look different from other people's in order to move closer to what I wanted. I had to pursue freedom more than I wanted security. I had to create choice more than I wanted comfort. That meant defying the notion that I couldn't generate fulfillment in my life beyond being a wife and a mother. I had to step into growth more than I wanted to stay the same. I had to embrace entrepreneurship more than I wanted employment. It was scary to have faith in believing my family's needs would be met. I had to practice restraint more than I wanted to react. I had to seek the truth more than I wanted to hide behind a lie. I had to accept my own identity more than I wanted my past to tell me who I was. The hardest thing I ever did was face myself in the mirror and tell myself *I forgive you, and you are deserving.*

If you desire to change deeply enough, *you* can make a choice. Just because it scares you doesn't mean it should stop you. You can decide to take action based on your purpose rather than on feedback from your surroundings. Even if what you want seems like the furthest thing from what society would define as the logical option, don't let people's opinions get in the way. Each choice you make could be your "big thing" in life, or it could just be another stepping stone along the way. If you don't choose to act on it, you'll never know how they fit. Don't stop at the sketches; let God grow your life into the full masterpiece he intends for you. Don't miss out on what gives you the confidence to embrace your joy because it's in this you'll find the courage to make worthwhile choices.

IGNITE ACTION STEPS

- Define who you are as a person without roles, titles, or positions. Don't pin your identity on anything that can be taken from you because those things aren't really part of who you ARE.

- Work toward defining your purpose. You can make lists of your non-negotiable values in life and what excites you, then see where they overlap. You might have to ask yourself "why" a couple of times to get to the root of it.

- Look at the places in your life where you wished you had made a different decision. Ask yourself if you decided to further your purpose or to keep yourself comfortable.

- Decide why you've been choosing logic over the pursuit of something. Is there a limiting belief under the surface that has convinced you that you 'can't' do it?

When you find something more important and persuasive than fear… listen. If you discover something that you MUST choose, despite logic or what initially seems right… recognize that is your purpose calling to you.

Jenette Longoria — United States of America
Copywriter, Editor, Ghostwriter, Co-Founder of Breakthrough Global LLC
🔲 jenette.longoria.56
🔲 thelongoriaj
🔲 jenette-longoria-738ai45sx

Ana-Maria Turdean

ANA-MARIA TURDEAN

"Keep applying yourself, for one day you will be abundant."

I desire to fill your heart with courage and instill in you the belief that you will discover the path to success. No matter how many setbacks you encounter, keep pursuing your dream. One day, everything will come together. Use every "No" to direct you to your "Yes." Every opportunity is a practice that will enable you to improve yourself. Everything is possible, you just need to believe in yourself, and the perfect endeavor will present itself.

PERSISTENCE IS THE KEY TO ABUNDANCE

On a warm day, at twenty-three years old, with the graduate hat in one hand and a bouquet of red carnations in the other, I walked toward a restaurant close to the festivity hall where the graduation ceremony had just taken place. It was wonderful to feel the fresh air on my face after the hot atmosphere in the hall. I started the day full of nerves, but now I was overcome with excitement and relief that my Bachelor's Degree in Business Studies was over. Together with some friends, colleagues, and my father, we took a seat on the terrace of a restaurant. We were eating, making plans for the summer, and discussing finding work. All of us graduates were happy to finally use the knowledge gathered during university and to be financially independent. I was ready to conquer the world.

I knew of a local newspaper in Romania, where I lived, advertising for positions, but felt alone and confused about how to tackle the job market. None of my family members had worked in economics. I assumed that I had the golden ticket with my degree, and that was all I needed. In my naivety, I was sure that all the companies would love to hire me and that I would receive an abundance of offers. I bought the newspaper, circled the ads for those things that interested me, and sent off multiple CVs. I waited, full of positive expectations. I occasionally got interviews, some were better than others, but none resulted in an offer.

For one interview, I traveled 45 km to a small company selling tractors. I was checking my notes on the way. I felt so prepared! I turned my head to the minibus window, full of excitement and anticipation, while gazing at the beautiful hills, forests, and blue sky, with puffy clouds at the horizon. I stepped off the bus, dressed in my best pink shirt and long black pants, ready to take on the world. After a twenty-minute walk, searching for the office, I was invited to a small conference room painted plain white. I liked the simple, tidy atmosphere. An older lady, plainly dressed, with dark hair, asked me firstly if I had experience with accounting software. *No, I didn't have experience.* A few accounting questions followed. 5 minutes later, I was outside. I was annoyed that I had traveled all that way for a 5-minute interview. 5 MINUTES! I felt angry. Almost 3 hours of traveling! *Did the person not see that I had no experience in my CV? Couldn't she have just kept me a little longer?* I would have felt so much better. *Could she not have just called?* I felt offended, but the search had to carry on. It was a great lesson.

My motivation dropped heavily as time passed without an offer. I didn't know what to do. I circled and replied to all the ads. I felt like a hamster running around on a treadmill, doing the same steps: print CV, send it off, wait for rejection. Finding an offer was the ultimate goal. I needed a solution.

I missed my sister living in the Netherlands, and thought that maybe spending some time with her would help. I flew to see her, and giving her a big hug was wonderful. I wished she could have helped me find a job, but she studied in a different field. In comparison to my sister, I felt useless. Like her, I wanted to be financially independent.

I loved being away from home and exploring a new country. I applied for a Bachelor's Degree in Finance. I thought, *if I can't get a job, maybe I should study more and get another diploma.* Living with my sister gave me a greater sense of freedom, which I had desperately wanted. After 2 years, and due to my lack of Dutch language skills, I returned to Romania to continue my job hunt. I was upset but still hopeful that an organization would hire me back home.

I returned refreshed and optimistic. I modified my CV, making it shorter and more attractive. I underwent some training for interviews, changed my wardrobe, and learned new questions to ask prospective employers. The confidence that had totally slipped away was starting to return. There was a definite improvement. I received more responses, the interviews lasted longer, and I felt sure something was around the corner.

One morning I was randomly looking at a website of a company that I dreamed of working for, and an internship in audit caught my attention. *What have I got to lose?* The salary was great, but the hours were long. I didn't mind the hard work. I was keen to start, so I looked up the company's location and went directly to the office, a courageous step I wouldn't have done at the start. It was small but trendy, clean, and a place where I could envision myself working. I left my CV with the employees from the office.

I had coffee with a friend telling her about my tragic job search a few weeks later. Her fiancé worked in the same company. She asked me, "Why didn't you tell me earlier you wanted to work there? My fiancé could have recommended you." It had never occurred to me to reach out for help earlier.

I told her, "I would love it if he could recommend me." She passed on my CV again. This time it was different, I was called for an interview a few days later. I put on my best outfit, had great questions, and had the knowledge they were looking for. I remember feeling happy, the atmosphere was comfortable—yet, part of me didn't want to get my hopes up.

The phone rang a few days later, and I was told that I was successful. SUCCESSFUL. As the details about the job offer just floated by, my joy increased quickly. I thought, *Finally, FINALLY, I have a job,* in my head! A full-time job in a fabulous environment with people I really liked. It felt like I was flying. I loved that the office was simple, but I knew that the job was challenging. I was using the knowledge I had worked so hard to accumulate at university. For the first time, I could see all the hard work, all the long travel for interviews, and the many applications that had resulted in somebody wanting to hire me.

For many years I had felt that I had received rejection after rejection; my confidence had been beaten so many times. But now I could see the courage

I found deep within to keep going and persevere. It takes great courage to get up when knocked back so often.

Now I see that the daily walks I used to do to keep my body fit were beneficial. The fresh air and the sweat kept my body alert. It meant I could take my mind off my bad situation. I wasn't sitting on my sofa, down and demoralized. There were definitely days when I just felt like doing nothing, listening to music, watching series after series on TV, but I knew that didn't help me.

I remember at the start thinking I could do it all by myself. I didn't reach out to others. Later, a cousin recommended me to work in tech support, and another cousin explained the different roles within companies, so I applied for the right position. I found it hard to imagine what it would be like in a cubicle or open plan. It seemed confusing and overwhelming at times, but my acquaintances supported me in understanding the job market. It is easy to think we don't need other people; now, I can see the most important element is the connections we make. It was because of a recommendation that I got my first job.

I remember walking through the doors in my white shirt and black boots, eyes alert and striding with confidence into my first day on my first full-time job. Inside I was bubbling with excitement. Everything was well organized, and I was proud to be part of that company. I noticed a coffee machine, a machine I got to use! The director showed me to a large white table, and I was given a laptop just for me. I felt so blessed and welcome. All the little things felt so big; a ballpoint pen, a notebook, a pencil, and an eraser, all mine. The rest of the day was fun.

I was a little nervous about lunchtime when a lady I didn't know came over to me. She was new also and suggested that we have lunch together. We went with another colleague to buy soup and even had time to play darts. It felt wonderful to be part of a team and accepted. That position only lasted a month, but it changed so much for me.

I was in touch with recruiters via LinkedIn™ throughout my continued job search. I received my first offer from a medical device company in Prague. I was enthusiastic to see that building the LinkedIn™ network was proving its worth! My stomach churned with excitement at an offer, but heading to a new country with a new language meant I really had to draw on the courage within.

With my head covered by a warm, furry hat, a scarf wrapped around my neck, and my knee-length purple winter jacket, I arrived early in the morning in Prague with 2 suitcases in my hands. My eyes were sleepy, as I hardly slept and was not used to traveling such long distances by bus. The real estate agent did not mention the flat number and was not answering my phone calls, so I went straight to the building where the room was supposed to be my temple of happiness. I walked to a restaurant nearby, ordered a drink, and called the recruiter and my family members. I opened my laptop and started writing desperate messages to my future flatmate. In a quest to kill time, I ventured out to open a bank account. I headed to a private clinic for the medical check required to start employment in the Czech Republic. I spent the rest of the day in Starbucks™, on a painful mission to ensure a roof over my head. Thankfully, my flatmate answered my messages and let me in, but by then, it was after 8 pm.

Moving to a new country was challenging, not to mention working in a foreign environment with different rules and expectations. The long hours required at the job soon became too much for me, and the stress played havoc on my well-being. I found myself once again searching for a new job as I was on a temporary contract. After enjoying a few wonderful months in Prague, with lots of events and gatherings, I decided to take on a new challenge in another unexplored paradise.

I had been connecting with companies from Luxembourg for almost 2 years. I visited there briefly to attend 2 interviews. One of the companies initially rejected me. While in Prague, I received a phone call saying I had been hired. Unfortunately, I rejected the offer as I spent a considerable amount and could not afford to relocate again, but deep in my soul, I was being called to work in Luxembourg. A second company from that unexplored paradise hired me during the happy summer after I turned thirty-one.

The arrival in Luxembourg was made in a rush. I left clothes and books dear to me in the old flat in Prague, so I knew that I would have to return there. My new role as Financial Officer proved to be something other than what I expected. One of the tasks was to open envelopes with a beautiful mail opener and sort documents, which made me feel valuable to the company. Unfortunately, my overcrowded accommodation, combined with false expectations of the role and lack of savings, resulted in having thoughts of leaving the job.

The thought of leaving the financial sector kept repeating in my mind. After all the rejections, I was grateful for opportunities, but most jobs were often totally different than my expectations. Every step forward came with challenges and growth. I began to consider if maybe I could draw on my other strengths.

I remember having long discussions with flatmates, family members, and friends about various career paths I could embark on.

I used to love going for long walks, jogging, and dancing regularly in Prague. I did not exercise in Luxembourg due to lack of time. I knew I needed to move to remain balanced. An idea was to take on a cleaning job temporarily. Some things broke in my accommodation, and I cleaned homes to cover the replacement. Cleaning was perfect; I could move my body and immediately noticed the results. I contacted the cleaning lady at our residence and she told me that an option was cleaning offices and banks. When she mentioned how much I would earn, I realized that it would not be sufficient to cover my expenses. I decided to go home to Romania and search for a job there.

In the winter, I visited Sicily to spend time with some friends I care about. Malta was on my list of places that I really wanted to visit, so with a deep breath and some courage, I booked accommodation there and scheduled a job interview. I wanted to move to a warm country after living in rainier lands. Throughout the stay, while visiting gorgeous places, I interviewed with various companies and improved my Italian language skills. I was already an expert in online and telephone interviewing by this time.

During one of my jobs, I connected with people willing to work in my field. I had a few calls with candidates from Italy, and I explained what we were doing, checked their resumes, and recommended them. Helping people searching for a job made my heart sing.

In recent years, my roles have included finance, customer service, and digital marketing, both in corporations and startups. I landed an amazing role in a great company last year. After fifteen years of continuously applying, my mission was finally accomplished. *ACCOMPLISHED*. An ex-colleague recommended me for the role, which I now love and adore.

For those searching and still wanting to find the right role for them, I recommend being in touch with others and letting them know your skills and aspirations. It is usually easier to land an offer if someone helps you out. Connections were the key to finding the next opportunity. Fortitude kept me going, and perseverance showed me that a *no* is only a no until it is a *yes*.

My advice to you, dear reader, is to keep applying and not lose hope. Sooner or later, a wonderful opportunity will knock on your door. Always ask for help, and spend time taking care of yourself. Exercise to keep yourself healthy, and travel to broaden your horizons as you may meet someone who can lead you to an unexpected work opportunity. My experience taught me that although I may have been through difficult situations, the job will show up eventually. Remain positive and believe in yourself every step of the way.

It takes courage to know that through hard work and determination the right job will ultimately find you.

IGNITE ACTION STEPS

- Work on self-love and reach out to family and friends for help and support.

- Connect with people in similar situations and encourage each other. You can find support groups on Facebook and LinkedIn.

- Go for a walk every morning as it helps clear your head, keeps you healthy, and is a great way to brainstorm ideas.

- Take a break and get out of your hometown, do something you've never done before; you never know who you will meet.

- Meditation is a great way to connect with yourself on a deeper level and bring more joy into your life.

- Reward yourself after each interview as you get closer to finding a job that you love.

Ana-Maria Turdean — Romania
NLP Coach, Designer at VIDA & Co. and Affiliate Marketer
www.anasmagicworld.blogspot.com
anasmagicworld
amturdean

Lameeka V. Harris

LAMEEKA V. HARRIS

"Your fears and challenges do not define you;
how you choose to respond is your
true defining moment."

I want you, the reader, to take from this story that you have everything in yourself to live your life boldly and courageously. No matter your story, choosing how you allow the world to see you is up to you. We are often taught that our fears protect us and stop us from doing things that hurt us. However, some of our fears are meant to push us out of our comfort zones, forcing us to rely on our courage. Yet courage looks differently for everyone. My story shows you that even when life puts you in situations that you don't understand or don't seem fair, there is always light at the end of the tunnel.

LOSING TO FIND THE WINNER IN YOU!

I have always been too much. *Too happy, too sad. Too quiet, too loud. Too nice, too mean. Too fat. Too black*. And now, *I am too disabled*. I have come to learn that being too much isn't necessarily a bad thing.

From as far back as I can remember, I always thought of my mom as Superwoman. She can go head to head with Superman, Spiderman, and the

Hulk, defeating them all without a flinch. She has always tried to instill power, strength, and courage in her daughters.

When I was five, it was Memorial Day weekend, and I had stayed the night at my Aunt's house. We were preparing for a family event. The phone rang, and my Aunt calmly said, "Oh no, Gwen, I'm on my way." Yet the moment she hung up, I sensed something was wrong. She quickly packed me and my cousin into the car and yelled, "We have to go, NOW!" She told us that our apartment was on fire, and my Mom, Gwen, and sister, Kisha were inside! I burst into tears, feeling that I would never see them again.

As we pulled up to my apartment building, firefighters and fire trucks were everywhere, flames were shooting out of the building, and people were hanging out of the windows. It was a very chaotic and active scene. We stood outside waiting for what seemed like forever. Waiting and not knowing. Tears streamed down my face. I watched, feeling helpless and frustrated.

Suddenly I remember hearing the best thing ever, "Jean, we are over here." I had never been so happy in my young life. I ran over to my mom and gave her the biggest hug ever. I was so relieved to see my mom and sister alive! My mom did an interview with the local news, and we left and headed for my Aunt's house. Once there, my mom and sister told us what happened.

As they waited for the elevator, the fire alarms began ringing. They headed for the stairs thinking it was a faulty alarm. As they descended the stairs, the stairwell filled with smoke. They exited the stairwell on one of the floors and realized it was quickly engulfed with smoke. They immediately banged on doors, and finally, someone opened; it was a young deaf woman and her newborn baby. The young woman was very scared. As they were in the apartment, other people banged on the door. There ended up being a group of about 10 of them, and the apartment was filling up with smoke fast. They needed to come up with a plan quickly, or they were not going to survive.

My mom took charge. She directed people to gather all the towels in the apartment, soak them in water and put them against the door to block the smoke. She then told them to get whatever they could find, put water on it and cover their mouths and noses. She alternated the people at the window so they could get fresh air. This quick thinking and courage kept them all alive that day. My mother had the will to do what needed to be done. Her courage inspired me. God ignited something in her to act courageously, and she did. Sometimes courage comes without us even thinking about it. It arrives by just doing what God has directed us to.

Despite having an incredible role model of courage, from my mother, I have never been one to define myself as courageous.

It wasn't until the second semester of my junior year of college that I had to summon up more courage than ever before. I was having the absolute time of my life, but suddenly, everything changed drastically. I was serving as the President of the Black Student Union, surrounded by a solid group of friends who did everything together, was really popular on campus, and excelled in all my classes. I woke up one morning, and my walking felt slightly off. I hadn't had any falls, accidents, or traumatic episodes, so I didn't think much of it. I figured I needed to do some exercises. I did a few stretches and got started with my day. However, as the days and weeks went on, my walking didn't get better; it worsened.

What started as a slightly uncomfortable drag of my left leg became severe and almost impossible to lift. I decided it was finally time for me to seek medical attention. It was the first appointment of many. It's important to mention here that I was on student health insurance, and it obviously wasn't worth much because I got the run-around. I sat in the appointment with the doctor and answered his questions. He asked about my family history and if I had had any accidents or falls. I answered everything he asked and mentioned nothing had happened to cause my difficulty walking. He then asked me psychological questions. At the end of his visit, he determined that nothing was physically wrong with me. In his opinion, it was clearly a psychological issue.

I knew that was far from the truth and needed to seek another opinion. I scheduled an appointment with a different doctor and got a better result. That doctor ordered an MRI and Physical Therapist (PT) evaluation. I went in for my MRI. The top half and the bottom half of my spine were scanned. The middle section of me was not scanned. I had my PT evaluation, and it was determined that physical therapy would be beneficial. Still, there was a long waitlist, and since I had that *good student* insurance, I was not able to go anywhere else.

I continued doing the work with my student organization and going to class while dealing with this gated walk that had me slightly unbalanced, yet thankfully there was zero pain. The MRI results showed nothing unusual. I found the courage to persevere, and I was determined to finish school and not let this 'unknown thing' get me off of my path. I completed school and got my degree, not letting my troubles with walking hold me back.

After college, I was passionate about working with children and got a job at my family's Day Care Center even though my movement was still compromised.

At the time, the Day Care Center was still fairly new and small, without many health care benefits. However, it just so happened that a new law had been passed stating if you had a certain amount of employees, you had to offer health insurance. I, of course, signed up immediately. The journey was now on to finally get to the root of my mobility problem. By then, I had been dealing with the issue for almost 2 years!

My mom and I went everywhere in Chicago to meet with different doctors. Neurologists, chiropractors, holistic, if you name it, we were there. Of course, by that time, my walk had become worse, and I was getting weaker. I had to walk using the assistance of a walker, which was a major lifestyle adjustment for me. I was a young woman and slightly embarrassed. Yet, I have always been surrounded by really good people who loved and supported me, especially my family. And even though my walk was bad, I could still take care of all of my basic needs on my own as far as toileting, dressing, and bathing, and I could still drive.

Until one morning, the unthinkable happened. I got up to prepare for work and fell to the floor. Not only did I fall to the floor, I lost control of my bladder. It was bad, really bad. I called out for my mom. When she saw me on the floor, her face said everything that I already knew. Superwoman was defeated. Tears started streaming down her face, and she began to talk to God, pleading to help her child. We knew I had to get to the hospital. I am unsure why we didn't call the ambulance, but I recall crawling to the front door. I had gathered enough strength, someway, somehow, to get down the stairs and into the car. I felt God had ignited something in me that said *I had to move*.

I made it to the emergency room at the hospital. I stayed a few days, and they ran some tests and, of course, the same result; *inconclusive*. Everyone was puzzled because all of the tests came up with nothing. I was going to be discharged. But God had sent me a little angel in the form of my primary care physician. He told the entire team working with me that I would not be discharged until they figured out the problem. He fought with my insurance company because they threatened not to cover my stay. Back to the MRI machine I went. That time they did a full spine scan, and they found it—the herniated disc that was hitting my spine in the T9 middle area.

I was excited that they had finally solved the mystery of what was wrong and knew the problem. I also was deeply upset that I had been in that machine 3 years previously, and they had missed it. I felt they could have found the issue sooner, yet I drew forth the courage to believe that it would all work out and that I would be fine.

Surgery was scheduled to shave the disc to release the pressure. I underwent the surgery and started intense physical therapy, full of hope. Unfortunately, I was *too optimistic. Too naive and hopeful. Too willing to believe* that everything would be okay.

The surgery took place, and the pressure was released, but I never regained the ability to walk again fully. I did receive some reprieve, and a few things got better: my bladder control, nerve damage, and knowing what was wrong and how to improve it. My mind could finally rest in, wondering what was wrong. With the surgeons' work, I know my condition could improve over time.

That could have been the end of my story, but it was just the beginning. When I went back home, my mom had a conversation with me. She looked at me and said, "Meeka, I can't imagine how you feel. I understand. I get it. I will take care of you." To this day, I don't know if that meant physical, mental, financial, or all of the above. I didn't ask her because the only thing I knew for sure was that I could not accept what she was offering me. I had to fight and find the courage to live without limits. And that's just what I did.

I continued to do my physical therapy. I mastered control of my wheelchair. I still used my walker and worked on my leg strength so that I could still have the ability to drive. I continued to go out with my friends. I continued to date. I chose to live my life to the fullest. I was devastated and left with so many questions, but I learned to accept that I may never be able to walk, and I chose not to question it.

I continued to work, elevated my career, and found joy in being the director of the Day Care Center, where I was able to train teachers and implement the strategies that would provide a healthy curriculum. I traveled, went on cruises, and swam with the dolphins. I found a new man and started dating after being introduced to him by a friend at a party. He was cute, tall, and we had a great conversation. He made me smile and didn't care that I was in a wheelchair.

I fell in love with him quickly, yet I didn't realize that loving him would be a turning point. I didn't label him as an abuser at first because it was only 2 or 3 times that he hit me during a 5-year relationship. But that's exactly what he was, and sadly I did love him. Maybe more than I loved myself. At the time, I didn't feel like I deserved more. I felt I should just be happy that someone wanted me. After all, I was in a wheelchair. Everything in me knew that I should not have stayed with him, but I silenced the voice with conviction that he only wanted me. I endured the abuse and the feeling of loneliness when you're living in a home with another person, yet you feel desperately alone.

I had a baby with him. It was the best thing that ever happened in our relationship. The pregnancy gave me the courage to leave that relationship forever. I knew that I could not bring a child into such a toxic situation. It was one thing for me as an adult to decide to stay, but my child could not make that decision—I had to make the decision for them. I packed up and left and never looked back. That day, I decided to be a single wheelchair mama! My unborn child became my superpower.

The most profound aspect of my being in a wheelchair is that it forced me to discover the essence of who I am and enabled me to fall in love with myself! I was no longer able to hide behind anything. False self-love, false confidence, no more shying away and hiding in the background. One thing you can not do when you're in a wheelchair is hide. I had never been so sure of myself until I knew I had forged my own way.

Today, I get accused of smiling *too* much, laughing *too* much. Others say I am *too* happy and *too* optimistic. I have an idea that everything in life happens for a reason. It depends on you to choose what that reason is. We create our own path, and we walk (or, in my case, roll) down that path with courage and earnestness. That is how courage works. You look at something that seems impossible, and you just do it. This is also why courage appears differently in everyone's life. It doesn't always show up in the form of running into a burning building. Most of the time, courage shows up in those everyday moments. Finding the strength and will to go on after a bad breakup or divorce that was meant to hurt you or finding the inspiration to quit your job and start the business you have always wanted. Courage is often silent. It is usually something between you and yourself. We are all 1 step away from taking the biggest, most courageous steps of our lives!

I encourage you to bet on yourself. Love yourself. Everything that you need to have the life you want is already inside of you. Let go of the fear of the unknown and trust that it is all meant to be. You will never know if you *can* unless you just do it. Be *too* bold, *too* brave, and *too* courageous. Be *too* much of who you are and more open *to* learning about yourself. Be your own superhero and be free to live a life you choose.

IGNITE ACTION STEPS

- **Be kind to yourself.** Life is sometimes hard. We all have days where it gets to be entirely too much. It's okay to take a moment and reset. Read a book, have a spa day, or whatever helps you feel good.

- **Be patient.** Life is not a sprint; it's a marathon. Just because something is not happening in the time frame you want does not mean it won't happen. Journaling is a great way to quiet the mind.

- **Embrace the unknown.** Find joy in experiencing new things. Try something that you have never done before—push beyond your comfort zone.

- **Recognise that some things are beyond your control.** This is life. *We just don't know.* Take support from your faith. I have felt much strength knowing that for me, God is always in control.

- **Define yourself.** Know that you have the power within you to define exactly what you want the world to see. Walk into the room and make people see YOU. Be your true, authentic self. When I roll into a room, people see a woman in a wheelchair. However, the way I present and show up for myself, when I leave, they see a woman who can climb Mt. Everest. Your attitude about your situation makes all the difference.

Lameeka Harris — United States of America
lameeka@itavschools.org
 lameekaharris

Felicia Brim Moore

Felicia Brim Moore

"Your vision, your dreams, your attitudes, you own the story."

I hope you will be encouraged to examine how you see those who you encounter. Be reminded that what you see is not always what it *is*. Everyone owns the script to their story, and finding the freedom to live without the scars of judgment is groundbreaking. Take the risk and master what life has to offer you. Hopefully, you will find your inner self, discover gifts and talents, and foster the creation of an improved and more authentic version of YOU!

On the Other Side of the Glass

The summers in New York made things really clear for me. My dad was a drummer, traveling back and forth between New York and North Carolina to study music. He went there with his drums and his determination, eager to explore and grow his career as a musician. Reflecting on his life and what he accomplished, it was a pleasure having a front-row seat, always observing his passionate, courageous pursuit towards success.

It was a journey that many around us did not understand. I grew up in a small tobacco town in the South filled with factories that produced common goods, such as cotton, textiles, and cigarettes. It was a tight-knit community that had many beautiful and not-so-beautiful things within. Everyone knew everybody, so it often felt like there was little room for mistakes. If you made a mistake, someone was almost sure to hear about it, and you would become the 'talk of the town.' But, of course, if you did something great, it was the highlight of everyone's week.

From a child's perspective, the beauty outweighed the bad. I had friends; we rode bikes, roller skated around the neighborhood, played sports, and danced, and most of us were active in our churches. I fondly remember that small quaint place that allowed kids to be kids. We all went to the same high school that our parents went to, and all the adults knew you because they were either related to you or knew your family from school, church, or work. We grew up wholesome and somewhat sheltered from many things that happened in larger urban areas. High crime and serious threats just didn't happen here, not in our town. Church was ever present in all our lives. Even if you hung out with your friends the night before, or were up late, you still went to church; it was understood, you better make it there before the preacher's sermon began.

Yet, traveling with my dad, I got to see what a *"big city"* was like. My dad was comfortable making twelve-hour trips back and forth, from NC to NY, repeatedly following the steps he learned in the 1950s from his childhood trips to the north with his godmother. In my early years, he made sure that my mom and I traveled with him to experience city life, and I remember each trip vividly. I recall visiting the university where he studied and being in a large music room for a showcase. The place was packed with people, and there were different musicians playing their instruments. There was a distinct pulse in the room full of percussion, there were gifted hands playing the bongos and drums, creating rhythmic, African melodies that stuck to my soul. Those beats were alive; I felt every sound as if it were my heartbeat. That music was beautiful and artistically crafted for everyone who came to listen and support them.

On another visit, we went all the way to the top of the Empire State Building, and it seemed like I could see what the top of the world looked like. I made that trip with Mom, Dad, and my godparents, who were natives of New York. They came along and spent the day with us. Later, at the age of thirteen, I began visiting them on my own. I would go from playing in tobacco fields and completing school activities to flying into LaGuardia Airport to shop and sightsee in Manhattan, Jamaica Avenue, and the Fashion District. I was surrounded by subways, tall buildings, and what appeared to be important people in my innocent eyes. Those images gave me something to hold onto. Those experiences, filled with amazement, were silently building courage. Those images fueled my instincts to live out my own dreams beyond what I knew as "home."

My parents were bold, and brave, and had big dreams for their future. But those dreams were deferred when my Mom was eighteen, and my Dad was twenty-one. In our small town, they were two well-known smart young people just beginning to navigate adult life. In high school, my mom was a cheerleader, and my dad was in the band and had hopes and dreams of playing drums at his preferred college. But, with me on the way, soon to be born, the discussion on the next steps shifted to getting married and caring for a baby. My mom changed her plans, and her new family quickly became her focus. Things weren't perfectly packaged, but I saw something very early in both of them that gave me a sense of self. It was their perseverance, beliefs, boldness, strength, and courage to face the unknown, a will to explore. The attitude in our family was *just keep going and get it done*. Others made judgments about how our story would unfold, how my parents would be, how I would be. Sometimes it seemed like I was looking through a glass, with the town on one side and my family and I on the other.

Years later, with my parent's guidance, I left for college, embarking upon the unknown and moving boldly with courage; I was willing to explore what I wasn't sure of. After completing my studies and graduating from my beloved Historically Black University (HBCU), North Carolina Central University, I celebrated with my family and began plotting out my next. I considered going to a familiar place like New York, but NYC was not at the top of my list. Instead, I moved about 4 hours away to Washington, D.C.

I had a desire to figure things out, my way. It was all about adulting, independently and wisely. I thought my plan would involve working in government since I pursued a criminal justice degree. After a few temporary jobs, I landed a position as a Criminal Investigator with a well known attorney's office in D.C. I had no intention of walking the streets of a major city to investigate criminal cases, yet that is where my career took me.

That unplanned experience somehow opened my eyes to newfound possibilities. I visited my clients at the jail; they were in for serious crimes like rape and murder. Through my investigative work, attorneys were able to build defense cases for the accused. In the United States, everyone has the right to an attorney and fair trial, so I was responsible for gathering key information that would be used for their defense. I visited jails and crime-infested neighborhoods to conduct investigations. During that time, my spiritual foundation came in handy. I used my faith and courage to work with people charged with heinous crimes.

Every day, I leaned in and relied heavily on the imparted wisdom that adults in my life shared with me. God gave me intuition and direction, I was able to navigate work safely. I went into dark places: run-down apartment buildings where it seemed like the only light coming in was from the sun, seedy back allies, and street corners looking for witnesses to alleged crimes. Sometimes, knocking on the door to see who would answer was the longest wait ever. The uncertainty of the environment made me question, whether *I should be here or not.* I always trusted the Holy Spirit to be my guide. Every visit, I entered with prayer, and courage followed.

After several years of investigating cases, my observations became more difficult to digest. The visits to the jail were disconcerting. This is where I saw the unimaginable. I came from a place where people made family 'work' in spite of hard times. However, in the jails, I saw people trying to make family 'work,' but it was quite different. There were glass separators with phones that transferred voices through divided conversations, unable to truly connect. There were the accused, mostly men, on one side of the glass and then, the visitors on the opposite side, typically wives, moms, kids, and grandmothers. Every visit was the same: the visits were difficult to watch, burdensome, and not easy for me to reconcile within.

Seeing those heartbreaking scenes over and over sparked a motivation to work even harder for people on both sides of the glass. I doubled down on my dedication as my investigative skills improved, and some of my toughest cases yielded a victory. I realized that connecting families was more fulfilling to me than winning a case. I began to dream about educating families and thinking of ways to reach young black men before they went to jail. I wanted to see families sharing the same side of the glass doing things like visiting the Empire State Building or visiting the Smithsonian Museum on the weekends. I asked myself, *How can I help them experience more stability and access, and prevent these unfortunate happenings?* I prayed for an answer, but the answer did not come right away.

These were very complex situations, and encountering individuals who were cast away by society was not a light task. As I spoke to them about being incarcerated, I saw their humanity and intelligence. The conversations with incarcerated teens grabbed my attention, they were products of an environment they did not create. I would see the innocent boy right behind their eyes, despite the fact they were making decisions that forced them into bravery that no kid could totally understand. The kids I met ignited a new sense of purpose. I felt the nudge to do something different, over time, my path revealed itself. While volunteering with youth programs at church, observers would always ask, "Are you a teacher?" I usually would respond and say, "No, and never wanted to be." But now, my answer was changing. Teaching was my gift, and I realized it was time to acknowledge that. With this conviction, came a swell of courage as I owned my new path toward my 'true love'; this discovery required a pivot in the early years of my career.

Once I realized it was time to make a change, I began my search. Internet-based job searches were not a thing, you just watched the newspaper for job announcements. As I have navigated professionally, I have found that when you search, you will often find what you are looking for. My thought was, *I wanted to work in the schools. But how would I do this without a license to teach?*

I stumbled across a job announcement for a new nonprofit seeking College Advisors who would serve students in the District of Columbia. It was as if God was shouting the answer at me. I immediately applied, went in for the interview, and got the job; the first Advisor they hired! Talk about affirming your life choices; it felt God-sent and the perfect fit for me. Our small staff launched a program that helped high school students complete college. My desire to educate others quickly became my reality.

In the inaugural year, the program supported six high schools in D.C. I ended up working in Southeast Washington, D.C. I was familiar with the neighborhood because of my days as an Investigator. Our program's leadership felt my background was a great match for that school community. I remember speaking to a school staff member during the first week of school, and they mentioned, "This high school is one of D.C.'s best-kept secrets." I would later find out how true the statement was, as I began forging a deeper examination of what was now "my" other side of the glass. I pulled from within, reflected on what I learned from my parents, and embraced the assignment. My dad's words echoed: "Be tough," "No time for crying, "What's the problem?", "Always be ready; you can do it." To my mom, those were harsh words for a girl, but her commitment to my spiritual development and his toughness meshed well, and I believed I could handle "it." The "it" was demonstrating the courage to help these beautiful souls discover what they could overcome and achieve.

At that time, D.C. students were struggling to find themselves in the midst of a crack cocaine epidemic within their communities. These kids did not ask to step into these strained conditions: neighborhoods that were infested by a foreign agent that presented confusion, crime, and loss. College attendance rates in the district were very low. The academic, social, and behavioral challenges were vast. On many occasions, the message to these students was, "College, college, college for sale!" It was strategic, we offered informative workshops, structured programs, and scholarship investments for qualified students. It was something that no one could imagine. A group of people showed up in an under-served high school to walk kids through the college process. The financial backing to support these students was unprecedented. It was aggressive and intentional; the information was priceless.

Even I, who was college-educated, learned something new every day. After a while, during lunch periods, the center was packed, and students just started coming from everywhere to express interest. As an Advisor, I was crafty and yet savvy, understanding each student case by case. The evidence suggested not every kid was going to college, but the truth was not every kid thought they COULD. So, the advising began, and I started learning about each student—their stories, their experiences, and their interests. I understood what most students had to endure seemed insurmountable and very complex. They saw dead bodies, overdoses, drug paraphernalia, heard gunshots on their way to school and after school. Some even lost friends or parents along the way. Yet here they were, stepping up and grabbing at a brighter future. I was constantly amazed by their courage, and the relationship enlightened my perspective.

Despite the challenges that students in this school district faced, there were enough of them who had good grades, test scores, and positive attitudes; who grabbed hold of the path forward. College became a part of their conversation—our conversation. I am still in amazement, as these students were trailblazers in their city. No one talks about this group as much as they should; these courageous young men and women who stood up and answered the call. Now the college-going culture has shifted tremendously in D.C. A huge push and a great amount of work was done to help these students, but more importantly, they had a will to help themselves, and that was key.

At a critical time in D.C. history, my colleagues, students, and I worked to change the landscape of higher education for families in the nation's capital. I believed in these students. We worked through many challenges together, building relationships, and empowering them to navigate using their potential and gifts. Bearing witness to their perspective was transformational. They were change agents! They influenced others in their families; even when there was doubt, they DID IT ANYWAY. Just like my dad, the traveling musician; like my mom, who was so strong and determined; my godparents, who were my constant supporters; in the face of adversity, they DID IT ANYWAY. And like me, the Criminal Investigator-turned-College Advisor, we are simply evidence of what can happen when you decide not to let fear dictate the outcome. In that uncomfortable place, I encountered many surprises; those students were the gifts that inspired me and others. They are now adults who have become educators, attorneys, coaches for high school and professional teams, premier chefs, engineers, entrepreneurs, librarians, and, most of all, great parents. So, on that Southeast side of D.C., there was value, intelligence, and giftedness contained in people with dreams and capability. They were found on the other side of the glass.

You never know what beauty you will encounter when you travel to uncomfortable places. Invite experiences that will alter your mindset and recognize that your process is preparing you for your next. Trust the process; it is your personal journey that does not need validation from anyone but you and God. Use courage to overcome hardships, and don't be afraid to struggle; your struggles are your launching pad toward personal growth. Be vulnerable and listen to your gut; you will end up where you are supposed to be. I encourage you to discover what exists on the other side of the glass in your life. You have already been given permission to experience it!

IGNITE ACTION STEPS

- Travel outside of what you know, meet new people, create new experiences, and embrace the differences in others.

- Trust God, even when your destination is unclear, he is your guide.

- Use your gifts to impact others, you are already equipped.

- Parents and teachers, believe in your students, and build relationships to better understand their dreams. Their path forward just might be different from yours.

- Students, find a mentor who will teach you and hold you accountable. Embrace the wisdom that others will share.

- Embrace your journey, accept your wins and losses; life is a classroom, you will never stop learning. Remain teachable.

- Devote yourself to personal growth, identify your fears, then work on replacing fear with courage…Go do it anyway!

Felicia B Moore, MSA — United States of America
Certified Change Practitioner/Advisor/Trainer/
Educational Advocate/ Motivator/Speaker
www.feliciabmoore.com
 Felicia B. Moore

Naomi Zion Mark

NAOMI ZION MARK

*"Take a leap so far outside of your comfort zone
that you come face to face with your destiny."*

**I want you to know that you were created to win, and if you bid farewell
to troubles and summon the courage to embrace new territories, there is
a chance of a brighter future. Dreams can come true despite turbulent
beginnings, and challenges of any type do not have to define or limit what
you can achieve in life. Rise above your obstacles and past, utilizing courage as your driving force toward your destiny. I hope my story helps you
see your current challenges are nothing but stepping stones on the path to
your greatest achievements and the greatest version of yourself.**

VOICE OF COURAGE

With amusement, my birth mother and stepfather frequently said, "You're
absolutely clueless and slow-witted, you're inadequate and stupid, and you
happen to be one of the least appealing individuals we've ever seen."

If you were with me 2 years ago, you would have witnessed someone
who found it extremely challenging, if not impossible, to speak in order
to present *me* in certain environments. For a substantial portion of my
life, I had hidden my true essence by habitually steering clear of specific

social circumstances, largely due to incapacitating anxiety about facing the same extreme rejection, mockery, and humiliation my neglectful parents made me endure. I feared being ostracized and left alone—the way they left me—for simply showing up as the truest expression of my unique self. You see, normally, a parent finds joy in contributing to the happiness of their beloved child. But the only actions that appeared to provide my abusive mother and stepfather with a deep sense of contentment were those that involved causing immense pain to me during my vulnerable years as a growing child.

As a little girl behind closed doors in the privacy of my childhood home, I faced my upbringing as a solo journey amid a profoundly damaging, often violent home. I endured an unrelenting stream of verbal, emotional, and mental abuse while grappling with chronic neglect, physical harm, and unceasing isolation. This torture concluded with the ultimate act of complete abandonment when I was left on the street at sixteen to navigate the vast world alone.

As a young girl, I was a bubbly, sweet, very sensitive, and caring individual who got on with everybody. I was a leader with many gifts who wanted everyone around me to be happy. However, I quickly grasped at home that displaying such behavior was unacceptable. And the abuse gradually led me to live in a constant state of fear and put my true nature in the background. I had begun to conceal my voice partly due to it being the safest and the least painful way to exist. As a little girl, I told myself, "If I'm invisible, no one can inflict harm. If I am invisible, all people will be satisfied." These limiting beliefs and more became an integral part of me. Ultimately, I became a selective mute, finding it impossible to present myself verbally in the majority of social environments. At school, I played the character of the jester and kept my true nature veiled. I wanted people to like me; I needed to survive. As an adult, not a single person alive was ever permitted to learn the truth about my thoughts—thoughts that constantly carried the burden of my neglectful parents, injurious comments, and incredibly harmful actions that tormented my weak psyche for decades beyond my childhood.

Their abuse had countless extremely serious ramifications on me, many of which took me decades to overcome. But what remained with me was the feeling of being uncomfortable in my skin and with my personality. It was nearly impossible for me to give a voice to any aspect of my existence: how I was doing, how my day might go, and what was happening within *and outside of me.* As a child, I had never been asked about my identity, my dreams, or my emotional experiences

As a selective mute, my existence was lonely and often painful. My world happened on the inside, inside my mind and heart, and it remained there for decades. I longed to be able to share myself, but for the most part, I felt scared that no one would care. Counselors and therapists were the sole individuals I felt safe speaking to openly. They were the only people who ever got to know *me* for the brief time that we encountered each other. In adulthood, I avoided challenging situations where I had to present the inner me. If I met people for professional reasons, I would speak in professional jargon only, and if I had to be in other social situations, I would simply be quiet. Around my birth mother and stepfather, for the most part, I didn't speak at all.

As a small girl, there *was* a glimmer of hope in me, a bright light within me that refused to die permanently. I was a top student at senior school, so a part of me knew I was good at some things. My English teacher often requested that I read aloud to the entire class. Each time I spoke, I couldn't help but notice that my voice had a remarkable ability to stun and captivate everyone present, and I would think to myself, *there truly must be something special about me.* Throughout my senior school years, each day, I put on a façade of being in a happy state. I was great at putting on a show, keeping everyone engaged, and receiving attention by masking how dead I was inside. But I was simply a good actress who had always enjoyed becoming lost in someone else's character. Concealing my identity is partly how I uncovered my talent for performance.

At the age of 7, I embarked on my path of acting. A primary school teacher asked who would like to perform in a play, and I raised my hand without thinking. I got the part of Jack's mother in Jack and the Beanstalk. By my early teens, I graced the stages of some of Birmingham's largest theaters, performing in professional musicals for crowds of up to two thousand people. The attention helped to temporarily fill the void within me. I also played 4 instruments as a child by ear and soon discovered I had a gift for songwriting. Acting, playing instruments, singing, and dancing became my outlets to express myself, and as a child, my ultimate dream was to be a star. Amidst the labels, fear, and suffering, I shone. Listening to music also played a pivotal role in giving me hope in my world growing up. Immersing myself in songs with powerful lyrics made me feel loved and empowered, briefly lifting my sadness and loneliness and arming me with a little strength to confront each day independently.

Indulging in music also helped distract me from the abusive life I was enduring. Whether I was moving to music, singing, or creating it from scratch, I could be ME for a while...

As I developed, I increasingly realized the value of my musical gifts. I wrote and recorded my first song at thirteen. At fifteen, an opportunity arose to be the lead vocalist for a band that had just completed a tour with the well-known Manic Street Preachers.

Decades later, I had written and recorded many musical compositions, and by a chance encounter, I reconnected with my dearest friend, Annie. We had shared a passion for music, but Annie had taken her career to new heights by becoming a signed recording artist. As in awe as I was of her, she reciprocated with a deep appreciation for my talent. "You've got a fantastic voice, Naomi; send some of your tracks to Michael." Michael was a Grammy-nominated record producer, as well as a celebrated music artist and the owner of a record label affiliated with another that ranked among the world's leading record labels. My jaw dropped. Michael listened to my songs and offered me a record deal.

The fact that I was being presented with this incredible opportunity seemed like a dream I hadn't woken up from. The visions I had in my early years of myself as a star rushed through my mind. I knew this once-in-a-lifetime opportunity could mean my music would be on all major streaming platforms and on CDs and distributed to potentially millions of people worldwide. I had to get my act together.

I have accomplished extensive transformation and growth since my youth. I had begun to trust again and emerge from my shell. But now was the time to get to my ideal self and my ideal destination with rapid speed. I looked at all of the things I needed to make it happen, for example, a unique image, performance skills, and recording equipment. I had never been a solo artist before; I needed confidence and, most of all, the ability to speak publicly. Singing had to be more than just me standing there with a mic and an instrument. I aspired to be a conduit to share not only songs but ME—my experiences, my truest self—to encourage, inspire, connect, and positively impact others' lives. But, the thought of speaking in public terrified me, and I was still grappling with selective muteness. *How can I stand up in front of crowds as a solo music artist if I'm scared of what people think of me?*

I shifted my focus to positive messages instead. I had taught myself that my voice could spark impactful shifts, hold significance and relevance, and should always be heard. I viewed and embraced my distinct qualities as strengths and not limitations. I believed that my sensitive nature was beautiful, and I firmly believed that I was created for a very special purpose. The road to speaking publicly and singing solo wasn't going to be easy, but I knew I had to go through this process so I could be exactly where I wanted to be, doing exactly what I wanted to do. I gave myself permission to create a space for me to shine. I wrote a list of everything necessary to speak *and* be a successful music artist. I visualized myself performing at Wembley Stadium, and I got to work.

Along that journey, I met Harmony Lawson. Harmony heard me sing and introduced me to 2 influential media experts and leading publicists. They had established a highly popular and safe platform to help individuals like me elevate their speaking careers and gain media opportunities. They also taught me how to overcome stage fright and be comfortable and confident while on camera. Through their boot camp, I made lasting connections and gained confidence, wisdom, and tools to further my journey.

Then Harmony sent me toward a Clubhouse™ room that was bursting at the seams. "Go in there and share your story!" she said, "I absolutely can't!" I said, but Harmony continued urging me, and I decided to go in.

Amongst a throng of hundreds of people, I immersed myself in the stories shared by seasoned and emerging motivational speakers. Among them stood the most influential motivational speaker of all time, the legendary Les Brown, and I felt like a small presence in comparison. The crowd eagerly anticipated his pearls of wisdom and queued up for their moment to share. With my own courage lacking, I didn't dare raise my hand to speak; I stayed hidden, diligently recording notes, ultimately condensing my life's journey into a concise form.

3 weeks later, I stumbled across a different room led by Les Brown and his son, John Leslie Brown. I was curious, so I entered. I didn't know then, but members of Les Brown's public speaker program, 'Hungry to Speak,' were presenting their speeches. The room was heaving with individuals as usual, eagerly listening, commenting in the chat, and being blessed by Les Brown's feedback.

"Would anyone in the audience like to comment and give the speakers feedback," said John Leslie Brown. A still voice within me said, *You can do that*. I felt courage building inside of me. During the speeches, I made sure I was far more intentional with my note-taking so I could potentially give feedback. Then, when the time came, I raised my hand to comment. Almost instantly, I began to feel fear and shake. I wanted to 'un-raise' my hand, but that tiny voice came back and repeated, *You can do it.* The moderator picked someone else, but I had a gut feeling I was supposed to speak. "No," said John Leslie Brown to the moderator, "Let's hear from Naomi Zion Mark." My heartbeat accelerated to the point where I thought it would beat itself out of my body. *You can do it,* the voice repeated. I began to speak. "I like the way you think," said John Leslie Brown, "Would you like to regularly share your feedback with us?" There was a pause in my heartbeat. My answer was yes, yet my voice went still for a moment. Refusing wasn't an option, however, and I let out a high-pitched, "Yes. please!" Suddenly, feedback time was over. "Les Brown would like you to share your life story now," said his son. I froze in fear. I thought *God help me.* There were in excess of 500 listeners. The still voice spoke a little louder. You *can do it; read that story over there, the one you were unknowingly writing to ready yourself for this moment.*

"Yes," I replied with uncertainty, "I'll share my story." Holding my story's pages, doubt crept further in. *I can't do this, why am I doing this?* I whispered inwardly. *You can,* the quiet voice affirmed. He calls my name; it's my turn to share my story. My heart raced, my stomach churned, and my palms were sweaty; the child in me felt terrified, inadequate, stupid, and unworthy. I experienced a lack of options. *I can't do this,* I said inside. *People are waiting for your story,* the still voice urged; you *can do it.* I inhaled what felt like the deepest breath in the Universe and whispered to myself, *Now or never,* and with conviction, I began to speak.

Afterward, cheering from attendees ensued. I noticed a surge of around one hundred new followers; audience members spoke up and expressed how touched and moved they were by my sharing. Les Brown liked it also, and my self-confidence skyrocketed.

Within a year, I joined Les Brown's public speaking program, *Hungry for Greatness.* I cried in front of everyone in my group when it was my turn to speak, just like I had in the other public speaking groups I attended the same year. Partially because I was scared of how people would see me. I was still a little girl inside my shell, still believing and behaving as if everyone was going to hurt me for presenting me. But, being honest about who I was, my fears, and where I was at the time, in front of rooms full of people at the top of their industries and seasoned speakers, helped me grow exponentially and ultimately feel comfortable presenting myself. Partly due to believing that if I could speak up in that nerve-wracking situation, I could present all of myself absolutely anywhere.

A year later, I co-hosted a live summit where I introduced notable speakers, including Les Brown. I delivered my speech live on KP Media TV and other platforms to an audience exceeding seventy thousand. Soon after, I became a certified motivational speaker under the mentorship and coaching of Les Brown.

The following year, I took the stage for the first time as a solo artist and captivated one hundred and twenty individuals with my presence. I felt like I was meant to be there. Encouraging feedback confirmed my ability to impact and uplift through performance, and those experiences propelled my confidence to embrace larger stages.

When once I never spoke, now speaking comes more easily. I believe my voice will be used to bring about change for the better. Speaking allows me to share my perspective in a way that allows me to be free and completely myself. It also enables me to inspire and encourage others in their transformation and motivate them in their lives. It helps me to connect with individuals on a deeper level. Having the courage to speak shows me that we all have something to say and can make a difference. How we use our words will change lives and make great things possible.

Dive deeply and look at what may be holding you back from speaking your truth. The only way you can become a good speaker is by the act of speaking. Take it one step at a time; every step is important, and pat yourself on the back. Keep the goal in mind, don't let anything deter you. Believe in yourself; your voice is special and powerful. Lots of people would love to hear what you have to say.

Courage is facing adversity, knowing that things may be against you, but you do them anyway. In taking that leap, you get closer to who you want to be.

IGNITE ACTION STEPS

How to grow in self-confidence:
- Look at yourself and your history without apology or guilt. Your past, including the person you once were, shaped you into a resilient survivor destined to flourish. Direct your attention to the present, your inner growth, your surroundings, and how you can craft a more radiant future.

- Construct a thorough list outlining the necessary steps to accomplish the very thing you find unachievable, and then take the first step. Keep progressing through the list, converting the unattainable into tangible achievements. Then, when the next hurdle surfaces, reassure yourself that you can smoothly overcome any adversity.

- Encircle yourself with individuals who embrace you as you are, and don't be ashamed of saying no to what doesn't contribute positively to your life.

- Jot down all your present skills, strengths, talents, and past successes. Acknowledge what challenges you've confronted and surmounted. No matter their scale, give yourself a big pat on the back for all you've achieved.

- Upskill. Acquiring new and improving existing skills helps prepare you for new challenges. This also helps to accomplish tasks with ease.

How to create a positive mindset.
- Work diligently to cherish your peace by doing everything in your power to stop the emotions linked to harmful language or a negative mentality from wreaking havoc on your reality. You can't control the thoughts that arise, so try to control how you react to them by just sitting with, listening to, and observing them. Avoid responding to them. Especially negatively.

- Acknowledge your distinctiveness. Accept your brilliance, accept the truth that you are wonderful and inspirational, your courage is unwavering, and you possess a collection of awe-inspiring qualities. *Yes, you do!*

- Adopt new helpful beliefs to help transform your reality. You could do this by jotting down 10 positive descriptors (e.g., *I am enough as I am, I am valuable, I am wanted, I accept myself*). Repeat these positive affirmations to yourself in front of the mirror as often as you can.

How to step outside of your comfort zone and reach difficult goals.
- Always keep your goals and dreams at the forefront of your mind, particularly amidst difficult times. Allow fear to take a backseat while you concentrate on your objectives. When fear tries to take center stage, let your goals and dreams eclipse it.

- Believe that you can move beyond your own limits to achieve your objectives and be willing to take the first step in the right direction.

- Step out with the belief that everything will be alright even though everything is/or appears to be falling apart all around you.

- Visualize the results you want. See yourself smiling at the finish line because of what you accomplished.

Naomi Zion Mark — Ireland
Motivational Speaker & Host of Naomi Zion Speaks,
Recording Artist, Author, Entrepreneur,
Fitness & Natural Healthcare Specialist
www.naomizionspeaks.com
www.wellnessgiant.ie
naomi.mark.98
thisisnaomizion

Michiko Couchman

Michiko Couchman

"We are all capable of powerful, illogical things:
like hope, like optimism, like courage."

May this story remind you that the simple act of opening your eyes to silver linings can be an act of courage. As you stare down the barrel of unexpected challenges beyond your comprehension or control, you must grant yourself the permission to defy logic and create optimism. When you decide to believe in miracles, you will see them everywhere. When you turn a deaf ear to doubt, you create a space to hear hope speaking to you. I warmly and sincerely encourage you to recognize and celebrate the courage you are showing every time you consciously choose to seek, see, and embrace the good in even the most dark and difficult of days.

Involuntarily Committed

"Should I pull over, Dr. Brenner?"

The Philadelphia skyline looms on the hazy horizon; buildings begin to glow with the light of the sunrise reflecting off their window panes. We've been making good time, and even with the growing line of red taillights, we can't be more than twenty minutes away from the doctor's office. The awareness that we are about to hear the news that couldn't wait sits like a lump of granite in my stomach. My husband finds a place alongside the highway to stop the car as the morning commuters are all too happy to cut in line on their way to work. He puts his phone on speaker.

"Unfortunately, your most recent scans show there are lesions in several bones, not just your jaw. The fact they are widespread means it has to be multiple myeloma, not a localized plasmacytoma."

The love of my life is the most unshakeable and confident person I know, a superhero to our 2 kids and me. But in that heartbreaking moment, destined to be etched in my mind forever, he is human. His voice is small as he breathily expels the words, "Oh. Okay." He mutes the mic on his phone as his face twists in agony and he slams his fist into the steering wheel. My eyebrows droop like a sad puppy's, an expression of sympathy he is used to seeing from me.

I have always been the emotional one in our relationship. Everything makes me cry: videos of helpless rescue kittens, the joy on new parents' faces, the mere thought of a child being bullied, and every Disney® movie made since 1998. But the empathy that makes me feel everyone's pain is also what helps me know, deep down, what my husband needs. When he is at his weakest, I must be at my strongest. The more upset my husband seems, the less likely I am to cry. Something in my heart quickly tells my brain to wipe dismay from my face, to display only love and reassurance for my husband. There is nothing deliberate or conscious about it; no digging or soul searching occurring. My fearless affect is instinctive and involuntary.

Dr. Brenner keeps things brief and tells us he will fill us in completely once we arrive. "Drive safely," he says with an unspoken apology rippling through his words. I wonder, *Why should he feel bad for telling us the truth; for giving us an answer?* We had been waiting five weeks for a conclusive diagnosis: test after test, theory after theory, in and out of the cancer center for one painful procedure after another. In the few quiet moments I'd had during those difficult weeks, I questioned every life choice I had made. I wondered if some 'bad karma' I might have accumulated was working behind the scenes to punish me by hurting my beloved partner. I had found every excuse to blame myself, feeling as though he didn't listen to his body because he was busy providing for me and my needs. Any night that I had the luxury of time to think I was completely mired in a sense of abject failure as if taking exclusive ownership of what was happening would give me the power to stop it. I was always on the brink of driving myself crazy.

5 weeks of physical and mental torture had finally ended with Dr. Brenner's words. But receiving the worst of the potential diagnoses we had been warned about

did not bring us relief. Yet, once again, through my commitment to my husband, the courage to play pretend—to seek the silver lining—arose in me involuntarily.

"At least we know now. That means we can finally take action and destroy this thing," I say, rallying my words and sending them forward to do battle with the questions hanging thick in the air. "You are going to be alright," I insist as we exit right off the highway. He lets out a sigh, then speaks his agreement. "I just have to fight this thing! Violent optimism, right?"

"Violent optimism" is a term he coined when we first began hearing the word "cancer" thrown around. He insisted aggressive optimism wasn't aggressive enough and that *violent* optimism was required. We still don't know how much quiet courage such dedicated boldness will take. Instead, we proceed 1 second at a time. We drive with our minds trained on only the next thing that has to happen. Decelerate to twenty-five miles per hour… change lanes to get around that annoying city bus… turn right… turn left… get in line for the parking attendant. We smile politely as we hand over the keys, knowing that however scared or bad we feel, it isn't the employees' fault.

The rush of warm air as we walk through the rotating doors brings us into the present, and we are suddenly very aware we have entered the cancer center. There is a gaunt older lady seated by the elevator, her bare scalp wrapped in a telltale silk scarf. Her husband somehow looks even more frail, as if love and a cane are the only thing holding him up. But he is smiling at her and reassuring her he can catch her if she falls. The love on his face looks a lot like courage, a lot like the instinctive reassurance I had shown my own partner. I am suddenly struck by how lucky I am to be young enough to care for my husband without actively fearing what the stress might do to my own body.

We make our way to the front desk, asking Tony, the receptionist, how his weekend was and waving a happy hello to Nurse Linda. Things feel comfortable, dare I say 'normal,' in the waiting area where patients vote on which department's Halloween pumpkin display is coolest. My hero sits next to me, bathed in warm yellow light and refusing to frown. I am struck by his courage and make sure my face matches his as we are called into Dr. Brenner's office.

Once we are in the room, though, staring at a blue leather chair covered by a thin sheet of paper made whiter by the stark fluorescent lights… our ability to shove reality aside fades. My lungs are searching for extra oxygen in the room, and I wonder if my husband sees everything going wavy like I do. I ponder whether the news that is coming would sound better in that warm, happy lobby. My thoughts are interrupted when the doctor enters. After quickly shaking our hands, he sits on his wheely stool and proceeds to let us know what multiple myeloma means. He is trying not to scare us while refusing to lie to us, a balance he has clearly had to find many times before as one of the leading myeloma specialists in the country. I am struck by how lucky we are to have him, of all people, as our oncologist. Yet a different feeling is about to strike me next, and our violent optimism is about to seem like violent delusion.

With a long, breathy exhale, Dr. Brenner begins. "So... I have to let you know that this cancer is considered incurable. This means there are treatments to put it into remission, but currently there is no way to make it go away completely."

This time a different expression involuntarily twists my facial muscles as hopelessness flickers inside my pupils, and my lips tighten in sync with my clenching jaw. I can't see a silver lining or a warm glow. I can't even turn my head to look at the man I love, knowing the sight of him framed by this new context will instantly bring forth tears. Without taking my eyes off the doctor, I fumble for and eventually find my husband's hand, giving it a tight squeeze, wondering who needs it more. Then the doctor cruelly, dutifully, continues with the hardest words I have ever heard:

"I also have to tell you the mean survival rate following diagnosis is about 10 years. This means about fifty percent of patients live longer than that, and fifty percent of patients unfortunately do not."

Dr. Brenner's most recent words are clanging in my skull, and I scrunch my eyes shut to try to force silence in my mind, knowing I need to hear what this professional lifesaver is saying. Though seated, my husband and I are in total lockstep, breathing each breath slowly and deeply in unison as we fight off tears. Neither of us wants to be the first one to break, to let the first tear or shuddering breath slip out, knowing it will destroy the other's stoic wall. The remaining 3 minutes of the doctor's explanation are an eternity as we both strain to hold the emotional dam in place. Somewhere in the mix is a restrained nugget of hopefulness as he mentions my husband is easily thirty to thirty-five years younger and in far better shape than the average myeloma patient. Then the doctor gets up to leave the room for a moment, and I finally look into the eyes of my best friend.

The pain moves like a mudslide, slow and thick, across our faces. Our eyes go wet and red, and there is a sharp sucking sound as we inhale desperately through half-closed mouths. He is the first to turn away, burying his face in his hands, and I see his shoulders shaking as he folds himself in half over his legs.

Game over. I sob desperately. A sense of impotence smothers me like a weighted blanket as I realize there is truly nothing I can do to make this all go away for him—no way for me to shoulder the burdens of treatment for him;

no world in which I can hit reset and make the cancer mine instead of his. *He never volunteered for this. He doesn't deserve this!* As images of a life without him flash across my broken brain, I don't know what emotion to give words to anymore. I can't call what I am feeling "sad," "confused," or "scared." What I feel now is deeper than all those combined. It is a complete emptiness, an absence of any light. I don't even realize I am rubbing his back with my left hand, comforting him again through sheer loving instinct. It gives me no sense of power or utility. *What does a comforting gesture matter when your world has just been sucked into a black hole?*

I sit in this darkness with him for a time, desperate to pull myself out so I can be his lifeline. Then suddenly, as fast as grief had thrown me to the ground, an inner rumble yanks me back to my feet. A baton passes from one thought to the next.

10 years left?...This can't possibly be our reality... It CAN'T... Okay. Then it won't be!

My next thought is spoken out loud, passing the baton to my husband.

"You know what? Those statistics don't matter because you're YOU, the guy who can overcome anything and always does. If anyone is going to beat the odds, it's you." I shove the baton more forcefully into his hands as I add, "Medical advances happen every day, so a cure is going to be found soon."

The daylight that had been streaming in through the window hits my consciousness as the black fog in my mind dissipates, and I declare with illogical hope that we will write our own story.

That is how we decide the tears are going to stop for now, though more will come on the long road ahead. Violent optimism takes the reins again. *We're going to be alright.* Seconds later, Dr. Brenner is back with papers in his hand and more to discuss. "Initial here to indicate you understand your cancer is categorized as incurable." It's a sentence filled with foreboding, but my husband puts pen to paper anyway. "Initial here to indicate you have designated Michi as your caretaker and emergency contact." I feel the weight of everything the word "caretaker" is about to imply, wondering momentarily if I am strong enough. Then I watch my superhero's cape flutter as he breathes deeply through each careful explanation and inks his agreement to whatever the medical gods recommend. *We're going to be alright.*

The doctor recommends we start with radiation first, let the burned cells heal, then do chemo after. But my husband has never been one to simply accept the safest option, constantly pursuing the thrill of extreme obstacle course races, roller coasters, and challenging work assignments. He asks, "You said I was younger and fitter than the average patient. Is there any reason I can't do radiation and chemo at the same time?" Dr. Brenner glances briefly my way to see if my face is telling him, "Say NO." I am not thrilled by the idea of my husband torturing himself, but his courage deserves to be kept afloat. So, I look the doctor in the eye with a pragmatic half-smile, signaling my desire to proceed. *We're going to be alright.* The doctor gives the go-ahead, and the dates for this Spartan approach to medical care are set. The ugly journey of discovering the simple beauties in life begins.

We are hungry when we leave the cancer center, wandering for a few blocks in search of food. We see Japanese characters on a wooden plank mounted to a black wall. Completely by chance, we had found the restaurant we had long been told served the best ramen in the whole city. It was 2 blocks away from the treatment center where we were about to spend the next 5 months.

"This is a sign," I say with a gleeful smile that boot-stomps all the fear sitting inside my heart. At this moment, I fully embrace that I am no longer going to settle for involuntary courage because violent optimism requires courage of a more deliberate sort. I decide that whether it makes sense or not, I will believe in miracles… the kind that will keep my husband with me for all my days. I pick up a penny on the ground and announce it is an omen that good luck is coming our way. I see a sparrow hopping from crumb to crumb on the city sidewalk and choose to believe it is a reminder from a higher power that we deserve to smile. Later, when I get letters soliciting donations for the Special Olympics®, Arbor Day Foundation®, and the ASPCA®, I decide these are chances to put some good energy out into the world, trusting that karma will bring it back. I assign meaning to every little thing that happens, doggedly determined to give myself reasons to hope and believe my husband is *going to be alright*. None of it is logical, but faith in miracles rarely is. As I commit to cultivating optimism, my superhero keeps me believing bravely because even on my most clouded days, keeping faith in him is second nature.

Weeks of daily radiation burned holes in my husband's throat. Courage then meant walking every inch of the grocery store in search of soft foods he could swallow and superfruit smoothie powders that might help him heal. Months of weekly chemotherapy took his hair, his muscle, and his energy. Courage then meant driving him to the cancer center and back in unfamiliar, aggressive city traffic; it meant trying to meet his gaze with an optimistic smile every time he sat in the infusion chair. Sometimes courage meant calling 911. Often, courage meant staunchly embracing normalcy, looking him right in his sunken eyes and saying, "Gah! You tracked shower water all over our kitchen!" Always, courage meant telling our kids, "Dad's going to be alright," with the hope that violent optimism was contagious.

It was. Our daughter was brave enough to persevere toward her own triumphs. She earned her second-degree black belt and became the highest-ranking student instructor at her Taekwondo studio (before she even turned thirteen) while helping lead her school's Gay & Straight Student Alliance and being selected for a program focused on empowering future female leaders... all while Daddy fought cancer. Our son finally decided to be social and make friends. He defied gravity by 'practicing parkour,' became a gaming legend, and triumphed in school while carrying a weight no 7-year-old ever should. He joked, laughed, and loved during times I was tempted to shut down and reminded me what courage lies in simply refusing to spend scary days stuck inside misery. I saw courage in each of them every day.

Indeed, I was shown throughout my journey that courage is everywhere, in everyone. It showed up in the furrowed eyebrows of a fellow mom who reached out before she even really knew me because she had just walked the same scary path as a mother and wife. It was in the glowing smile of a friend who raises her autistic daughter with incomparable grace in a country that constantly misunderstands her. It glistened in the eyes of a neighbor who dried her tears to tell her child *they are going to be alright* even if Daddy isn't living in the same home anymore. Each day I feel the warmth bred by courage in the soft cheeks of a boy and girl who hug me tight from both sides to let me know we are all in this together. I see courage, most of all, in the fuzzy hairs on the head of my superhero, who has come through hell and back to reclaim his life.

We are 1 year into this involuntary adventure, and I am grateful to say he is currently in remission. Though circumstances have changed the shape of our lives forever, our violent optimism remains unscathed. I don rose-colored glasses like armor to shield me when others express their concerns and doubts, trying to remember the compassionate source of people's worries. I laugh and make jokes about cancer, however inappropriate, because sculpting reasons to laugh from things that make your heart cry is courageous in its own right. I live every day insisting on putting hope, positivity, and self-esteem out into the world. I tell women they are extraordinary, I tell men they are kind, I tell authors they are brilliant, and I tell children they are brave. I tell everyone they matter and *they are going to be alright*. And even if I should know that it is illogical to think this can be guaranteed, that anything in life can be guaranteed, I keep tapping into the courage it takes to believe anyway. Because I know the power of embracing illogical things: like hope, like optimism, and like courage.

When circumstances force you to pull over and confront seemingly impossible things, you have the power to defy logic and embrace hope. Every time you reach out a hand toward the people you love, you will find strength and comfort in the instinctive connection you find there. We all struggle with moments of deep darkness, but we can create pathways for the light to get through by giving new labels to simple things: a penny is a lucky charm, a storefront is a good omen, and a statistic is just a rule waiting to be broken. We can accept that being illogical is the quickest road to being hopeful and recognize that love can be another name for courage. As we celebrate the courage we show by consciously choosing to seek, see, and embrace the good in even the most difficult days, we weave the hero's cape that will set us alight.

IGNITE ACTION STEPS

- Take note of the things that make you smile involuntarily, and recognize there is a reason they were put in your path. Sparrows make me smile because they make the best of any place; a floral meadow or a trash-covered city block. They are the very embodiment of optimism.

- Write a thank you note or letter, at least once a month, to someone who has created a bright spot in your life. Don't limit it to those in your closest circle. If there is a barista who always makes your coffee just right, or a bus driver who gets your kid home safe each day, let them know you appreciate them.

- Engage in "compassionate capering." Buy a bunch of flowers, and hand them out to random people who look like they deserve a smile. Yes, some people will question your kindness but have courage. The difference you will make in the day of the person who accepts your flower will ripple positively in untold directions.

Michiko Couchman, M.Ed. — United States of America
Editor, Writer, Mother & Wife
michi.couch

Ignite is proud to present two courageous
souls that came together in such a beautiful and unique way.
Their stories are intertwined and interlaced with magical beauty and destiny. Please enjoy these next two stories as they show the courageousness of
two amazing women stepping into igniting each other's lives. Their stories
are of the powerful Ignite Moment that brought them both together.

Lillian Skrovig Dooies

LILLIAN SKROVIG DOOIES

"PERSEVERE, be STRONG, be POSITIVE."

You are stronger than you realize. Rely on your inner strength, stamina, and courage when unexpected positive or negative events occur. Challenging events require a positive mindset. I hope my story will inspire you to find peace, meaning, and strength in your life.

7:00 AM

The large lingering bruise on my thigh was obvious, a reminder of a recent slip down my stairs. Before the fall, I felt extremely tired, but I wasn't concerned as my yearly medical exam was scheduled in a few weeks. I had my bloodwork taken 2 weeks before in preparation for my appointment. Not concerned anything was seriously wrong, I continued working, preparing my lessons for my 7th-grade social studies students. I was happy to reconnect with my students following the winter break and hear about their holidays. I received a phone call from the doctor's office during my planning hour. With a kind and calm voice, the nurse said that I needed to get to the emergency room right away. Perhaps due to her gentle demeanor, her words didn't really sink in, and I responded by saying that

I couldn't leave because I had another class to teach. Then she said, "You're in heart attack and stroke territory, and you need to go RIGHT NOW." That got my attention, and I left school within 10 minutes. I would never return.

The emergency room was quite busy for a Tuesday at 3 PM. After waiting 2 hours, I was escorted to a little curtained space where staff immediately began by taking my blood pressure, and drawing my blood. Still lying on the bed, I was rolled into the emergency room hallway, across from the nurse's desk, where I waited for hours until a doctor insisted I shouldn't be in such a germ-ridden and exposed space with the health risks I faced. I was moved to a glass-enclosed room and at 11 PM, finally admitted to a 5th-floor hospital room. I was incredibly scared as my mind wandered through all the possible things that could be wrong with me. While I waited in that cold, hard ER bed, 2 friends came to visit. One brought prayers; the other brought chocolate and socks at my request! We commiserated and collectively decided I was probably anemic, and that's why I had been feeling so tired.

After 3 days in the hospital, I was sent home with quite a different diagnosis than anemia. I was instructed to pack for thirty days of treatment at a larger, more specialized, and experienced (as in, they do this every day) hospital. My diagnosis was Acute Myeloid Leukemia (AML), an aggressive blood cancer. My doctors told me that my life was about to change. My health was now my top priority, and due to my severe condition, I was placed on a special diet to avoid coming in contact with any life-threatening germs. AML can kill you within 3 months, and after hearing this, I was fearful and uncertain about where to begin.

It took 3 weeks to get an appointment at a leading cancer hospital. A dear friend drove my oldest daughter, Shannon, and I from Florida to Houston, Texas. You might call it an uneasy journey, as we had no idea what to expect. We arrived to find an enormous clinic and hospital encompassing multiple buildings and towers, floor upon floor, up to eighteen stories high. Learning to navigate that enormous facility would take many months. Thank goodness for all the kind people who helped me along the way!

My daughter, friend, and I nervously arrived for my first appointment at the clinic within the Leukemia Department at 7 AM on a Tuesday. It took most of the morning to get checked in, complete forms, provide insurance information, and have my picture taken. After lunch, my vital signs were recorded, blood work was done, and we met the first doctor. He and his team greeted us graciously. They took time to explain treatment options, including a chemotherapy regimen, a clinical trial, and a stem cell transplant. They also welcomed our questions. But honestly, we didn't even know what to ask. The medical terms, medication names, and confusing treatment options swirled around in my head; a tremendous amount of information to absorb all at once. As we walked to the building across the street for my CT-scan, my friend said, "We are 3 very intelligent women, and yet I don't know what's going to happen. Are you having chemotherapy for a year or a transplant?" My daughter and I were just as perplexed as we didn't know which treatment would be the solution.

We soon found out the first step of my treatment *had* to be chemotherapy and the goal of going into remission. After chemotherapy began, the doctor determined that chemotherapy alone would not ensure my survival and I would need a stem cell transplant. I was thankful that they had a plan on how to help me but also surprised and a bit disappointed as I had hoped chemotherapy would be the answer. I was fortunate to be selected for a clinical trial that would offer additional treatment for me while providing valuable information for improving future cancer care.

The first week at the University of Texas M. D. Anderson Cancer Center was consumed with a whirlwind of doctors, exams, lab work, tests, and incredibly painful bone marrow biopsies to confirm my original diagnosis of AML. Tests would start at 7 AM and often not end until late at night. Once the clinic had gathered all the necessary information, I was admitted to the hospital to start chemotherapy. I was exhausted and scared. We all were. Our hopeful trio exited the elevator at 11 PM and walked onto the eerily quiet oncology floor; the only sounds came from the nurses who were preparing rooms. The stark space needed to be cleaned from top to bottom to avoid any potential infections. I felt as if I was walking into another world, one that I hoped would save my life.

A nurse met us at the elevator and led us to a sterile white room where I was instructed to shower from head to toe and don a hospital gown when done. I was frightened. Turning to my daughter and friend, I said, "I can't do this." My friend quickly responded, "Do you want to live?" reminding me to tap into whatever courage I could muster. I finished my shower with renewed strength, realizing this was my only hope to survive—non-compliance would seal my fate. I would likely die within the year. I had not experienced painful tests and driven 1100 miles to give up easily.

After my shower, we were escorted to my new home, a large corner room with a single exterior window. With trepidation, I entered the room, wondering what was going to happen, and thus began my isolation. Now I knew why the doctor had told me to pack for thirty days.

My protocol began at 1 AM. The technician and I quarreled as he insisted on putting the IV in my right arm. I argued, saying he should use my left arm as I'd had clotting issues with my right arm while in Florida. He wouldn't budge, so finally, I said, "Fine. Go ahead." The IV was withdrawn and placed in my left arm within an hour. Deeply drained from the ordeal, I eventually fell asleep.

So it went for the next thirty days: doctors, nurses, and technicians came in throughout the day and night. Different chemotherapy regimens: all administered through IV. One for 1 hour, another for 3, some overlapping. In addition to the chemotherapy drugs, I was given other medications to protect my eyes and organs. My vital signs were monitored 6 times daily, and although I knew I was in the best hospital for my disease, I couldn't help but be anxious, wondering from one day to the next if I would survive.

My physical response to the initial chemotherapy was relatively mild, with medication keeping me from feeling too ill. Yet I vividly recall my stomach churning when the nurse pointed out to me that my hair was beginning to fall out. I was disheartened, knowing this was a visual sign of what my body was experiencing. I asked if we could wait to shave my head until my daughter was with me. My family could not enter my room but were visible through a window to a small connected room, and we spoke by telephone. The nurse shaved my head as Shannon watched from the next room. It was a heartbreaking experience for both of us. It was heartbreaking but worth it, as the hair loss indicated the chemotherapy was doing its job.

My disease went into remission, and over the following months, I was in and out of the hospital for continued chemotherapy. When not in the hospital, I visited different clinics in preparation for the next phase of the process; my transplant. I had memorized my patient number and became accustomed to the routine of checking in and waiting, often for hours, for tests and procedures. I eagerly waited to hear my name called. The days were long, and the process tiring. The clinics would often see over one hundred patients daily.

My overall health was extensively monitored, including dermatology, eyes, dentistry, pulmonary function, CT scans, MRI, and frequent bone marrow biopsies. The doctors needed assurance that I was in good health and could undergo the rigors of a transplant. It took every fiber of my being to persevere through the incredibly painful and intrusive testing I had to go through.

The time came to find a matching DNA donor. I was scheduled to have an allogeneic stem cell transplant: a transplant in which stem cells from an unrelated donor are collected and infused into my body. A qualified stem cell donor had to match my DNA 'markers' or characteristics at a minimum of 10 markers. I was very fortunate to find a match within a few weeks. My donor was found on the 'Be The Match' registry (National Marrow Donor Program), and my transplant occurred 4 months after my initial diagnosis.

The term "transplant" might conjure up fear and images of styrofoam ice chests and intricate surgery. In reality, a stem cell transplant is a simple IV infusion, something I had become accustomed to at this point. That was the easy part. The hard part tested my strength and that of my family in unimaginable ways.

My transplant regimen was a 3-day process. The night before the procedure, I slept poorly and was restless; I was terrified of what would come.

Day 1 started with the administration of extremely high-intensity chemotherapy used to kill any remaining cancer cells in my body. I thought that alone was going to kill me. The procedure was designed to weaken my immune system, making it easier for the infusion of donor stem cells to reach my bone marrow and not be rejected. The ultimate goal was 100% engraftment, where my body would accept the stem cells and begin creating white and red blood cells and platelets. If successful, this process would give me an entirely new immune system. It was a full day filled with continual hallucinations and vomiting in a way never experienced or imagined in my life. A half-day had passed when I said to the doctor that I wished we could stop. He said we could not.

After the torturous day of chemotherapy, Day 2 was a day of rest. I was completely drained.

Day 3 was the actual day of my transplant: an infusion of stem cells so freely given by an anonymous donor. I distinctly recall my transplant nurse coming in at 7 AM saying, "Your stem cells have arrived, and we're just waiting for them to thaw." She returned at 1 PM and began my infusion. Late afternoon when it was done, my children, who had been there all day, crowned me with a tiara, had my favorite pastries waiting, and my son was playing celebration songs on his ukulele! Joy!

Post-transplant, I was required to stay near the hospital for 135 days and have a caregiver. I had a severe response to my transplant and struggled with Graft versus Host Disease (GVHD). GVHD affected my skin and eyes: my eyes were dry and itchy, requiring visits to an oncology ophthalmologist, and my skin would break out in an itchy rash. Treatment seemed to be a never-ending cycle; it took months of clinic visits and medications to resolve these issues. At 7 AM, I would take my first pill of the day, taking twenty-two medications daily. Ultimately, I became fully engrafted.

Upon discharge from Houston and my return to Florida, I was under the care of local doctors. Also, I continued quarterly visits to M. D. Anderson Cancer Center for a number of years. I was extremely fatigued, receiving weekly 4-hour infusions and many medications. I was alive, but my life had definitely changed. Because of my weakened immune system, I was unable to return to teaching, but did visit with my students to share my journey and wish them well as they continued on to high school. My departure a year earlier had been so sudden and unexpected that we all welcomed the opportunity for reconnection.

My family spent an indeterminable amount of time in medical waiting rooms with me from the first till the very last day, and now my donor was with me also. I carried someone else's kindness and courage directly in my veins, but I didn't know who they were. My donor was completely anonymous, which is done by design to make sure both of our anonymity is preserved.

I wondered who my donor was. What was their name? Man or woman? Where did they live? And so much more. My donor and I could communicate by giving our letters to the hospital liaison. We could not divulge any personal information: no names, no states, no family information, or anything that might hint at our identities. Our letters were even censored! I recall writing about my son's dog, Molly, and her name being marked out; it could have been a person, a clue!

Guidelines allow that one year after a transplant, a donor and recipient can meet if they choose. The hospital coordinator knew how eager I was to meet my donor and provided contact information sooner than expected. I was so excited to call my donor, and her name was Jenny.

Jenny and I called each other, and within 3 weeks, she and her friend came to Florida to meet me and my family. My heart was racing and my palms clammy as I waited, and saw Jenny driving down the street to my home. I met her on the driveway with a huge hug! This beautiful young woman had given me a chance at life! We all chatted and laughed the first night while sharing a special homemade dinner. We gave them a tour of our town the following day and, that evening, had a party honoring these wonderful ladies, inviting all the friends who had been so important in my journey. A few years later, my friend, who had driven me to Houston, flew with me to meet Jenny's lovely family. I was filled with anticipation to meet my donor's family, knowing that they had raised her to be the incredible person she is and that they would be the same. Not surprisingly, we were welcomed like royalty, enjoying a rooftop party, dinner in a private room of a beautiful restaurant, driving through the gorgeous mountains, lunch at a famous resort, and more. It was a memorable time with Jenny, and her family and friends. I recall these events with fondness.

Jenny has become a dear, true friend, a loving, giving person, and someone I would gravitate to and befriend if I had met her at a party. I believe we have the same outlook on life, with similar values and perspectives. We are both givers and try to make life good for others. My family and I are truly blessed and grateful to have Jenny in our lives and a part of our family. We are more than a DNA match; we are lifelong friends and 2 people committed to giving the most we can. To encourage others, Jenny joined me at M D. Anderson, where we recorded a video sharing our story and friendship.

At the time of this writing, I am a 10-year stem cell transplant thriver! Woo hoo! In enduring my hardships and discovering my courage, I have drawn inspiration and courage from God, my doctors, my dear friends, and above all, my family: my parents who endured their own hardships and taught perseverance by example, my intelligent, brave, and compassionate children and my lifegiving donor Jenny. I am so grateful to them all for the life they have given me. My children were with me every step of the way, making sure I was never alone, a reminder of my reason to be brave.

I'm a survivor but refer to myself as a THRIVER! Thriving means I strive to make the best of every day and give back what I can. I volunteer to speak with patients going through a similar cancer journey. I also volunteer with my local 'Be The Match' group encouraging potential stem cell donors. I have ups and downs like anyone else, but I have no complaints in the big picture. When in a quandary, I channel the courage and strength of my family, which has grown so beautifully over the years. They are why I get to start with a fresh slate each time 7 AM rolls around.

Ignite Action Steps

1. Be strong, stay positive, and advocate for yourself and others.

2. Plan your day, have a purpose, set goals. Enjoy the accomplishments.

3. Be a good patient. Follow all the instructions from your doctor and contribute to a positive outcome.

4. 'BE THE MATCH' that saves a life!

Lillian Skrovig Dooies — United States of America
Educator and Writer
Lillianwritestoday@gmail.com
www.mdanderson.org/cancerwise.html

Jenny Salimi

JENNY SALIMI

"Live to give."

I have one goal—it's to challenge the assumption that courage must come out of a traumatic, hard, or scary situation. I share my story hoping to shift the perception of courage by emphasizing that even the tiniest effort can unleash a profound and far-reaching effect. My wish is for you to discover the power in tiny acts of courage that ripple through the lives of others, leading to remarkable outcomes.

THANK YOU FOR MY LIFE

I was in the perfect nap position, stretched out on my comfy, leather recliner thumbing through the pages of one of my favorite magazines. It was self-care Sunday, and I was enjoying some downtime preparing for a busy work week. In search of ways to feel more grounded and balanced, I learned reading was the best way for me to unwind and recharge. I came across a 2-page spread article about a courageous young girl in her early twenties, sharing a story that no one should go through, let alone someone who had yet to embark on her journey of life. As a woman in my mid-thirties, I felt I was just barely scratching the surface of my own adventure and still in the pursuit of my purpose.

The young girl in the article was going through medical hell: unexplainable bruising, indescribable pain, skin turning pale, and no energy to do more than sleep. Repeated misdiagnoses and rapid symptom progression had her friends and family worried. It was after 2 years of grueling and painful tests that the truth unfolded—she was diagnosed with an uncommon form of leukemia. I couldn't stop reading even though sadness was starting to consume me. I felt sickened, and my stomach started to turn. Her escalated stage of leukemia meant that it was too late to go through a trial of radiation or chemotherapy as a first step. She needed to find a bone marrow donor. Disappointingly, none of her biological relatives were a suitable match. The family desperately turned to the national registry of donors where weeks went by—still no match. I was in tears and felt completely heartbroken as I read the last few sentences which were her public plea for anyone and everyone to register with the national bone marrow registry, Be the Match™, to become a bone marrow donor, and possibly save her life.

My emotions were swirling, and my pulsing blood hummed in my ears. One moment, I was infuriated at fate and every God out there that this could happen. Then the next moment, I suddenly had an unexpected and fierce determination ignite within me. I tossed the magazine onto the floor and ran to my laptop. With trembling hands, I looked up the Be the Match website. I scrolled through every single page, reading stories about the struggles other people of all ages had gone through, and the pictures of the young kids hurt me the most. I reached the final page that shared instructions on how to be added to the registry. I found myself typing in my information as fast as my brain and fingers could communicate. The last step was to click the Register Now button and receive an expedited swabbing kit in the mail. My heart was pounding as I watched that annoying loading icon just circling, circling… *what's wrong with my wifi*? Finally, the "Thank for Registering" page popped up. *Phew*.

I had an overwhelming desire to see if I could have an effect on someone by being courageous and trying to help a stranger. I wanted to be the girl in the magazine's donor! I didn't know that the chances of matching are exceptionally low, especially if the donor and/or recipient has a mixed ethnic background. I didn't care. Miracles happen every day. Time wasn't on her side, so I didn't waste any. If I could help save that girl's life, I would have chopped off my right arm. Okay, maybe not my arm, but for sure my pinky finger.

I happened to be going through some life changes that were taking me down a road toward personal development and self-awareness. I was thirty-six years old and had been blessed with a beautiful and unbreakable bond with my parents. My circle of friends was like a garden of flowers with no weeds. And according to my standards, my career was fairly successful. But I had a tendency to always play it safe, which teetered on the border of being delightfully boring and mundane. Don't get me wrong, I was living it up as a single girl living in the city, but I was slowly becoming unfulfilled. I felt stuck.

Being at the tail end of a very monotonous and fizzling 3-year relationship, I became determined to live a little more intentionally. I wanted more moments that were meaningful, where I could feel things in my heart and not just go through the motions. I was hungry to feel things I'd never felt, which meant I had to do things I'd never done. *What things?* I didn't know. But all I could do was just show up in life and try harder.

I had a revelation that creating a 'bucket list group' would be a good start. I reached out to 7 of my closest girlfriends who I thought would enjoy and benefit from a nudge that would hopefully lead to a greater sense of fulfillment and accomplishment. I was pleased with the easy sell, and shortly after, we had our first bucket list group meeting. The one and only rule to start was that you had to show up with a list of at least fifteen aspirations. Trust me when I say you have to dig deep to come up with fifteen different ideas to try, explore, and experience. I thoughtfully crafted a list of things I'd always been curious about, even things that seemed out of reach. I wanted to test the theory that if you write it down, it can manifest and become a reality. One of my 'out of the ordinary' items was to save a life. I wanted to offer the most selfless and courageous act I could think of. The magazine article about the young girl sparked the idea that one person *could* make a life-saving gesture. Since I didn't know what it entailed to be a donor, I broadened my goal to be more general; save one person's life somehow.

A few months passed after joining the bone marrow donor registry. Then one day, while I was at work, I got a call from the organization that I registered with saying I was a match on six out of ten markers which was a positive indicator. On that very call, I booked my first of several medical appointments. Slowly, I put the phone down and sat there staring at the wall with a big, wide-toothed smile.

In order to be considered a true match, the donor must be close to 10 markers, a near-perfect match. I needed a special blood test analyzing specific proteins, or markers, on my white blood cells. Truth be told, I was a little scared. My emotions left me flushed and dizzy. *Am I going to be able to truly help someone? Is my potential recipient a young child who hasn't had the chance to live a life? Or is it for someone who has built a life and needs to fight for it so they can be around to meet their grandchildren?*

After more blood tests, an EKG, and the most thorough physical I've ever had, all the required tests were complete. I proudly received a clean bill of health on all fronts. Now I would have to wait patiently to hear back on the results. One week went by. Then another. By the third week, I had grown anxious with anticipation. *Why hadn't I gotten a call back yet? Was I not a match?* As much as I tried to tuck it away, discouragement was setting in. I had no idea I was prematurely attached to my potential recipient and would be devastated if I couldn't help. My heart was already invested, and wanted to be a match so badly!

Then the phone call finally came in, again while I was at work, and I WAS A MATCH! Not only did this mystery recipient and I match on all 10 markers... we were off the charts, matching on thirteen... a beyond-perfect match. This time I slammed down the phone and started skipping down the office hall to share the good news with a work buddy who was everyone's best friend. I felt like I'd just won the lottery.

Next step—schedule the donation date at least 4 months out. It would have to allow for enough time for the recipient to undergo high-intensity chemotherapy, which completely destroys their immune system. This was the only way my cells could take over and have the chance to replace the donor's cancerous cells. It's a truly miraculous process and one I am simplifying here, but what mattered most was I was getting the opportunity to potentially save a life.

I had a big decision to make. I had to either fully commit or walk away. Once the recipient started the excruciating process of chemotherapy, there was no turning back for them. Welling up with all the courage I had in me, I resoundingly said, *HELL YES!* There was no earthly way I was turning away this incredible opportunity. I was given a special gift, having the honor of donating part of me to a stranger. My excitement must have been contagious, as the nurse on the other line started giggling. And there it was set in stone—donation date: April 13, 2013.

Let me clear up the stigma that you always have to go through a surgical procedure where the doctors use huge needles to withdraw liquid marrow from the back of your pelvic bone. That is not the case! You can also donate through a stem cell transplant which is a non-surgical procedure. That is the route I was able to take.

Over the course of 4 months, I lived by the 4 pillars of health (nutrition, exercise, relaxation, and sleep). I was already a vegetarian at the time, so that helped eliminate all the toxins and chemicals that came with that territory. I stopped using lotions and potions and found shampoos with the simplest basic ingredients. No food coloring, artificial flavors, sweeteners, and so on entered this body. I tried living as pure and clean as humanly possible. It was the least I could do for my recipient. And surprise, surprise, it resulted in me feeling my best, so it was a win-win.

Leading up to the last week before the scheduled donation date, I was given injections of a specific medication for 5 days in a row to increase my blood-forming white blood cells (WBCs). The donation day came, and boy, was I ready. There were a slew of possible side effects, but I was fortunate enough to only feel a little achy with bouts of insomnia. I don't know if the anticipation or insomnia kept me up the night before, but by 2 AM I was sitting on my parents' couch in a comfy black sweater dress, ready for them to take me to the hospital for my 6 AM appointment. They've always trusted my judgment, and I'm thankful for that, but I could tell they were a little leery of everything going on, hoping that there would be no long-term side effects for me.

I'll save the details of my experience of the stem cell transplant for another day, as that could be enough for its own chapter, but I must give props to modern technology and medicine. *Simply outstanding.*

After the procedure was complete, my cells were put on ice in a small, white and red medical cooler. Within an hour, they were on their way to my recipient in Florida with a hand-written card of my good wishes and prayers that I had what he or she needed to survive. It was a fascinating feeling to have shared something so intimate with someone, yet be forced to remain anonymous. Per some regulations that I don't quite understand, my recipient and I couldn't have direct contact with each other for twelve months. After one year, our contact info would be released with mutual consent. The only way we stayed connected was through letters in the mail which would be delayed at least 2 months because they first had to be sent to Be the Match. The organization would read our letters, black out any identifying details, and then forward them to the intended recipient. It was kind of funny reading a letter with black lines that would leave incomplete sentences and unfinished thoughts. I wasn't even allowed to know the recipient's dog's name!

Then, the real magic of my act of courage began. Exactly one year and one hour after our info was released, my recipient took me by surprise and called. She was soft-spoken and had the sweetest and most gentle voice. "Hi, this is Lillian. You were my donor." Hearing her voice for the first time was like a sweet melody, which I soon came to learn matched her personality. We shared excitement, laughter, and bursts of tears with an instant connection that's indescribable. I was on cloud 9, flooded with emotions I'd never felt before. The effects of my small act of courage were starting to unfold.

Within a month, I was on a plane with my best friend with me for support because I was nervous! As we pulled up to the house to meet Lillian and her spectacularly lovely family, I had wild and out-of-control butterflies fluttering inside me, like when you're really excited yet a tad nauseous for a first date with someone you've had a major crush on. My bestie and I sat in our rental car in the driveway for what seemed like 3 hours (it was really 3 minutes) just looking at each other. It was time. Time to see what the universe had in store for me. Slowly walking up to the door, I reached out my shaking hand and rang the bell. The door immediately swung open, and we were warmly greeted like long-lost family members despite being virtually complete strangers. I don't know what does if that doesn't play games with your psyche.

Seeing Lillian and being able to hug her for the first time after weeks of anticipation was a relief. She had so much gratitude in her eyes. We all sat in the living room for hours, telling stories and getting to know each other through laughter and tears. An unbreakable bond was blossoming. A couple of times, I had to pinch myself *hard* to see if I'd wake up from this beautiful dream. My heart felt so full, and I was in awe of how fate could bring our 2 worlds together.

4 months after that, I was on a plane again as a guest at Lillian's youngest daughter's wedding. I looked for my name tag on every table, trying to find my seat. The last table I walked up to was the table for immediate family, and there it was—I had a seat with my name on it at the family table. *I was now family*!

When Lillian's turn came to visit me, there were so many moments where we were giddy and smiley. It felt so serendipitous, and there was no doubt we were meant to meet. Our being brought together was a miracle in itself.

The last day of her visit arrived, and we dragged our feet, knowing we'd soon have to say our goodbyes. We used up all of our minutes until it was time to roll her suitcase into the elevator, through my lobby, and send her on her way. I was dreading giving her a hug as I knew we'd both be sobbing because this wasn't just a hug. This extraordinarily special hug would be between 2 people who share more than just good memories. We were connected at a cellular level; my DNA was in *her* blood. Her once straight hair had even grown back curly, just like mine. My heart started to feel heavy as, with open arms, we pulled each other in. Then as she slowly pulled away, I was given the gift of hearing 5 words that changed me forever. It was a defining moment that took my breath away. She whispered, *"Thank you for my life."*

BOOM! Her sentiment hit me hard like a ton of bricks, leaving me speechless, becoming the standard on how I want to show up in this world. I could feel my eyes welling up with tears and my knees beginning to tremble. I had done it. I now know what it felt like to take a small step of courage and experience the tremendous impact it can make. Saving a life is now checked off my bucket list!

One of the bone marrow organizations caught wind of our story and quickly involved me in their drives to get people to register. What better way to spread awareness than having someone onsite who has lived through and could share the entire experience? Their approach was unique in that they would set up tents at concerts and festivals. As people passed by, we'd wave them in to give them a quick spiel about being a donor in hopes they'd agree to get swabbed then and there to join the registry.

People's reactions were a big awakening for me. The misconceptions about being a donor were many, and the mere thought of needles sent people running. I was baffled… no, wait, I was mortified at the responses. This made me more determined to explain that their selfless act of courage could help save a life. Imagine the effect on a struggling family with a loved one whose only hope is YOU. My challenge to them, and to you, is to have the courage to volunteer to help others in ways you never have before. You can volunteer your time, financially, or through your health. How could it not lead to deeper connections and enriching experiences, which are key elements to our happiness?

I'm living proof that the smallest act of courage can have a far-reaching impact that can change the lives of one and of many. Each new day creates an opportunity to awaken the possibility that we *can* make miracles happen when we find courage. We're all in this life together and can be the hope and help someone needs. If you're curious about saving a life, let me share that it's true, miracles do happen every day.

IGNITE ACTION STEPS

Courageously live by a simple set of rules:

- **Give love** when you're feeling down, and give your heart when yours is broken.

- **Give time** when you have none; give help when you don't know how.

- **Give hope** when someone has lost theirs, and give your hand when someone reaches out.

Jenny Salimi — United States of America
Inventor and Author
www.jennylynnebooks.com
🔲 *jennysalimi*
🔲 *jennylynnebooks*
🔲 *jennylynnebooks*
🔲 *jennylynnebooks*

RESOURCES OUR *IGNITE YOUR COURAGE* AUTHORS RECOMMEND

Ana-Maria Turdean
- https://anasmagicworld.blogspot.com/2023/08/increase-your-chances-of-getting-new.html

Cheryl Rafter
- Until I Become, Sir Darren Jacklin
- www.healyourself.ca

Christina Sommers
- Loving Your Life Again Podcast https://www.buzzsprout.com/2107832, Apple Podcasts, Spotify, or your favorite podcast platform
- https://reloadinchrist.com/contact/ Sign up for my newsletter to get the latest updates and offerings
- National Domestic Violence Hotline https://www.thehotline.org/ or 800.799.SAFE (7233)
- National Institute of Mental Healt https://www.nimh.nih.gov/health/find-help

Lameeka Harris
- Shirley Ryan Ability Lab https://www.sralab.org
- Shirley Ryan Day Rehab https://www.sralab.org
- Rush Hospital https://www.rush.edu
- It Takes a Village Family of Schools https://itavschools.org
- Village Leadership Academy https://www.vlacademy.org

Lillian Dooies
- https://www.mdanderson.org/cancerwise.html
- https://bethematch.org/

Michi Couchman
- The Multiple Myeloma Research Foundation www.themmrf.org
- Leukemia & Lymphoma Society www.lls.org

Nolan Pillay
- Online Program: https://www.udemy.com/course/obstacles_make_you_stronger
- Book: https://www.amazon.com/My-Covid-Journey-Techniques-through-ebook/dp/B09GPXTXSK

Sandra Von Hollen
- www.allinalignment.com
- www.bethhaley.com
- www.ignitethelight.ca

PHOTO CREDITS

Ana-Maria Turdean - *Viorica Cernica*
Ashira Karps - *Aimee Pozniak Photography*
Cheryl Rafter - *Hamid, Perfect Shot Studio, West Vancouver, B.C*
Christina Sommers - *Daniel McGarrity Photography*
Deborah A. Ellis - *Alston M. Walker, AMW Photography*
Farah Smith - *Jasmine Lord*
Felecia Moore - *Hyon Smith*
Gina Trimarco - *Kathy Strauss*
JB Owen - *Janine Marek*
Jenette Longoria - *Doten Photography*
Jennifer Salimi - *Jorge Castillo*
Jermaine Brantley - *Charles Holloway, Jr.*
Karen R. Rosser - *Joshua Alfonso*
Lameeka Harris - *Daryl James*
Lillian Dooies - *KG*
Marcia Klostermann - *Kris Roberts Photography*
Michi Couchman - *Anthony Barnes, Innovay Studios*
Peter Giesin - *JB Owen*
Sandra Von Hollen - *Jesse & Danielle Von Hollen*
Stephanie Drummond - *Terri Baskin Photography*

THANK YOU

Thank you for being a part of the magical journey of IGNITE!

Everything we do is for you, the reader, and we thank you for taking the time to enjoy and cherish these stories; and for opening your hearts and minds to the idea of igniting your own lives. We know that when one person touches the life of another, we create a ripple effect of change. That change will uplift hearts, awaken minds, and transform ideas into empowering action steps. We commit to being the leader in empowerment publishing and making sure our message inspires others in a way that will positively impact all of Humanity.

A deep appreciation also goes to each and every author who made *Ignite Your Courage* possible. It is their powerful and inspiring stories, along with their passion and desire to help others, that will *Ignite Courage* within each and every one of us. It takes courage to share a vulnerable part of yourself, and each one of the people in this book exemplifies that. They stepped up to share their stories for the very first time. They courageously revealed the many layers of themselves and exposed their weaknesses as few individual leaders do. Additionally, they spoke authentically from the heart and wrote what was true for them. We could have taken their stories and made them perfect, following every editing rule, but we chose instead to leave their unique and honest voices intact. We overlooked the exactness to foster individual expression. These are their words, their sentiments, and their explanations. We let their personalities shine in their writing so you would get a true sense of who each one of them is. That's what makes IGNITE so unique. Authors serving others. Stories igniting humanity.

A tremendous thank you goes to all those on the IGNITE team who have been working tirelessly in the background, teaching, editing, supporting, and encouraging the authors to reach the finish line. These individuals are some of the most genuine and heart-centered people I know. Their dedication to the vision of IGNITE, along with their integrity and the message they convey, is of the highest caliber possible. They each want you to find inspiration and use the many Ignite Moments in this book to rise and flourish. They all believe in you, and that's what makes them so outstanding. Their dream is for all of your dreams to come true.

Production Team: JB Owen, Peter Giesin, Katie Smetherman, Mimi Safiyah, Kristine Joy Magno, and Carolina Gold.

Editing Team: Alex Blake, Michiko Couchman, JB Owen, Mimi Safiyah, Zoe Wong, and Sarah Cross.

Project Leaders: Steph Elliott, Stacey Yates Sellar, and Karen R. Rosser

A special thanks and gratitude to the entire team for their support behind the scenes and for going 'above and beyond' to make this a wonderful experience. Their dedication made sure that everything ran smoothly, and with elegance.

We welcome you to share your story and become a new author in one of our upcoming books. Your message and your *Ignite Moment* may be exactly what someone else needs to read to Ignite their life. Readers become authors, and we want that for you. Go to www.igniteyou/life to apply to write your story.

WRITE YOUR STORY
IN AN IGN TE BOOK!!

**THE ROAD TO SHARING YOUR MESSAGE AND BECOMING
A BEST-SELLING AUTHOR BEGINS RIGHT HERE.**

We make YOU a best-selling author in just four months!

If you have a story of perseverance, determination, growth, awakening, and change...
and you've felt the power of your Ignite Moment, we'd love to hear from you.

We are always looking for motivating stories that will make a difference in someone's life. Our
fun, enjoyable, four-month writing process is like no other—and the best thing about IGNITE is
the community of outstanding, like-minded individuals dedicated to helping others.

With over 700 amazing individuals to date writing their stories and sharing their Ignite Moment,
we are positively impacting the planet and raising the vibration of HUMANITY. Our stories inspire
and empower others and we want to add your story to one of our upcoming books!

Go to our website, click How To Get Started, and share a bit of your Ignite transformation.

JOIN US TO IGNITE A BILLION LIVES WITH A BILLION WORDS.

Apply at: www.igniteyou.life/apply   Find out more at: www.igniteyou.life

Inquire at: info@igniteyou.life

.

Milton Keynes UK
Ingram Content Group UK Ltd.
UKHW021335201023
430989UK00008B/30